SPELLING DEMONS

WEEK BY WEEK

Elizabeth Hagner

J. WESTON
WALCH
PUBLISHER
PORTLAND, MAINE

User's Guide
to
Walch Reproducible Books

As part of our general effort to provide educational materials which are as practical and economical as possible, we have designated this publication a "reproducible book." The designation means that purchase of the book includes purchase of the right to limited reproduction of all pages on which this symbol appears:

Here is the basic Walch policy: We grant to individual purchasers of this book the right to make sufficient copies of reproducible pages for use by all students of a single teacher. This permission is limited to a single teacher, and does not apply to entire schools or school systems, so institutions purchasing the book should pass the permission on to a single teacher. Copying of the book or its parts for resale is prohibited.

Any questions regarding this policy or requests to purchase further reproduction rights should be addressed to:

Permissions Editor
J. Weston Walch, Publisher
321 Valley Street • P. O. Box 658
Portland, Maine 04104-0658

1   2   3   4   5   6   7   8   9   10
ISBN 0-8251-2874-9
Copyright © 1986, 1997
J. Weston Walch, Publisher
P.O. Box 658 • Portland, Maine 04104-0658
Printed in the United States of America

CONTENTS

(Reproducible student pages are noted with an **R**)

FOREWORD

Rabbit, in A. A. Milne's *The House at Pooh Corner*, says Christopher Robin respects Owl because "you can't help respecting anybody who can spell *Tuesday* . . . ." Later, Kanga reprimands Roo for Roo's tone in speaking to Owl, explaining, "That's *not* the way to talk to anybody who can spell *Tuesday*."

Away from Pooh Corner, one may not be praised for spelling *Tuesday* correctly, but misspelling of it will certainly be noted: "Why, that person can't even spell *Tuesday*!"

There comes a time when we must learn to spell the demons like *Tuesday*. To do this, we will work with, not just memorize, the spelling rules so they will help us with the demons. We'll consider the various ways to spell the sounds of English so the demons don't look so strange to us. We'll learn to manipulate prefixes and suffixes around the roots of words. We'll use memory tricks if they make sense to us. Finally, we'll recognize when we need to verify our own spelling by using the dictionary, and we'll make our own special lists of words.

We will have to do better than Owl, however, who "could spell *Tuesday* so that you knew it wasn't *Wednesday*." We can tame those demons so that they won't defeat us any longer. We will be able to spell *TUESDAY*—even *WEDNESDAY*!

TO THE TEACHER

A demon a day—more or less—is the object of *Spelling Demons Week by Week*.

Ways to Use This Book

If you are already using a spelling curriculum, *Spelling Demons* can supplement it in the following ways: You might use the bare essentials of this book to ensure that your students know the demons. Or, using the subject index (*i* before *e* words, words ending in *y*, final silent **e** before **-ing**, etc.), you could select demons to reinforce a lesson from your curriculum. Another possibility is to duplicate individual lessons for students with persistent problems with a particular demon.

These lessons can also constitute a spelling curriculum in themselves because the basic demons (and many related words) are covered, as are the spelling rules.

Organization of This Book

Spelling Demons is divided into four units of ten lessons each to correspond to the school year, so you can easily work the lessons into the standard school calendar.

Each of the **40 two-page lessons** contains an average of eight words for students to study. Short exercises follow the rather thorough discussions of the demons. These exercises are in the form of questions, crossword puzzles, word searches, mazes, light-hearted story writing, sentence writing, sentence completion, and so on. Sentences in the exercises use words from other lessons to reinforce the instruction. You may occasionally want to dictate some of those sentences as a review exercise.

Each lesson finishes with a page of **additional activities** if you think reinforcement is necessary.

Answers to the exercises follow each two-page lesson plus additional activities.

Each student will need a copy of the **pronunciation key** on page *xix* to use with some lessons. Discuss this page with them to make sure they understand the markings of the sounds.

Quarterly quizzes follow each group of ten lessons. You may use some of these for class or home work rather than as quizzes. There are oral tests, of varying lengths, on the words themselves; "sound to spelling" quizzes for which the students will probably want to have the pronunciation key at hand; and other quizzes to test their understanding of the demons and rules. You can have your students do all of the quizzes or choose ones you find appropriate to your group.

Subject quizzes follow the four quarterly units, drawing upon many different lessons: contractions; doubling final consonants; final, silent **e**; homonyms; **i** before **e** rule; plurals; **y** words; and verb tenses. You might use these as review quizzes, or you could assign them as homework, using the text as a reference.

Final tests follow the subject quizzes. They are similar to the quarterly quizzes, except that they cover the material in the whole text. Again, you may choose whichever tests you want to use—or parts of them. There is no reason to feel you have to do *all* of everything. The choice is yours according to what you believe your students need and will benefit from and what you have time for. *Spelling Demons* wasn't written with the idea that every teacher would use every exercise and quiz for every student.

Full **answers** are provided after all quizzes and tests. A **listing** by lesson of subjects covered follows. A complete **index** of the demons is at the end of the book.

SUBJECT INDEX
(BY LESSON NUMBER)

SPELLING DEMON WORDS
COVERED IN EACH LESSON

LESSON 1

Words Covered: certain; minute; spinach;
genuine; privilege; average; biscuit

LESSON 2

Words Covered: one; only; once; soldier;
forty; nine, ninety, nineteen,
ninth; hundred; two, to, too

LESSON 3

Words Covered: come, coming; take, taking; make, making;
have, having; give, giving; receive, received;
write, writing; smile, smiling; lose, losing;
real, really; usual, usually; sincere, sincerely

LESSON 4

Words Covered: mayonnaise; cauliflower; broccoli

LESSON 5

Words Covered: neighbor; weigh; weigh, way;
reign, rein, rain; foreign; eight; freight

LESSON 6

Words Covered: life, lives (noun); live, lives (verb);
belief, beliefs;
roof, roofs

LESSON 7

Words Covered: study, studies (noun);
study, studies, studied, studying (verb);
try, tries, tried, trying;
cry, cried, cried, crying;
reply, replies, replied, replying;
fly, flies, flew, flown, flying;
country, countries;
company, companies; enemy, enemies;
county, counties; ally, allies; story, stories

SPELLING DEMON WORDS
COVERED IN EACH LESSON (Continued)

LESSON 8

Words Covered: plan, planned, planning; hop, hopped, hopping; big, bigger, biggest; plan, planner; begin, beginning; commit; control

LESSON 9

Words Covered: efficient, sufficient, deficient, proficient, omniscient, conscience, species, glacier, ancient

LESSON 10

Words Covered: enough, through, although, thought, trouble, about, cough, doughnut

LESSON 11

Words Covered: know, knew, known, knowing; no; knew, new; knowledge; acknowledge, acknowledgment; tired; jewelry; judge, judgment

LESSON 12

Words Covered: kaleidoscope, Fahrenheit, reveille, onomatopoeia, weird, etc., they (them, their), very, while, chihuahua

LESSON 13

Words Covered: ceiling; receive, receipt; deceive, deceit, deceitful; conceited, perceive, conceive

LESSON 14

Words Covered: do, does, doing, done, doesn't, don't, did; go, goes, going, gone, went; does, does not, doesn't; do, do not, don't; seize; did, did not, didn't; was, was not, wasn't; had, had not, hadn't; have, have not, haven't; is, is not, isn't; can, cannot, can't; will, will not, won't

SPELLING DEMON WORDS
COVERED IN EACH LESSON (Continued)

LESSON 15

Words Covered: carry, carries, carried, carrying;
marry, marries, married, marrying;
worry, worries, worried, worrying;
library, libraries;
lb., oz.;
happy, happier, happiest, happily, happiness;
lazy, lazier, laziest, lazily, laziness;
easy, easier, easiest, easily, easiness;
busy, busier, busiest, busily, business

LESSON 16

Words Covered: hope, hoping; hop, hopping;
happen, happened (and related words:
summon, gallop, utter, parallel, channel,
differ, offer, suffer, quarrel);
benefit, benefited, benefiting (and related
words: travel, label, ravel, cancel, marvel,
parcel, rival, quarrel, shovel, enamel,
channel, counsel, model, equal, level)

LESSON 17

Words Covered: prefer, refer, transfer, confer;
occur, concur;
vacuum; color;
quit, quite, quiet; let's; circus, circuses

LESSON 18

Words Covered: clothes; close, closes, closed, closing; close; often;
rhyme; rhythm; principal, principle

LESSON 19

Words Covered: lose; loose; until; surprise; build, built;
guess, guest, nickel, choir, ocean

LESSON 20

Words Covered: pretty; been; woman, women; manila folder;
any, many; says, said; again, against

SPELLING DEMON WORDS
COVERED IN EACH LESSON (Continued)

LESSON 21
Words Covered: Wednesday; Tuesday;
ache; stomach; August; school

LESSON 22
Words Covered: potato, potatoes; tomato, tomatoes;
mosquito, mosquitoes;
radio, radios; auto, autos

LESSON 23
Words Covered: colonel; picnic; silhouette; somersault;
I; because; used to

LESSON 24
Words Covered: of; could, would, should; which;
beautiful; busy

LESSON 25
Words Covered: a lot; polka dot, polka dotted; February; library;
all right; all ready; already;
all ways; always; *al*-words

LESSON 26
Words Covered: success; seem; true; truly; toward;
awful; speak, speech; blue; whole, hole; wholly, holy

LESSON 27
Words Covered: excitement; except; excel; excel, excels, excelled, excelling;
excellent; sure, surely; sugar; weather; whether

LESSON 28
Words Covered: children; straight; practice;
off; some; something

LESSON 29
Words Covered: mean, meant; hear, heard; read;
please; pleasant; early;
break; breakfast; caught, taught, daughter, naughty;
tonight; tomorrow

SPELLING DEMON WORDS
COVERED IN EACH LESSON (Continued)

LESSON 30

Words Covered: probably, answer, people, separate
interesting, picture, with, different

LESSON 31

Words Covered: *Special Days I:* Abraham Lincoln's Birthday,
Leap Year Day, ides, April Fools' Day, National Birthday Day,
National Spelling Day, Memorial Day
Special Days II: Independence Day, Bastille Day,
Friday the 13th, Columbus Day, Halloween,
Veterans Day, Indian summer

LESSON 32

Words Covered: think, thought; bring, brought; buy, bought, bought;
say, pay, lay; lay, laid, laid, laying;
lie, lay, lain, lying; lie, lied, lied, lying

LESSON 33

Words Covered: stop, stopped; fish, fished; laugh, laughed; ask, asked;
choose, chose, chosen; before; America; tongue

LESSON 34

Words Covered: since; science; our, are;
pass, passed; past;
write, right, wright, rite

LESSON 35

Words Covered: suggest, suggestion; buried; keep, kept; doctor;
raspberry; suppose, supposed, supposing; purpose

LESSON 36

Words Covered: it's, its; your, you're; yourself, yourselves;
there, they're, their

LESSON 37

Words Covered: want, wanted; when; went; than, then;
machine; onion, union; animal; problem

SPELLING DEMON WORDS
COVERED IN EACH LESSON (Continued)

LESSON 38

Words Covered: enjoy, enjoyed, enjoys, enjoyment, enjoying;
journey, journeys, journeying, journeyed;
turkey, turkeys; alley, alleys;
who; whom; how; whose, who's; who'll

LESSON 39

Words Covered: decide, decision; Caesarean section; scissors;
afraid; among; across; above

LESSON 40

Words Covered: where; wear; were; (we're plus ware);
believe; friend; piece

PRONUNCIATION KEY: DICTIONARY MARKINGS

Accented Vowels

ă	at
ĕ	get
ĭ	it
ŏ	got
	(ä in *Webster's Collegiate*)
ŭ	but
ou	out, now

ā	ate
ē	feet
ī	ride
ō	rode
o͞o	rule
	(ü in *Thorndike* and *Webster's*)

ô	soft, or, paw
oi	oil, boy
o͝o	put, foot
	(u̇ in *Thorndike* and *Webster's*)
yo͞o	music
	(yü in *Thorndike* and *Webster's*)
ä	father

Unaccented Vowels:

a	about
e	item
i	edible
o	gallop
u	circus
y	martyr

Vowels Before *r*

âr	care
är	car
ûr	her, fur, sir
îr	pier

Consonants

j	jam, gem
g	go
k	cat, skate, tack
s	city, see

ch	church
sh	show
zh	television
th	thin
th	this
ng	sing
hw	what

---

1. Most dictionaries now don't mark the short vowels, but you should know the markings, because some do.

2. I point out *Thorndike* and *Webster's Collegiate* dictionary variations because so many schools use these dictionaries. My preference is for the *American Heritage Dictionary.*

 Spelling Demons Week by Week

FIRST QUARTER

LESSON 1

certain

Pronunciation: sûrt′ən

Syllables: *cer* -   c sounds like **s** because it's followed by an **e**. (If it were a **u**, you'd have to pronounce the **c** as a **k**—and you'd have *curtain*!) The most common spelling of the **ur** sound is **er**.

tain -   unaccented vowels—spelled **ai** (think of **certain rain** when you're climbing the moun**tain**, and pronounce it that way when you're spelling it.)

If you can't spell *certain*, can you spell *sure* instead?

minute

Pronunciation: mĭn′ĭt

Syllables: *min* - **mĭn** (sounds the way it's spelled)

ute - **ĭt** The **u** and final silent **e** don't make this syllable sound **ūt** in this word—a noun meaning a measure of time, such as 60 minutes in an hour—because this syllable is un-accented.

　　If you're talking about *minute* particles of matter or the *minute* details your teacher wants, then you want the adjective. The adjective is spelled the same way as the noun but pronounced **mī nūt′**—accented on the second syllable with a long o͞o sound. Maybe that will help you spell it even when it's pronounced **mĭn′ĭt**.

spinach

Pronunciation: spĭn′ĭch

　　Your favorite! Have you ever tried dipping spinach in pancake batter and French frying it? You can hardly taste the spinach.

　　But remember to put that **a** in the word. A? What **a**? The **a** after *spin*. **Spin a** plate 'a **spinach**! Unfortunately, the **a** sounds ĭ.

　　If you can spell the *spin* part of *spinach*—and that's easy—you have to look through only a couple of dictionary columns to find the rest of the spelling. That doesn't take long.

A.　Write the words for those spelled with dictionary markings:

1.　I eat **spĭn′ĭch** every **mĭn′ĭt** I can.

2.　Are you **sûrt′ən**?

3.　I **sûrt′ənlē** am.

4.　On the average, how many pounds of **spĭn′ĭch** do you eat in one day?

5.　Actually, only very **mī nūt′** quantities.

B.　Fill in the missing letters in the sentences, using the following words: *average, minute, spinach, bargain, certain(ly), captain, mountain.*

1.　The capt _____ n was cer _____ n to find a barg _____ n at that store.

2.　The mount _____ was _____ rtainly sending up a fount _____ n of steam!

3.　On the average, one eruption a min _____ .

4.　Better steam than spin _____ !

5.　Spin _____ gives me a stomachache.

6.　Those clouds will bring cert _____ n rain.

7.　Better rain than _____ ach!

8.　Would you rather eat orange squash?

LESSON 1 (Continued)

genuine
Pronunciation: jĕn′ yōō ĭn
Syllables: *gen* - **jĕn**   **g** with **e** after it has the **j** sound.
   u - **yōō**   a long **u** sound; as if there were a consonant **y** sound before the long double **o**.
   ine -   final silent **e**, but unaccented syllable, so **i** isn't long.
My diamond earrings are not *genuine*; they are fake.
Her concern for him is *genuine*.

privilege
Pronunciation: **prĭv′ ə lĭj**
Syllables: *priv* -   you can hear these letters. If you can find those in the dictionary, you have only one column of words to look through to find the rest of the word.
   i -   unaccented; hard to remember; think of yourself—think **I**; **I** like to have **privileges**, **I** do, especially if one of them is staying out late on Friday night.
   lege -   unfair spelling; It's the **lĭj** sound—**ij** like the **ij** sound in *average*, but this time it's spelled with an **e**. Remember how easy it is to find the word in the dictionary if you can't remember the spelling of this last syllable.

average
Pronunciation: (1) ăv′ rĭj (2) ăv′ ə rĭj
How's your batting *average?* What's your cumulative *average* in school? Are you an *average* student? or above *average?* What's the *average age* of the students in your class?
   The word has three syllables: *av er age.*
   av -   You hear both those letters.
   er -   You hear the **r**, but you may not pronounce the **e**. You don't have to, but you must *spell* the word with the **e**.
   age -   Can you remember: ave**rage** age? It could help. It's pronounced **ij**. The **e** makes the **g** a **j** sound.
   Many words with an **-age** ending are pronounced **ij**: *marriage, voyage, village, carriage, manage, encourage, damage.*

biscuit
Pronunciation: **bĭs′ kĭt**
   The **u** is silent. If we're going to spell the word with a **c**, then the **u** keeps the **k** sound (**c** followed by **i** would give an **s** sound). That **u** is silent in a number of words: *guess, build, buy, guard.*

C. Fill in the blanks to make the words: *encourage, carriage, damage, village, marriage, manage, voyage, privilege, genuine, biscuit.*

1. Will you ride in a carr _____ ge to your marr _____ ge ceremony?

2. Yes. Then we're taking a voy _____ to a vill _____ .

3. I encour _____ you to man _____ your finances so they don't dam _____ your marri _____ .

4. Finances are no problem. I make millions growing spinach.

D. Answer the questions, using the following words: *privilege, genuine.*

1. Is this the real diamond? Yes, it is the _____ one.

2. Seniors have the _____ of being first to get tickets.

LESSON 1
Additional Activities

1. In the following words, the first syllables are spelled correctly; the last syllables are written in dictionary pronunciation, the sounds being shown between slanted lines. The vowel sound in each syllable is a short **i** sound. How is the last syllable of each word *really* spelled?

   cer / tin / _____   genu / in / _____

   min / it / _____   privi / lij / _____

   aver / ij / _____   bis / kit / _____

2. What spelling do *certain* and *mountain* have in common?

3. How does thinking of the phrase "average age" help you to spell *average*?

4. If the **u** were not after the **c** in *biscuit*, how would you have to pronounce the word?

5. Some commercial establishments spell *minute* as "minit." What part of the word are they spelling incorrectly?

6. What is another way to pronounce *minute* to indicate its correct spelling? Mark the dictionary pronunciation of this word, which means "very small."

7. In *stomach*, the **ch** is pronounced **k**; in *spinach*, it is pronounced **ch**. What letter is before the **ch** in each word?

8. The letter **u** is in the middle of *genuine* as a separate syllable. What are the first and last syllables of that word?

9. How will you remember that *privilege* is spelled with **-ege** at the end? How will you remember that *privilege* has an **i** in the middle of the word? Write the word.

10. The pronunciation of the **c** in *certain* and *biscuit* and the pronunciation of the **g** in *average*, *privilege*, and *genuine* follow the rules for pronunciation of **c** and **g**. What are those rules?

Answers

LESSON 1

A. 1. spinach, minute
2. certain
3. certainly
4. spinach
5. minute

B. 1. **ai, ai, ai**
2. **ai, ce, ai**
3. **ute**
4. **ach**
5. **ach**
6. **ai**
7. **spin**
8. Yes, would you?

LESSON 1 (continued)

C. 1. **ia, ia**
2. **age, age**
3. **age, age, age, age**

D. 1. genuine
2. privilege

LESSON 1: Additional Activities

1. *tain* (*certain*)   *ine* (*genuine*)

   ute (*minute*)   *lege* (*privilege*)

   age (*average*)   *cuit* (*biscuit*)
2. the **-tain** ending
3. The word *age* makes up the last three letters of *average*.
4. **bis-sit**
5. **-ute**
6. mi nute′ mī nūt′
7. **a**
8. *gen* and *ine*
9. I might think that the two **i**'s come first and then the two **e**'s. I might mispronounce the last syllable as lē gē.

   I will pronounce the second **i** carefully as a short **i** when I spell the word. I may remember that the two **i**'s are the first two vowels in the word.   *privilege*
10. The letter **c** followed by an **e**, **i**, or **y** is pronounced as an **s** (*certain*).

    The letter **c** followed by an **a**, **o**, **u**, a consonant, or nothing is pronounced as a **k** (*biscuit*).

    The letter **g** followed by an **e**, **i**, or **y** is pronounced as a **j** (*average*, *privilege*, *genuine*).

    The letter **g** followed by an **a**, **o**, **u**, a consonant, or nothing is pronounced as a **g** (*go*).

LESSON 2

one   wŭn
Most of us can spell *one*. Although the word does not sound the way it looks, we can spell it probably because it is the first number we ever learned to spell. Look at it carefully, though, because it has a homonym (*won*) and because *once* and *only* are related to it. *One* is the number. I have **one** head, two feet, and ten toes.

only
Pronunciation: ōn′lē
It is an adjective and an adverb.
Meaning: alone in kind; sole
He was here *only* once before.
Think of: *one* plus *-ly*, but the **e** has been dropped from the word.
The word does not come from *own*.

once
Pronunciation: wŭns
The pronunciation doesn't seem to fit the word, does it? But think about the word:
1.   **o** is often pronounced short **u**:
     one, come, mother, of, none, done, Monday, from, onion
2.   An **e** (or an **i** or **y**) after a **c** makes the **c** soft—the **s** sound.
3.   The **n** *does* sound like an **n**.
4.   The **w** sound to begin the word is unexplained. Sorry!
Once means "one time only." Think of *one* when you spell *once*.

A.   Children's fairy tales often begin: "**Once** upon a time . . . " Can you write a preposterous tale on a separate sheet using the following words (or most of them) in which the **o** sounds **ŭ**? Begin with "Once upon a time."

once, onion, Mother, Monday, color, company, discover, governor, honeybee, money, somewhere, stomach, tongue, sponge, wonderful, dozen, ton, months, front, another, of, won, comfort, uncover, nothing, son, one

B.   Fill in the correct word: *one, once, won, only.*

1.   I ran in _____ race; Jimmy ran in two races.
2.   I came in last. I did not win. I have never _____ a race.
3.   I came in second. That happened to me _____ _____ .

C.   Fill in the crossword puzzle:

Across

1.   possess, have
4.   one time

Down

1.   number before two
2.   not any
3.   alone in kind

soldier
Pronunciation: sōl′jər
The first three letters are easy; the last four are not. The **d** has a **j** sound as in *individual, education, schedule,* and *gradual.* It is an **i** before **e** word, but all you hear is an unaccented vowel before the **r**.
British *soldiers* fought the Americans in the Revolutionary War.
In the woods you may see British *Soldiers,* the name given to gray-green lichen about an inch high topped by a tiny scarlet fruit.

LESSON 2 (Continued)

forty fôr′tē

This word is simply not fair! *Four* is spelled "fo**U**r," *fourteen* is spelled "fo**U**rteen," but *forty* is spelled "forty," without a **u**. If you can think of a mnemonic (memory trick) to help you, fine; otherwise, just learn the word.

I drove *forty* miles to *Fort* Washington for my *fortieth* birthday.

nine, ninety, nineteen, ninth

Here's another number group that is unfair. *Nine, ninety,* and *nineteen* all keep the **e**; *ninth* drops it. And all the **i**'s are pronounced as long **i**'s.

I suppose that if you put an **e** in *ninth*, you might have to pronounce the word in two syllables: **ni′neth** or **nin′eth**. Maybe that's why the **e** is dropped.

If you did *not* have the **e** in *ninety*, it would divide as *nin ty*, and then you would be pronouncing that word as **nĭn′ty**, not **nīn′ty**. Whatever; if you are keeping a list of difficult words, add *forty, ninety,* and *ninth*. They are already on my list.

hundred hŭn′drĭd

Pronounce it correctly and you will probably spell it correctly:

$\qquad$ *hun **d**red*, not *hun **d**erd*.

If I live to be one *hund**red*** I will paint my house **red**.

$\qquad$ *hundredth*—How's that for a word? It's hard to pronounce the

$\qquad$ **d** before the **th**, but that is the way to spell it.

This is the *hundredth* penny I have counted.

D.   Use words to fill in the correct numbers in the blanks:

1.   Four times ten equals _____ .
2.   Nine times ten equals _____ .
3.   After eighth comes _____ .
4.   After ninety-nine comes one _____ .
5.   After ninety-ninth comes _____ .

two, to, too

Two is another funny-looking one, isn't it? It is, however, so familiar to most of us that we don't misspell it. What we misspell are the other two words pronounced the same: *to* and *too*. Maybe we don't misspell them, but we aren't sure which one to use when.

$\quad$ *two*:   the number *2*:   Our family has *two* birthdays in February.

$\quad\;$ *to*:   (1) in the direction of: I go *to* the library on Wednesdays.

$\qquad$ *To* is a preposition in the above sentence. It is followed by an object (*library*). The object may have an adjective or an article before it (*the*).

$\qquad$ (2) *To* plus a verb equals what we call an infinitive:

$\qquad\qquad$ You have *to pass* a driving test in order *to get* your license.

$\quad$ *too*:   also, in addition: I want to play in the orchestra, *too*.

E.   Use the correct word (*two, to, too*) in each sentence:

1.   You are supposed _____ have only one dessert.
2.   I don't care. I want _____ .
3.   Do you want _____ helpings of spinach, _____ ?
4.   I do not want _____ eat any spinach.
5.   Then you may not go _____ the kitchen _____ get your dessert.
6.   Pass the spinach _____ me, please.
7.   I'll be glad _____ .

LESSON 2
Additional Activities

1. What two letters begin *one*, *only*, and *once*?

2. How is the **on** pronounced in *one* and *once*? How is it pronounced in *only*?

3. I saw this sign: "For Sale By Oner." How should that have been spelled?

4. What letter in *four* has been omitted in *forty*?

5. How do you form *ninety* and *nineteen* from *nine*?

6. How do you form *ninth* from *nine*?

7-14. Write the correct word (*two*, *too*, or *to*) in the following:

It is (7) _____ tiring (8) _____ do (9) _____ jobs.

I want (10) _____ take Russian, (11) _____ .

You'll have (12) _____ practice your tuba sometime other than 6 A.M.

(13) _____ bad! I like (14) _____ practice then.

15-18. Write the following numbers in words:

149 _____

291 _____

the year 1942 _____

the year 1492 _____

19. How is the **j** sound in *soldier* spelled?

20. What are the vowels in the last syllable of *soldier*? Does the order follow the rule for **ie/ei** words?

Answers

LESSON 2

A. Sample preposterous tale:

Once upon a time my mother made me eat an onion in front of the governor. He told my mother on Monday that it would be better to buy a honeybee so that my tongue could taste honey before it went to my stomach. I thought that was a wonderful idea, so we bought a dozen honeybees, and in a month, we had a ton of honey for comfort.

B.
1. one
2. won
3. Once; only once

C. Crossword Puzzle:

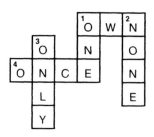

D.
1. forty
2. ninety
3. ninth
4. hundred
5. one-hundredth

E.
1. to
2. two
3. two, too
4. to
5. to, to
6. to
7. to (understood infinitive *to pass*)

LESSON 2: Additional Activities

1. **on**
2. **wun, ōn**
3. Owner
4. **u**
5. Add **ty** for *ninety* and add **teen** for *nineteen.*
6. You drop the **e** and add **th.**
7. too
8. to
9. two
10. to
11. too
12. to
13. Too
14. to
15. one hundred forty-nine
16. two hundred ninety-one
17. nineteen (hundred) (and) forty-two
18. fourteen (hundred) (and) ninety-two
19. **di**
20. **ie**; yes

10

LESSON 3

come, coming
A word ending in a final silent **e** drops that **e** before adding the suffix **-ing**.
Will you *come* out to my costume party?
Sure, I'm *coming* as a zombie. Remember?
The **o** sounds like a short **u**.

take, taking
A word ending in a final silent **e** drops that **e** before adding the suffix **-ing**.
Take your turn on the swing.
I'm *taking* turns. It's *my* turn.

make, making
A word ending in a final silent **e** drops that **e** before adding the suffix **-ing**.
Want to *make* a sand castle with me?
No, I'm *making* a sand monster.

have, having
A word ending in a final silent **e** drops that **e** before adding the suffix **-ing**.
I'm *having* a hard time learning to ride this bicycle.
I *have* a tricycle. Want to take that?

give, giving
A word ending in a final silent **e** drops that **e** before adding the suffix **-ing**.
Give me a push on the merry-go-round, will you, please?
I'm *giving* my little brother a push on the swing right now.

A. Use the **-ing** form of the verb in parentheses to fit in each sentence:
1. (come)   When will your brother be _____ home from college?
2. (take)   My little sister is always _____ my lipstick.
3. (make)   I'm _____ paper flowers for the school float.
4. (have)   Are you _____ a good time in the pool?
5. (give)   She's not _____ me my turn on the computer!

receive, received
When a word ends in a final silent **e**, then you need add only the **d** of **-ed** to make the past tense.
    re
  ceive   -   **e** before **i** after a **c** (the **c** sounds **s**)
    d   -   just **d** added rather than **-ed** because *receive* already ends in an **e**
I *received* a surprise when I brought in the mail.

B. Write the **-ed** form of the words in parentheses:
1. I was (surprise) _____ when I (receive) _____ a package. I
(believe) _____ the package was sent to me for my birthday by my Aunt
Margaret. The book (arrive) _____ the day before my birthday. I (notice)
_____ the postmark said Milwaukee. I (decide) _____ to open the
package early.
2. I'm going to play in a piano recital. My mother has (invite) _____ my
cousins, who should have (arrive) _____ by now. I've (practice)
_____ and (practice) _____ and (practice) _____ . I think
I'm really (prepare) _____ now.

LESSON 3 (Continued)

write, writing

When a verb ends in a final silent **e**, drop that **e** before adding the suffix **-ing**.

Write also begins with a silent letter: **w**. **W**rite, **w**rote, **w**ritten have the silent **w**. Will you *write* a thank-you letter to your aunt for that book?

C.   I'm _____ Grandma now to thank her for the computer games. I've already *written* Aunt Meg. I *wrote* her yesterday.

smile, smiling

When a verb ends in a final silent **e**, drop that **e** before adding the suffix **-ing**.

D.   That boy always has a *smile* on his face. He is always _____ at me. I wonder if he wants to ask me out.

lose, losing

When a verb ends in a final silent **e**, drop that **e** before adding the suffix **-ing**.

This word is pronounced lo͞oz. If you **lose** something, you can't find it. Don't mix it up with *loose*, pronounced lo͞os, meaning "not tight."

E.   Did you *lose* your homework? You are always _____ things.

real, really
usual, usually

The usual way to make an adverb from an adjective is to add **-ly**. If the word already ends in **l**, you still add **-ly**, which will give you two **l**'s in the word. Think what the adjective looks like before you shortchange the adverb. (It's *real* that you add **-ly** to, not *rea*!)

  usual/usually   real/really   original/originally   typical/typically

If the word *already* ends in two **l**'s, just add **y**: *full/fully*. You don't need three **l**'s.

Some words that end in **-le** or **e** drop that **e** before adding **-ly**:

  whole/wholly   true/truly   probable/probably   terrible/terribly

sincere, sincerely

Pronunciation: sĭn sîr′

The second **s** sound is spelled with a **c** (followed by an **e** to give it the soft **s** sound). The îr sound is spelled **ere**, like *here*.

Remember to keep the last **e** when you add **-ly**.

F.   Make the adjective following each sentence into an adverb by adding **-ly** and making any other necessary spelling changes. Write the adverb in the blank:

1.   This is a real treat. I _____ like these scissors. (real)

2.   The usual scissors are for right-handed people. I _____ have to use those. (usual)

3.   I _____ hope we will always have left-handed scissors for left-handed people. (sincere)

4.   It is _____ difficult for a left-hander to use right-handed scissors. (terrible)

5.   A right-hander can _____ not _____ appreciate the troubles left-handers have. (true/full)

6.   They _____ have never thought about it. (probable)

7.   It is a _____ new concept for them. (whole)

LESSON 3
Additional Activities

1. Words ending in a final silent **e** drop that **e** before adding **-ing**. Add **-ing** to *come*, *take*, *make*, *have*, *give*, *write*, *smile*, *receive*, and *lose*.

2. If a verb is "regular," it adds **-ed** to make the past tense. If that regular verb already ends in **e**, you will just add **d** to the word. Make the past tense of *receive*, *arrive*, *decide*, *practice*, *believe*, and *prepare*.

3. To make an adjective (*quick*) into an adverb (*quickly*), you usually add **-ly**. If the word already ends in **l**, you still add **-ly**. That will give you two **l**'s in the word. Make adverbs from the adjectives *real*, *usual*, and *sincere*.

4. There are two commonly used adjectives ending in **e** or **-le** that drop the **e** before adding **-ly**. They are *whole* and *true*. In two other adjectives, *probable* and *terrible*, a consonant precedes the **l**. Drop the **e** and the **l** before adding **-ly**.

5. Sign a letter "Sincerely yours,". Remember to capitalize the first word of that closing but not the second. Remember the **e** before the **-ly**, too. Write it again to be sure you have it correct.

Answers

LESSON 3

A. 1. coming
   2. taking
   3. making
   4. having
   5. giving

B. 1. surprised, received, believed, arrived, noticed, decided
   2. invited, arrived, practiced, practiced, practiced, prepared

LESSON 3 (Continued)

C. writing
D. smiling
E. losing

F. 1. really
   2. usually
   3. sincerely
   4. terribly
   5. truly, fully
   6. probably
   7. wholly

LESSON 3: Additional Activities

1. coming
   taking
   making
   having
   giving
   writing
   smiling
   receiving
   losing

2. received
   arrived
   decided
   practiced
   believed
   prepared

3. really
   usually
   sincerely

4. wholly
   truly
   probably
   terribly

5. Sincerely yours,
   Sincerely yours,

LESSON 4

mayonnaise

Syllables: *may on naise*

Pronunciation: mā ə nāz′

For me, *mayonnaise* is another one of those words that requires me to remember whether it has two **n**'s or two of something else—like these words: *questionnaire, accommodate, recommend.*

(1) *questionnaire* - I want to answer "**No, no!**" to filling out a questio**nn**aire.

(2) *accommodate*: When you a**cc**o**mm**odate someone, you go all out, so you have both two **c**'s and two **m**'s.

(3) *recommend*: You're not going *all* out; you're just re**c**o**mm**ending something, so you have only one **c** and two **m**'s. I'd **recommend M & M**'s to anyone, especially myself!

Back to *mayonnaise* and *broccoli*—tricks, mnemonics, whatever will help you remember— use them. I'll tell you mine in case they are helpful to you. If not, make up your own.

I use **mayonnaise** on   **broccoli**

2   1   **2   1**

And how do you remember which is two and which is one? You can take all your broccoli and throw it into the two seas (**c**'s)—the Atlanti**c** and the Pacifi**c**. Can you think of a pi**cc**olo when you think of bro**cc**oli—two **c**'s, one **l**? I'd rather listen to a **piccolo** then eat **broccoli**. Can you think of some other ways to remember the two **c**'s and one **l**? We could all eat spinach, instead!

cauliflower

Pronunciation: kô′ lĭ flou ər

If you have seen a cauliflower, you can see why the "flower" is part of the name. It certainly looks like a flower, not the flour you make a cake from. The part you eat is actually made up of undeveloped flowers. If you let it keep growing, the flowers open up. A head of broccoli turns into yellow flowers. What color do you suppose cauliflowers are? Where will you find out?

It's the **cauli** you have to remember:

    cau   -   the **au** sound as in *daughter*
    li   -   like the **li** in *broccoli*

broccoli

Pronunciation: brŏk′ ə lē

It is related to **c**abbage and **c**auliflower, so it has two **c**'s. I put mayo**nn**aise on bro**cc**oli—the double letters come in the middle of the words.

This word confuses a lot of people. Learn it!

A.   On a separate sheet (or the back of this sheet), write a very serious or a very funny story using the words below in the order they are written. Of course, you will have to insert a few other words, also. Have a friend write a story using the words in the opposite direction.

> beginning, broccoli, could've, written, February, lb., answer, hundred,
> mayonnaise, separate, surprise, a lot, library, busy, cauliflower,
> beautiful, oz., until, polka dot, write, etc., business, ampersand,
> beauty, people, wrote, end

LESSON 4 (Continued)

Vegetables! Crossword Puzzle

Across

3. long and orange (plural form)
7. not a vegetable; you put it on broccoli or on BLT sandwiches
8. green flower head; rhymes with Monopoly
9. small, round, red; often used in salads (plural form)
10. small, round, green (plural form)
11. long green, long yellow, acorn, huge, all kinds
12. grows on ears (not yours, I hope)
15. water is one kind of them (a fruit; plural form)
16. not a chicken egg! It's purple, although it can be white, too
17. green or red, used in tomato sauce; sometimes hot! (plural form)
19. red, round, juicy (plural form)
20. animal who ate everything in my garden but eggplant and tomatoes

Down

1. green; leafy or in heads
2. green; used in pickles, too
4. white flower head
5. green, tightly packed; used for cole slaw
6. thin, long, green (plural form)
8. small, light green; look like tiny cabbages growing up a stalk
13. leafy, green; Popeye eats it.
14. French fried _____ rings are good!
18. white, grown underground; used for French fries and chips, too (plural form)

Spelling Demons Week by Week

LESSON 4
Additional Activities

1. In what way is *piccolo* spelled like *broccoli*?

2. In what way is *broccoli* spelled like *mayonnaise*?

3. How do you get the long **e** sound in *broccoli*?

4. What is the sound of each **o** in *broccoli*?

5. How would spelling *Donna* help you to spell *mayonnaise*?

Answers

LESSON 4

A. Sample Stories:

In the beginning, people should have considered broccoli to be a flower, not a vegetable. We could've written the praises of its yellow flower in February and never had to eat it by the lb. The answer to the dilemma of eating broccoli is to have it as one hundred flowers instead. We now put mayonnaise on the separate parts of broccoli. Sometimes you even get a surprise of a green worm that is just the color of broccoli. There are never a lot of worms, but one is enough. I went to the library and was very busy writing a term paper about cauliflower, which I think is more beautiful than broccoli. An oz. of broccoli goes a long way. I was working hard until a girl in a polka dot dress walked into the library to write a paper on broccoli, beans, peas, etc. It was none of my business what she was writing about, but I saw her use an ampersand in her title. She had such beauty that I was surprised people wrote about her as the cauliflower queen. That put an end to my interest.

In the end, I wrote people about the beauty of cauliflower. I used an ampersand in my letter. I told them about the business, the marketing, etc., and asked them to write me if they had polka dots on their vegetables. Until yesterday, I had not received an oz. of mail about the beautiful cauliflower. But today I am busy in the library answering a lot of mail, which came as a surprise. I will separate the letters because someone spilled mayonnaise on one of them. I must have one hundred letters. How can I answer them all? I'll need a lb. of paper. By February, I shall have written all I could've, and I'll start asking about broccoli for another beginning.

LESSON 4 (Continued)
Vegetables! Crossword Puzzle:

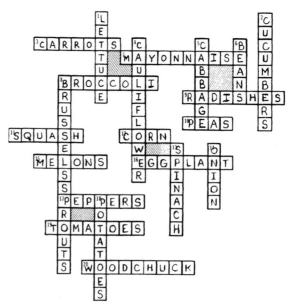

LESSON 4: Additional Activities

1. It has two **c**'s in the middle of the word and only one **l**.
2. It has its double consonant (**c**) in the middle of the word, like *mayonnaise* (**n**).
3. from the **i**
4. The first **o** is short; the second **o** is long.
5. *Donna* has **onna**, and so does *mayonnaise* (*Donna/yonna*).

18

LESSON 5

neighbor
Pronunciation: nā′bər
    i before **e**
    except after **c** (unless **c** sounds **sh**)
    and except when it sounds long **a**
    as in *neighbor* and *weigh*,
    plus lots of exceptions you should learn or keep in a list

    I've changed that rule slightly, but one part of the rule that's always true is that if the vowel sound is long **a** (ā), then it will be spelled **ei**, not **ie**.
    There's the word from the jingle: *neighbor*.

A.   Write the correct spelling for the words written in dictionary pronunciation. Remember, they are all **ei** words. A list of them follows.

      You say your (nā′bər) _____ (nāz) _____ ? But only horses (nā) _____ . She's not a horse. It does sound as if she's (nā ′ĭng) _____ doesn't it? Hm! How much does your (nā′bər) _____ (wā) _____ ? You say she rides the (frāt) _____ elevator? And she pulls a (slā) _____ ? And there are (rānz) _____ on her? Better carry out a little more (sûr vā′ləns) _____ . Maybe your (nā′bər) _____ *is* a horse.

    neighbor, weigh, neigh, neighs, neighing, surveillance, sleigh, freight, reins

weigh
Pronunciation: wā
    There's the other famous word from the jingle: *weigh*.
    ei when it sounds long **a**
    as in *neighbor* and *weigh*
Silly bug says: Oh, I thought it was *way*!
No, no, no—we're talking about **ie** and **ei** words. *Way* is another word. We're talking about *weigh*.
    It's **w ei** with a **gh** on the end to make it harder. Think *GHost*—I weigh nothing, like a **gh**ost.

B.   Fill in one of the following words to make sense in the sentence: *weigh, neighbor, overweight, eighty, weighed, eight, eighteen, weight, weighs.*

      My (nā′bər) _____ (wāz) _____ 300 pounds. She is (ō vər wāt′) _____ . She should lose (wāt) _____ for her health. She (wāz) _____ so much she can take only (āt) _____ steps at a time. When she was (āt) _____ years old, she (wād) _____ (āt′ ē) _____ pounds; when she was (āt ēn′) _____ , she (wād) _____ one hundred (āt′ ē) _____ pounds. I wonder if my (nā′bər) _____ likes butter on her popcorn. Maybe I should go (wā) _____ myself.
    Don't forget the **gh** after the **ei**: *weigh*. (**Wei** alone would look funny, wouldn't it?)
    To spell *weight*, put a **t** on the end of **weigh**.
    Wait is the homonym for *weight*.
I lifted *weights* during my *waits* for doughnuts.

weigh/way
    When you **weigh** yourself on the scales, you're trying to find out how many pounds you have gained or lost. You want to find out your **weight**.
Way means "manner of doing something" or "the route."
This is the *way* to my house.
Shall we *weigh* ourselves on the *way* to dinner?

LESSON 5 (Continued)

reign, rein, rain

The word you'll use the most is *rain*—that wet stuff falling down on your umbrella, or on your head if you forgot your umbrella.

The other two are **ei** words sounding **a**, so they fit the rule.

Rein (usually plural *reins*) is used with a horse or a pony. That's what you hang onto to make the animal do what you command.

Reign refers to rule. A king **reigns**. *King* has a **g**; so does *reign*. Think of the word *regal*, which refers to kings and queens. That has a **g** in it, also.

C. Fill in the blanks with the correct word: *reign(s)*, *rein(s)*, *rain*.

1. What king _____ in this foreign country?
2. Hold the reindeer's lines (_____) while I fill the sleigh.
3. I don't want to get wet in the _____ , holding the reindeer.
4. The _____ (ing) king held the _____ (s) in the _____ .
5. The government was trying to put the _____ (s) on inflation.

foreign

Pronunciation: fôr´ən

It comes from a word meaning "outside." That helps with the meaning but not with the spelling. Look at the last part of the word: *reign*. Think of a **reign** of a fo**reign** king, and maybe that will help you with the spelling. Think **rān** in *reign* for a long **a** sound to spell it **ei**.

eight

Pronunciation: āt

The vowel sound is long **a**, so it is spelled **ei**.
Related words:

eighty	*eight y*	just add a **y**
eighteen	*eight een*	just add **-een**
eighth (8*th*)	*eight h*	just add **h**. The **t** is already there to make the **th** sound with the final **h**.

freight

Pronunciation: frāt

The vowel sound is long **a**, so it is spelled **ei**.

It rhymes with *eight* and *weight*.

A passenger train carries people; a **freight** train carries things: hogs, cars, oil, logs, popcorn. A **freight** elevator carries goods, although people can ride in it, too. A **freighter** is a ship that carries cargo such as grain or oil.

Don't forget the **gh**: *freiGHt*.

D. What can you do with **eigh**?

1. Put **w** in front of it: _____ .
2. Keep the **w** in front and add a **t** at the end: _____ .
3. Keep the **t** at the end; subtract the **w**: _____ .
4. Now add **-een** at the end: _____ .
5. Take off the **-een** and add a **y**: _____ .
6. Take off the **-ty**; put an **n** on the front: _____ .
7. Keep the **n** on the front and add *-bor* on the end: _____ .
8. Now add *-ly* to that word: _____ .
9. Go back to **eigh** by itself and add **fr** to the beginning and **t** at the end: _____ .

                   Spelling Demons Week by Week

LESSON 5
Additional Activities

1. How is the long **a** sound spelled in *neighbor*, *weigh*, *reign*, *rein*, *eight*, and *freight*?

2. How does knowing the spelling of *reign* help you to spell *foreign*?

3. What are the silent letters in *neighbor*, *weigh*, *eight*, and *freight*? What is the silent letter in *reign* and *foreign*?

4. Write a sentence using the words *reign*, *rein*, and *rain*.

5. Write a sentence using the words *weigh* and *way*.

6. What are some incorrect ways to spell *neighbor*? Why would someone misspell the word in those ways?

7. Spell the words for the numerals 8, 80, 18, and 8th.

8. How does thinking of the word *king* help you to remember the spelling of *reign*?

9. Write the words for the years 1800, 1880, 1818, and the 1800s.

10. What are the homonyms for *rein*? for *eight*? for *weigh*?

Answers

LESSON 5

A. neighbor, neighs, neigh, neighing, neighbor, weigh, freight, sleigh, reins, surveillance, neighbor

B. neighbor, weighs, overweight, weight, weighs, eight, eight, weighed, eighty, eighteen, weighed, eighty, neighbor, weigh

LESSON 5 (Continued)

C.
1. reigns
2. reins
3. rain
4. reign(ing), rein(s), rain
5. rein(s)

D.
1. weigh
2. weight
3. eight
4. eighteen
5. eighty
6. neigh
7. neighbor
8. neighborly
9. freight

LESSON 5: Additional Activities

1. **ei**
2. The letters of the word *reign* are at the end of *foreign.*
3. **gh**
   g
4. Sample sentence: I will **reign** with a **rein** in the **rain.**
5. Sample sentence: Which **way** will I **weigh** the most: with shoes or without?
6. Nabor, nabur, naber, nieghbor
   Someone might hear the long **a** sound and spell it as an **a**; someone might not know how to spell the schwa/**r** sound; someone might not know that it was an **ei** word, not an **ie** word.
7. eight, eighty, eighteen, eighth
8. The word *king* has a **g** in it; so does *reign*. A **king reigns**.
9. eighteen hundred, eighteen (hundred) eighty, eighteen (hundred) eighteen, the eighteen hundreds
10. reign, rain; ate; way

LESSON 6

life, **lives** - noun
live, **lives** - verb

noun: (one) *life* for singular;   (two) *lives* for plural;
               Pronunciation: līf   Pronunciation: līvz

verb: I, you, we, and they *live*;   he, she, it *lives*
               Pronunciation: lĭv   Pronunciation: lĭvz

You have memorized lists of plurals, and you have looked at the principal parts of verbs. Have you considered noun plurals and verb parts together? It *could* help you in your spelling.

The plural for *life* is *lives* (līvz). The **f** changes to **v**. The third person singular form of the verb *live* to go with *he*, *she*, and *it* is *lives* (lĭvz): he **lives**, she **lives**, it **lives**.
The wolf has fourteen *lives*. (līvz)
She *lives* in an orange house. (lĭvz)

belief, beliefs

Belief is a noun. The plural is *beliefs*. That word does not change the **f** to **v** in the plural. How will you find out which words change and which don't? Use the dictionary. It is user friendly, and it will tell you. If it doesn't tell you a special plural, you can correctly assume that the word just adds **s**.
Believe is the verb. I *believe*; you *believe*; he or she *believes*.

A. Follow the directions:

1. A group of words ending in **-lf** change that **f** to **v** before adding **-es** for the plural:
             half, calf, shelf, self, elf, wolf
    Write the plural of each of those.

2. Some one-syllable words with two vowels before the **f** change the **f** to **v** before adding **-es** for the plural: *leaf, loaf, thief.*
    Write the plurals for those words.

3. Write the pronunciation of the italicized words in each of these sentences:
    a. Do you believe a cat has nine *lives*?
    b. If a cat has nine *lives*, how many *lives* does a dog have?
    c. Who *lives* in that house?
    d. I *live* there.

4. Write the part of speech for the italicized words. (Are they nouns or verbs?)
    a. I *believe* in eating chocolate cake for breakfast.
    b. That's a crazy *belief*.
    c. I know. Want to hear some of my other *beliefs*?
    d. No, thanks; I *believe* not.
    e. Where do you *live*?
    f. I *live* in Farmington. My sister *lives* in Barrington.
    g. How many *lives* does a frog have?

5. Write the plural of the words in parentheses:
    On our farm we raise (elf) _____ , (calf) _____ , and wolf _____ . (Thief) _____ have sometimes tried to steal our (elf) _____ , but we are careful to hide them under (leaf) _____ . To feed these special creatures, we need one hundred (loaf) _____ of bread a day. Our (elf) _____ help make the bread. With (knife) _____ , they cut the (loaf) _____ into (half) _____ for themselves. They store the (loaf) _____ on special (shelf) _____ . Our (life) _____ on the farm are busy.

        Spelling Demons Week by Week

NAME _____ DATE _____

LESSON 6 (Continued)

roof, roofs

one *roof*, two *roofs*   You just add **s** for the plural.

Pronunciation: (1) rōof, rōofs
                (2) ro͝of, ro͝ofs

The **roofing** contractor told me that he has put four **roofs** on houses on our block. He also said that people in the Middle West tend to say **rōof** and people in the East tend to say **ro͝of**. However you say it, you spell it the same, and you need one on your house.

If you have a horse instead, you will be talking about a **ho͝of**. You can talk about **hoofs** or **hooves**—you have a choice of spelling. And you have a choice of pronunciations, too: **ho͝ofs, hōofs, ho͝ofz,** or **hōofz**. No matter, the horse still needs a **hoof**.

Scarf and *wharf* can also take either plural. It's nice to have a choice, isn't it? Just be consistent. Don't speak of **scarves** in one sentence and **scarfs** in the next.

Look at the lists:

Just add s for the plural	**Change f to v then add -es**	**Choice of plural**
roof, roofs	life, lives	hoof, hoofs, hooves
dwarf, dwarfs	wife, wives	scarf, scarfs, scarves
bluff, bluffs	knife, knives	wharf, wharfs, wharves
proof, proofs	half, halves	
turf, turfs	calf, calves	
skiff, skiffs	wolf, wolves	
chef, chefs	elf, elves	
belief, beliefs	self, selves	
chief, chiefs	shelf, shelves	
handkerchief, handkerchiefs	leaf, leaves	
sheriff, sheriffs	loaf, loaves	
	thief, thieves	

B.   That's quite a list of words. Check the ones you're likely to use. Do you know the plural form—for sure? If not, add them to that list you're keeping of difficult words. For me, other than *belief*, most of the words I'll use change the **f** to **v** for the plural.

C.   Use *roof* or *roofs* in the blanks:

1.   We have put two new _____ on our house in all the years we've lived here.

2.   When did you last put a new _____ on your house?

D.   Find the correct spelling in the puzzle of the plurals of *wife, belief, shelf, self, roof,* and *leaf.*

```
w  i  v  e  s  h  e  s  s
r  s  i  h  a  l  f  s  e
o  i  e  l  o  a  f  s  v
o  l  v  v  e  f  a  e  l
f  e  m  l  a  a  r  i  e
s  b  e  l  i  e  v  e  s
e  b  s  f  e  i  l  e  b
i  s  h  e  l  v  e  s  s
```

LESSON 6
Additional Activities

1. A cat has nine **lives**. How do you pronounce the plural of *life*, which is *lives*? Mark it with dictionary markings.

2. My cat **lives** dangerously. How do you pronounce the third person singular verb form of *live*, which is *lives*? Mark it with dictionary markings.

3. To make the plural of *life*, you change the **f** to **v** and add **-es**. How do you form the plural of *belief*?

4. *Belief* is a noun. What part of speech is *believe*?

5. Write the plurals for these words ending in **-lf**: *wolf, elf, self, shelf, calf, half*.

6. Write the plurals for these words ending in **f** preceded by two vowels: *thief, leaf, loaf*.

7. *Belief* ends in **f** preceded by two vowels. Do you form its plural like *thief, leaf, loaf*? How do you form its plural? How do you form the plurals of *chief* and *handkerchief*?

8. What statement could you make about the plurals of the **-ief** words of *belief, chief, handkerchief*, and *thief*?

9. Write the plurals of *wife* and *knife*.

10. What are the choices of plurals for *scarf*?

Answers

LESSON 6

A. 1. halves, calves, shelves, selves, elves, wolves

    2. leaves, loaves, thieves

    3. a. lĭvz

       b. lĭvz, līvz

       c. lĭvz

       d. līv

    4. a. verb

       b. noun

       c. noun

       d. verb

       e. verb

       f. verb, verb

       g. noun

    5. elves, calves, wolves, thieves, elves, leaves, loaves, elves, knives, loaves, halves, loaves, shelves, lives

LESSON 6 (Continued)

B. *belief, handkerchief, life, knife, half, self, shelf, leaf,* and *loaf* are the words I will use the most.

C. 1. roofs

    2. roof

D.   Puzzle

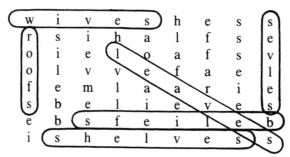

LESSON 6: Additional Activities

1. līvz
2. lĭvz
3. Just add **s.**
4. a verb
5. wolves   shelves

   elves   calves

   selves   halves

6. thieves

   leaves

   loaves

7. No, you just add **s.** Again, you just add **s:** *chief, chiefs; handkerchief, handkerchiefs.*
8. You form the plural of *belief, chief,* and *handkerchief,* all **-ief** words, by just adding **s.** To form the plural of *thief*—even though it's another **-ief** word—you change the **f** to **v** and add **-es.**
9. wives, knives
10. scarfs, scarves

26

LESSON 7

study, **studies** - noun
study, **studies**, **studied**, **studying** - verb

1. A noun will change that **y** to **i** before adding **-es** for the plural.
2. A verb will change that **y** to **i**:
   a.) before adding **-es** for the third person singular
      I is called the first person.
      You are called the second person.
      All the other people are considered the third persons.
      Third person singular is one person: he, she, it, the dog, the cat—anyone but you or me.
      The third person singular adds **s** to a verb.
   I *walk*; she *walks*. I *type*; he *types*.
      When the verb ends in **y** preceded by a consonant, you change the **y** to **i** and then add **-es**.
   I *study*; she *studies*.
   b.) before adding **-ed** for the past tense (for any person).
   I *study* today; I *studied* yesterday.
3. A noun *or* verb ending in **y** after a consonant will *keep* the **y** before the suffix **-ing** or **-ist** (to avoid two **i**'s coming together).
She worked as a *lobbyist* for civil rights.

try, tries, tried, trying   **reply, replies, replied, replying**
cry, cries, cried, crying   **fly, flies,** (Surprise:) **flew, flown** (!), **flying**
Note that the **y** at the end of these words sounds like a long **i**.
I will *try* to *reply* without a *cry* when the *fly flies* by.
I *tried*, but I *cried* when I *replied*.
I am *trying* to *fly*. *Flying* looks like fun. If I jump out of this tree and I am not able to *fly*, I will be *crying* when I fall.
Don't jump, silly!

A. Substitute the plural for each word in parentheses:
1. I'll give you three (try) _____ to guess what I have in my hand.
2. Two (fly) _____ .
3. No.
4. Three (fly) _____ .
5. No.
6. An elephant.
7. Yes. What color?

country, countries
Pronunciation: **kŭn′trē**
The **k** sound is spelled **c** as in *cousin, county, copy*.
The short **u** sound is spelled **ou** as in *cousin, enough, rough, trouble*.
The long **e** sound is spelled **y** as in *library, copy, February*.
When **y** is preceded by a consonant, change **y** to **i** and then add **-es** to make the plural: *country, countries*.
Countries are usually divided into smaller governmental units.
Canada divides into provinces; our *country*, into states. Our states are then divided into *counties*.

The Soviet Union was once one powerful country. After 1991, it was divided into several independent countries.

LESSON 7 (Continued)

company, companies
Pronunciation: kŭm´pə nē
> The **o** sounds like a short **u** as in *brother, son*.
> The word ends in **any**, pronounced ĕn´ĕ.
A word, noun or verb, ending in **y** preceded by a consonant changes the **y** to **i** before the suffix **-es**.
My mother is having *company* next Monday for dinner.
My brother and my dad work for different *companies*.

enemy, enemies
Pronunciation: ĕn´ə mē
> Sound the word carefully, so you put the **n** and the **m** in the right places. The final **y** sounds long **e**.
> A word, noun or verb, ending in **y** preceded by a consonant changes the **y** to **i** before the suffix **-es**.
A country tries to get along with its neighbors so it won't have *enemies*.

county, counties
Pronunciation: koun´tē
> The only spelling difference between *county* and *country* is an **r**. In the United States, a **county** is a division of a state, which is a division of a **country**.

ally, allies
Pronunciation: ăl´ī
Meaning: close associate; one united with another in some formal or personal relationship.
In World War II, the United States, Great Britain, France, Russia, and China were the *Allies* against the Axis countries of Germany, Italy, and Japan.

story, stories
Pronunciation: stôr´ē
> Don't forget to change the **y**, sounding long **e**, to **i** before you add the **-es** for the plural.

B.   Use the correct plural spelling of the words in the parentheses in each sentence:
1.   (library, study)   You may use any of the town's _____ to do your social _____ reading.
2.   (lady, reply)   The _____ sent their _____ by mail.
3.   (sky, country)   The _____ of many _____ were affected by the volcano.
4.   (try, story)   How many _____ do you need to guess the titles of the _____ ?
5.   (supply, country)   We get our _____ from three different _____ .
6.   (story, ally)   We wrote _____ about our _____ in the war.
7.   (county, country)   How many _____ are in our entire country? How many _____ are in the entire world? Where will you find out?

C.   All the following nouns end in a consonant before the **y**. Write their plurals, changing the **y** to **i** before adding **-es**:

baby	_____	lady	_____	copy	_____
strawberry	_____	raspberry	_____	butterfly	_____
penny	_____	jelly	_____	sky	_____
dairy	_____	diary	_____	candy	_____
laundry	_____	history	_____	party	_____
supply	_____	family	_____	sissy	_____
city	_____	puppy	_____	lily	_____
factory	_____	cherry	_____	county	_____
duty	_____	story	_____		

LESSON 7
Additional Activities

1. The past tense of *try* is *tried*. The past tense of *fly* is *flew*. If you don't know what the past tense of a verb is, look in the dictionary. Most dictionaries will tell you the past tense of a verb right after the pronunciation, while others place it at the very end of the entry. It will say for *fly: flew, flown, flying*. It may say "pt" for "past tense." If the verb is regular, but the spelling of the past tense changes, the dictionary will still tell you. It will have for *try: tried*—to show you that the **y** changes to **i** before adding **-ed**. What is the past tense of fry?

2. Why do you keep the **y** before adding **-ing** to words ending in **y** like *study, reply,* or *cry*?

3. What is the difference in spelling between *country* and *county*?

4. Write the singular of *studies, companies, allies, stories, tries, cries, replies,* and *flies*.

5. Write the plural of *baby, candy, history, family, city,* and *lily*.

6. What is the rule for forming the plurals of words ending in a consonant before the **y**?

7. Why would you *not* form the plural of the name *Mary* by changing the **y** to **i**? How would you form the plural of the name? What's another way you could indicate the plural?

8. What do we mean when we talk about the "person" of a verb? What person is *I? you? he, she,* or *it? we? they? popcorn? doughnuts?*

9. How is the short **u** sound in *company* spelled? in *country*?

Answers

LESSON 7

A. 1. tries
2. flies
4. flies

LESSON 7 (Continued)

B. 1. libraries, studies
2. ladies, replies
3. skies, countries
4. tries, stories
5. supplies, countries
6. stories, allies
7. counties, countries

C. babies, strawberries, pennies, dairies, laundries, supplies, cities, factories, duties, ladies, raspberries, jellies, diaries, histories, families, puppies, cherries, stories, copies, butterflies, skies, candies, parties, sissies, lilies, counties

LESSON 7: Additional Activities

1. fried

2. We rarely have two **i**'s together in English. The **y** retains the long **e** sound, and the **i** in the **-ing** has the short **i** sound.

3. Country has an **r** between the **t** and the **y**.

4. study
company
ally
story
try
cry
reply
fly

5. babies
candies
histories
families
cities
lilies

6. If a noun has a consonant before the final **y**, change the **y** to **i** and add **-es** to form the plural.

7. It would change the name of Mary to Marie. The plural is formed by adding an **s**: two Marys. Another way to indicate the plural would be to say two women named Mary.

8. "Person" refers to the distinction between the speaker, the one spoken to, and the one spoken about. *I* and *we* are the first person; *you* is the second person; *he, she, it,* and *they* are the third person. *Popcorn* and *doughnuts* are the third person.

9. In the word *company*, the short **u** sound is spelled with an **o**; in *country*, the short **u** sound is spelled **ou**.

LESSON 8

plan, **planned**, **planning**
hop, **hopped**, **hopping**

These are one-one-one words:
1. *one*-syllable words . . .
2. ending in *one* consonant that is . . .
3. preceded by *one* vowel.

Before you add a suffix beginning with a vowel to a one-one-one word, double the consonant. That keeps the pronunciation of the short vowel sound.

Today I *plan*; yesterday I *planned*; I have been *planning* all this week.

The bunnies *hop* today; they *hopped* yesterday; they have been *hopping* so long they're tired.

If you didn't double the **n** in *plan*, you'd have **plāned**, which is not the word you want at all. *Planed* means you took wood strips off or you zoomed along the ground like an airplane.

If you didn't double the **p** in *hop*, you'd have **hōped**. You may *hope* for a sunny day, but the bunnies are *hopping*.

Which of the following are one-one-one words?

  run   scream   swim   come   jump   walk   rob   carry

Run, *swim*, and *rob* are.
Jump and *walk* have two final consonants.
Scream has two vowels before the consonant.
Come and *carry* have no final consonant.

A. Use the **-ed** or **-ing** form of the word in parentheses in each sentence:
1. (get)   It is _____ dark before dinner now.
2. (stop) It _____ raining before noon.
3. (swim) _____ is good exercise.
4. (drop) _____ trash on the highway is inexcusable.
5. (run)   The buses are_____ late this morning.
6. (drop) He _____ the car trash into the container.
7. (stop) She _____ the car and waited for the train to pass.
8. (plan) We are_____ for a crowd of 100.
9. (hop)   The kangaroos _____ over Australia's grassy plain.
10. (hop)   _____ on one foot is hard work.

big, **bigger**, **biggest**

Two other suffixes beginning with vowels are **-er** and **-est**. They form the *comparative* and *superlative* of adjectives. What do those words mean? They're big words for "more of something" and "the most of something."

My *big* toe is *bigger* than your *big* toe.   (comparative)
My *big* toe is the *biggest big* toe of all.   (superlative)

When you add **-er** and **-est** to one-one-one words, be sure to double the final consonant first. Do that with the following adjectives:

B. *red, hot, sad, thin, mad, fat*

If you add the suffix **-ish** to a one-one-one word, double that consonant also: *red, reddish*.

plan, **planner**

You can add the suffix **-er** to some verbs to make nouns. He **plans** every hour of his day; he is a real **planner**.

With one-one-one words, be sure to double the final consonant before you add the **-er**. Do so with the following verbs:

C. *stop, bid, rob*

LESSON 8 (Continued)

begin, beginning

Begin is a *two*-syllable word, so it's not a one-one-one word. But, two-syllable words with the one-one spelling (one final consonant preceded by one vowel) double the final consonant before a prefix beginning with a vowel *if the accent is on the last syllable. Begin* is accented on the last syllable.

be gin   be ginning
1 1   doubled

Beginning is one of the top ten words misspelled. Watch out!

commit

Commit is a two-syllable word, ending in one consonant preceded by one vowel, with the accent on the last syllable; therefore, the **t** is doubled before a suffix beginning with a vowel.

Don't let the two **m**'s in the middle keep you from doubling the **t** before **-ed** and **-ing**: *committed, committing.*

Commitment, however, does not have a doubled **t** because **-ment** does not start with a vowel.

The **o** in *commit* is unaccented. Pronounce it as an **o** when you spell it.

D.   Use the correct form of the word in parentheses in each sentence:
1.   (begin)   I'm _____ to like hot butterscotch sundaes, too.
2.   (commit)   Are you _____ to losing weight? Or are you _____ to exercise? Some of us are _____ to eating sundaes.

control

Control is a two-syllable word, ending in one consonant preceded by one vowel, with the accent on the last syllable; therefore, the **l** is doubled before a suffix beginning with a vowel: *controlled, controlling.*

Because so many two-syllable words (ending in one consonant preceded by one vowel) that end in **l** have the accent on the first syllable (for example: *travel, model*), we may forget that *control* is accented on the second syllable. The **l** in *control* is doubled before a suffix beginning with a vowel: *controlled, controlling.*

The first **o** is unaccented, so you don't hear it as an **o**, as in *contribute, continue, construction*, and *commit.*

The beginning **k** sound is spelled with a **c**. There are relatively few words in our language that begin with a **k**. Look at the dictionary to see the number of pages devoted to **c** as opposed to **k**.

The original word has one **l**: *control*. Save the two **l**'s for *controlled* and *controlling.*

E.   Find the *incorrect* spelling of *beginning, committed, commitment, forgotten, control, controlled*, and *controlling* in the word search.
There are nine misspellings.
Why are they wrong?
Can you also find some correctly spelled fruits and vegetables in the puzzle?

c	b	e	g	i	n	i	n	g	f	c	g
c	a	j	l	l	o	r	t	n	o	c	n
a	o	r	o	n	i	o	n	m	r	b	i
b	x	m	r	a	e	p	m	y	g	e	n
b	q	u	m	o	z	i	h	z	o	a	n
a	c	o	m	i	t	t	e	d	t	n	i
g	c	o	n	t	t	r	o	l	e	d	g
e	o	j	m	k	z	e	w	v	n	a	g
h	r	e	b	e	e	t	d	x	q	e	e
w	n	z	u	c	c	h	i	n	i	p	b
t	c	o	n	t	r	r	o	l	i	n	g

LESSON 8
Additional Activities

1. Explain what is meant by a one-one-one word. Give an example.

2. Once you know what a one-one-one word is, what do you do with it before adding a suffix beginning with a vowel?

3. What are two very common suffixes beginning with vowels?

4. Why are *scream* and *walk* not one-one-one words?

5. Adding **-er** and **-est** to an adjective makes the adjective "more" or "most." What must you do with a one-one-one adjective before adding **-er** or **-est**?

6. Circle the words correctly spelled:

   hoter,   hotter,   thinner,   thiner

7. With two-syllable words (ending in one consonant preceded by one vowel), you have to know where the accent is. If it is on the last syllable, you will double the final consonant; if the accent is not on the last syllable, you will not double the final consonant. Most dictionaries show the accent at the end of a syllable; *Webster's* shows it before the syllable. Where is the accent in *begin*? in *commit*? in *control*? Add **-ed** to *commit* and *control*. Add **-ing** to each of the three words.

8. When you add a suffix not beginning with a vowel, like **-ment**, you don't have to double that final consonant. Add **-ment** to *commit*.

9. Add **-ful** to *forget*. Add **-en** to *forgot*.

10. *Beginning* is one of the most frequently misspelled words. How is it usually misspelled?

11. What are the past tenses of *begin*?

Answers

LESSON 8

A.
1. getting
2. stopped
3. Swimming
4. Dropping
5. running
6. dropped
7. stopped
8. planning
9. hopped
10. Hopping

B.
red, redder, reddest
hot, hotter, hottest
sad, sadder, saddest
thin, thinner, thinnest
mad, madder, maddest
fat, fatter, fattest

C. stopper, bidder, robber

LESSON 8 (Continued)

D.
1. beginning
2. committed, committed, committed

E. Puzzle

The misspellings are for *beginning* ("begining" and "begginning"), for *committed* ("comitted" and "commited"), *controlled* ("conttroled"), *controlling* ("contrroling"), *commitment* ("committment"), *forgotten* ("forgoten"), and *control* ("controll"). The fruits and vegetables are *pea, bean, zucchini, cabbage, pear, onion,* and *beet.*

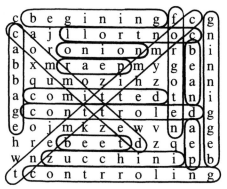

LESSON 8: Additional Activities

1. A one-one-one word is a one-syllable word ending in one consonant that is preceded by one vowel. One possible example: *plan*
2. You double the final consonant before adding a suffix beginning with a vowel.
3. **-ed** and **-ing**
4. *Scream* has two vowels before the final consonant; *walk* ends in two consonants.
5. You double the final consonant.
6. hotter, thinner
7. *Begin, commit,* and *control* have the accent on the second syllable. *committed, controlled; beginning, committing, controlling*
8. commitment
9. forgetful; forgotten
10. It is usually misspelled by not doubling the **n.**
11. began, begun

LESSON 9

efficient
Pronunciation: ĭ fĭsh´ənt
Because the **c** is pronounced **sh**, the word fits a special part of the **i** before **e** rule: If the **c** is pronounced **sh**, it is **i** before **e**, not the **e** before **i** that you would expect after **c**.

One who is *efficient* produces well, is effective. If I am *inefficient*, I am not effective. I am an *inefficient* dishwasher. I am *efficient* at putting sufficient butter on the popcorn.

sufficient
Pronunciation: sə fĭsh´ənt
Because the **c** is pronounced **sh**, the word fits a special part of the **i** before **e** rule: If the **c** is pronounced **sh**, it is **i** before **e**, not the **e** before **i** that you would expect after **c**.

If I have enough, it is *sufficient*. If I don't have enough, it is *insufficient*. The book space in a school locker is always *insufficient*.

deficient
Pronunciation: də fĭsh´ənt
Meaning: lacking something; incomplete
Because the **c** is pronounced **sh**, the word fits a special part of the **i** before **e** rule: If the **c** is pronounced **sh**, it is **i** before **e**, not the **e** before **i** that you would expect after **c**.

If you eat nothing but popcorn, your diet will be *deficient*. You will have a *deficiency* of vitamins. You will have a deficit. All that because you ate so much popcorn!

proficient
Pronunciation: prə fĭsh´ənt
Meaning: If you are proficient, you are good at something.

He is *proficient* in riding a unicycle. He has *proficiency*.

Because the **c** is pronounced **sh**, the word fits a special part of the **i** before **e** rule: If the **c** is pronounced **sh**, it is **i** before **e**, not the **e** before **i** that you would expect after **c**.

omniscient
Pronunciation: ŏm nĭsh´ənt
Because the **c** is pronounced **sh**, the word fits a special part of the **i** before **e** rule: If the **c** is pronounced **sh**, it is **i** before **e**, not the **e** before **i** that you would expect after **c**.
Meaning: **omni-** means "all"; **-scient** comes from *scientia* = "science," or "to know"

An *omniscient* one knows all. Who could possibly have *omniscience*?
Related words: *omnipotent*: "all-powerful"   *omnivorous*: "eats everything"

A.   Write the first part of the following words:

1.   _____ cient — enough

2.   _____ cient — not enough, lacking in

3.   _____ cient — good at something

4.   _____ cient — very old

5.   _____ cient — skilled at getting things done

6.   _____ cient — all-knowing

LESSON 9 (Continued)

conscience

Pronunciation: kŏn´shəns

Because the **c** is pronounced **sh**, the word fits a special part of the **i** before **e** rule: If the **c** is pronounced **sh**, it is **i** before **e**, not the **e** before **i** that you would expect after **c**.

The syllables are: *con science*.

The second one, **-science**, is pronounced as **-shəns**, one syllable in this word. You know the syllable as two syllables when it stands as a word alone: *sci ence*.

When you spell it, think: *con sci ence*.

Here's another word that is made from *conscience* that may help you remember it: *conscientious*. It divides into syllables: *con sci en tious*. The **i** and the **e** are in separate syllables; you hear both the **i** and the **e**.

species

Pronunciation: 1. spē´shēz   2. spē´sēz

Because the **c** is pronounced **sh**, the word fits a special part of the **i** before **e** rule: If the **c** is pronounced **sh**, it is **i** before **e**, not the **e** before **i** that you would expect after **c**.

Meaning: biological classification; a kind

There are many *species* of roses. This *species* is nearly extinct.

Here are some words related in meaning to *species*: *special, specific*.

glacier

Pronunciation: glā´shər

Because the **c** is pronounced **sh**, the word fits a special part of the **i** before **e** rule: If the **c** is pronounced **sh**, it is **i** before **e**, not the **e** before **i** that you would expect after **c**.

It is a special treat to see the *glaciers* in *Glacier* National Park. My cousin who studies ancient *glaciers* is a *glacialist* studying *glaciology* in *Glacier* National Park. *Glacious*!* *I mean: Gracious!

ancient

Pronunciation: 1. ān´shənt   2. ān´chənt

Because the **c** is pronounced **sh**, the word fits a special part of the **i** before **e** rule: If the **c** is pronounced **sh**, it is **i** before **e** not the **e** before **i** that you would expect after **c**.

Meaning: very old

"We will study the species of roses found under glaciers."

"There aren't any roses under glaciers!"

"How do you know? Anything is possible."

B. Answer the questions:

1. What is the rule for spelling the vowels **i** and **e** fter **c** when the **c** sounds **sh**?

2. What is the usual spelling of the vowels **i** and **e** after **c**?

3. What does your **conscience** tell you to do when dishes need to be washed?

4. How many **species** of flowers can you name?

5. Where in the United States can you find **glaciers**? Where is the most **ancient** tree in the United States? Where can you find out?

LESSON 9
Additional Activities

1. Why do we spell *efficient, sufficient, deficient, proficient, omniscient, conscience, species, glacier,* and *ancient* with **ie** after **c**?

2. Write a sentence that contains both *sufficient* and *deficient*.

3. Write a sentence that contains both *efficient* and *inefficient*. (The prefix **in-** means "not" in *inefficient*.)

4. What word do you know that is part of *conscience*, besides *on*?

5. What is a **glacier**? Where do we have them in the United States? What is an iceberg? Where might you see one? Which are more **ancient**—**glaciers** or icebergs? Explain. If you can't answer any of these questions, spell *omniscient*, which you are not. Why aren't you?

Answers

LESSON 9

A. 1. suffi
   2. defi
   3. profi
   4. an
   5. effi
   6. omnis

LESSON 9 (Continued)

B. 1. When **c** sounds **sh**, you spell the words **cie**.
   2. **cei**
   3. wash them
   4. maybe a dozen or two
   5. in Montana, Wyoming, Alaska; in California; in an encyclopedia

LESSON 9: Additional Activities

1. If the **c** sounds **sh**, then the word is spelled **ie**, not **ei**, after **c**.
2. Sample sentence: The artificial snow was **sufficient** for skiing; the area was **deficient** in natural snow.
3. Sample sentence: I am **efficient** at doing housework; I am **inefficient** at managing my allowance.
4. science
5. According to the *American Heritage Dictionary*, a glacier is a huge mass of laterally limited, moving ice originating from compacted snow. An iceberg is a massive floating body of ice broken away from a glacier. Glaciers in the United States would be found in Alaska and in other western mountainous states such as Montana and Wyoming. Tiny icebergs would be found in water below the continental glaciers; most, however, would be found off the northern coasts of North America. Glaciers are ancient; icebergs are made of the same ancient matter as glaciers, but have formed more recently. *Omniscient* means "all-knowing." No one can be all-knowing.

38

LESSON 10

enough

-**ough** has four sounds:
1. With a **t** after it, it sounds ôt as in *thought* and *bought*.
2. It sounds long **o** as in *though* and *doughnut*.
3. It sounds o͞o as in *through* and *throughout*.
4. It sounds ŭf as in *rough*, *tough*, and *enough*.

Enough is an -**ough** word pronounced ə nŭf´, which makes you want to spell the word "enuf." Don't. It's wrong. It's spelled with **ough**, the same as *rough* and *tough*.

This ski trail is a *tough* one—it's *rough*. I've had *enough*.

through

Through is another -**ough** word. It is pronounced thr o͞o.

"Over the river and *through* the woods, to Grandmother's house we go."

Traffic signs such as "No Thru Traffic" have not helped us learn the real spelling of this word, although that spelling saves space. Maybe in one hundred years, everyone will spell *through* that way. In the meantime, if you want your nontraffic spelling to be correct, spell the word as *through* throughout your writing.

although

Pronunciation: ôl thō´

Note that there is just one **l** in the word. Here are some sentences with -**ough** words sounding long **o**:

Although I made the *dough* for biscuits, I may fry some of it for *doughnuts*.
We have done a quick, *though thorough*, search for the *thoroughbred's* records.
My brother is home on *furlough* from the army.

thought

Pronunciation: thôt

A fair number of -**ought** words sound ôt. Fill in these sentences with the correct -**ought** word:

A. 1. ought - I _____ to do my spelling!
   2. __ought - I _____ my homework in my messy room.
   3. ____ ought - I even looked on my _____ iron bookshelf.
   4. __ought - My search came to _____ .
   5. __ought - I _____ a new spelling book.
   6. ____ ought - I _____ that was a lousy idea.
   7. ____ ought - That _____ my allowance balance to nought.

B. Make a chart of the -**ough** words to keep in your notebook. Write them according to the sound of -**ough**:

$$\bar{o} \qquad \overline{oo} \qquad \breve{u} \qquad \hat{o}$$

Here are the words to put in the chart:

enough, although, though, through, cough, brought, throughout, thorough, dough, tough, doughnut, ought, sought, rough, fought, nought, furlough, wrought, thoroughbred, bought, thought, overwrought

LESSON 10 (Continued)

trouble
troubles, troubled, troubling, troublesome
Pronunciation: **trŭb′əl**
The **ou** sounds short **u**, as it does in *country, cousin, enough, double, rough, tough, touch, young,* and *southern.* Those are most of the **ou** words sounding short **u** that you'll run into.

A common ending is **-le**. The final **e** is silent, and you have a schwa sound between the **l** and the consonant preceding it:

trouble, double, people: **trŭb′əl   dŭb′əl   pē′pəl**

A. Write a form of the word *trouble* in each sentence; more than one form is correct:
1. I have _____ spelling words with double consonants.
2. They are _____ for many people.
3. Is your young cousin _____ you?

about
Pronunciation: **ə bout′**
The first letter is an **a** pronounced as a schwa. It is almost a short **u** sound, but it is not spelled with a **u**.
The **ou** is the **ou** sound as in *out*: **ab**out.
Meaning: approximately, almost, on every side.

D. Use *about* in the following sentences to show different meanings of the word:

1. What's all the excitement _____ ?
2. She is _____ 5′5″ tall.
3. I'm _____ finished with my spelling homework.

cough
Pronunciation: **kôf**
Cough is like *rough* in that the **gh** sounds **f** in both words. They are different in the sound of the vowel combinations:

cough — ô   rough — ŭ

Cough is like *thought* in the sound of its **ou**.

I *coughed* and *coughed* all night with my cold. *Cough! Cough! Cough!* I *thought* I would never stop. It was a *rough* night. Although I took *cough* medicine, apparently it was not *enough* to stop my *coughing.* Maybe I can stay home from school!

E. Answer the following questions:
1. What is the sound of the **c** in *cough*?
2. What is the sound of the **gh**?
3. What is the sound of the vowels **ou**?
4. Which of the following has the same *vowel* sound as *cough*? Circle one: *rough, although, thought.*
5. With what word does the **gh** in *cough* rhyme? Circle one: *tough, banana, New York.*

doughnut
Pronunciation: **dō′nŭt**
Meaning: a small ring-shaped cake made of rich, light dough that is fried in deep fat.
How does that sound? How many different kinds of **doughnuts** can you name? How else is *doughnut* spelled? That's easier to answer, isn't it? Although *doughnut* can be spelled "donut," it is made from *dough*. Have you ever made **doughnuts**? No? Donuts? No? Why don't you try?

LESSON 10
Additional Activities

1. Write the spellings of the following dictionary-marked words:

   ə nŭf′   kôf

   thrōō   ə bout′

   ôl thō′   trŭb′əl

   thôt

2. *Trouble* ends in a final silent **e**. What do you do with it when you add the suffixes **-s**, **-ed**, **-ing**, and **-some**?

3. Which tastes better, a chocolate doughnut or a chocolate donut?

4. What is the consonant sound of **gh** in *cough*, *rough*, and *enough*?

5. What is the difference in spelling between *though* and *through*? between *though* and *thought*?

6. Do any of the following words give you spelling problems: *enough, through, though, although, thought, trouble, rough, about, cough, double, tough, ought, doughnut*? How can you resolve those problems?

7. Group the rhyming words: *ought, rough, through, fought, tough, thought, trouble, enough, sought, though, nought, bought, double*.

   What words do not rhyme with any others in this list?

8. What is the meaning of *thorough*?

9. What is the meaning of *wrought*? What is the relationship of the word *wright* to *wrought*? What is **wrought** iron? What does it mean to be over**wrought**? Tell your teacher that you need to do this for homework, not for a quiz.

10. Do your homework.

Answers

LESSON 10

A.
1. ought
2. sought
3. wrought
4. nought
5. bought
6. thought
7. brought

B.

ō	o͞o	ŭf	ô
although	through	enough	cough
though	throughout	tough	brought
thorough		rough	ought
dough			sought
doughnut			fought
furlough			nought
thoroughbred			wrought
			bought
			thought
			overwrought

LESSON 10 (Continued)

C.
1. trouble/troubles
2. troublesome
3. troubling

D.
1. about
2. about
3. about

E.
1. k
2. f
3. ô
4. thought
5. tough

LESSON 10: Additional Activities

1. enough, through, although, thought, cough, about, trouble
2. When you add the suffix **-s**, you keep the **e**: *troubles.*
   When you add the suffix **-ed**, you drop the **e**: *troubled.*
   When you add the suffix **-ing**, you drop the **e**: *troubling.*
   When you add the suffix **-some**, you keep the **e**: *troublesome.*
3. I think they'll taste the same.
4. **f**
5. *Through* has an **r** after the **th**; *thought* has a **t** at the end of the word.
6. If they give you trouble, you might try listing them under headings indicating the sound of the **-ough**. You could write them in sentences and ask someone to check the correct spelling and meaning. You could always look them up in the dictionary to be sure.

7.

ôt	ŭf	ŭb′əl
ought	rough	trouble
fought	touch	double
thought	enough	
sought		
nought		
bought		

   Through (thro͞o) and *though* (thō) do not rhyme with any others in the list.
8. fully done, finished
9. *Wrought* means "put together; shaped by hammering with tools," said of metals or metalwork. A *wright* is a person who constructs something. The word is used chiefly in combination, such as *shipwright, wheelwright. Wrought iron* is easily welded or forged iron. A person who is *overwrought* is excessively nervous or excited; agitated; worked up over something.

   Teacher, I need to do this for homework.
10. I just did it.

First Quarter Quizzes

As part of each quarter's quizzes, you will find oral tests of various lengths to dictate to your students. It is your choice: 10 words, 20, 50, or 100. Your choice may depend on the time you have, which and how many words you feel are important for each quarter, and what you want individual students to do. If the word is a homonym, I have provided a sentence.

The oral quizzes are followed by three reproducible written quizzes: Sound to Spelling, General, and Spelling Rules.

Oral Quiz

Test I: 10 Words

1. privilege
2. soldier
3. sincerely
4. broccoli
5. neighbor
6. believe
7. countries
8. beginning
9. conscience
10. through (I walked through the field.)

Test II: 20 Words

1. privilege
2. minute
3. soldier
4. hundred
5. sincerely
6. received
7. broccoli
8. mayonnaise
9. neighbor
10. foreign
11. believe
12. halves
13. countries
14. studying
15. beginning
16. bigger
17. conscience
18. sufficient
19. through (I walked through the field.)
20. cough

Test III: 50 Words

1. privilege
2. minute
3. certain
4. average
5. biscuit
6. spinach
7. soldier
8. hundred
9. once
10. only
11. ninth
12. too (This is too much!)
13. to (I want to go to the circus.)
14. sincerely
15. received
16. coming
17. writing
18. having
19. smiling
20. losing
21. really
22. usually
23. broccoli
24. mayonnaise
25. cauliflower
26. neighbor
27. foreign
28. weigh (How much do you weigh?)
29. eighth
30. reign (The queen will reign for life.)
31. believe
32. halves
33. lives (He lives in Butte now.)
34. lives (She read about the lives of the saints.)
35. countries
36. studying
37. tried
38. allies
39. beginning
40. bigger
41. planned
42. committed
43. conscience
44. sufficient
45. ancient
46. efficient
47. through (I walked through the field.)
48. cough
49. enough
50. doughnut

Oral Quiz (Continued)

Test IV: 100 Words

1. certain
2. minute
3. spinach
4. genuine
5. privilege
6. average
7. one (There is only one Godzilla.)
8. only
9. once
10. soldier
11. too (I am too late for the bus.)
12. two (I walked on my two feet.)
13. to (I walked to school.)
14. fourteen
15. forty
16. nine
17. ninth
18. ninety
19. hundred
20. come
21. coming
22. take
23. taking
24. make
25. making
26. have
27. having
28. give
29. giving
30. receive
31. write (I will write a letter.)
32. writing
33. smile
34. smiling
35. lose
36. losing
37. real (That's a real diamond.)
38. really
39. usual
40. usually
41. sincere
42. sincerely
43. mayonnaise
44. cauliflower
45. broccoli
46. neighbor
47. weigh (How much do you weigh?)
48. reign (It happened during the reign of Louis XIV.)
49. rein (I will rein in the horse.)
50. foreign
51. eight (She is eight years old.)
52. freight
53. eighty
54. eighth
55. life
56. lives (We are studying the lives of the presidents.)
57. live (Where do you live?)
58. lives (He lives in Seattle now.)
59. belief
60. believe
61. roof
62. study
63. studies
64. studied
65. studying
66. tries
67. trying
68. cries
69. replied
70. flies
71. country
72. countries
73. companies
74. county
75. ally
76. allies
77. story
78. planned
79. hopped
80. bigger
81. beginning
82. forgotten
83. commit
84. committed
85. commitment
86. efficient
87. sufficient
88. deficient
89. proficient
90. conscience
91. species
92. glacier
93. ancient
94. enough
95. through (I walked through the field.)
96. although
97. thought
98. trouble
99. about
100. doughnut

FIRST QUARTER
Sound to Spelling Quiz

In the following test, spell the word correctly from the sound of the word given by the dictionary markings.

1. sûr′tən

2. mĭn′ĭt *or* mī nūt′

3. spĭn′ĭch

4. jĕn′yo͞o ĭn

5. prĭv′ə lĭj

6. ăv′rĭj

7. bĭs′kĭt

8. wŭn (I still have **wŭn** library book out.)

9. ōn′lē

10. wŭns

11. sōl′jər

12. fôr′tē

13. nīn

14. nīn′tē

15. nīn′tēnth

16. nīnth

17. hŭn′drĭd

18. to͞o (I am **to͞o** late for the bus.)

19. to͞o (I walked **to͞o** school.)

20. to͞o (I walked on my **to͞o** feet.)

21. kŭm

22. kŭm′ĭng

23. tāk

24. tāk′ĭng

25. māk

26. māk′ĭng

27. hăv

28. hăv′ĭng

29. gĭv

30. gĭv′ĭng

31. rē sēv′

32. rē sēvd′

33. rīt (I will **rīt** a letter.)

34. rīt′ĭng (I am **rīt′ĭng** a letter.)

35. smīl

36. smīl′ĭng

37. lo͞oz

38. lo͞oz′ĭng

39. rē′əl *or* rēl (That's a **rēl** diamond.)

40. rē′əlē *or* rē′lē

41. yo͞o′zho͞o əl

42. yo͞o′zho͞o əl lē

43. sĭn sîr′

44. sĭn sîr′lē

45. māy ə nāz′

46. kô′lĭ flouər

47. brŏk′əlē

48. nā′bər

49. wā (I **wā** more than you do.)

50. rān (The king will **rān** forever.)

FIRST QUARTER
Sound to Spelling Quiz (Continued)

51. rān (I lost one **rān** while I was riding the horse.)

52. fôr′ən

53. āt (I am **āt** years old.)

54. frāt

55. līf

56. līvz

57. lĭv

58. lĭvz

59. bĭ lēf′

60. bĭ lēfs′

61. bĭ lēv′

62. bĭ lēvz′

63. ro͞of *or* ro͝of

64. stŭd′ē

65. stŭd′ēz

66. stŭd′ē ĭng

67. stŭd′ēd

68. krīz

69. rĭ plī′ĭng

70. flīz

71. kŭn′trē

72. kŭn′trēz

73. kŭm′pə nē

74. koun′tē

75. ăl′ ī

76. ăl′īz

77. stôr′ēz

78. plănd

79. plăn′ĭng

80. hŏp′ĭng

81. hŏpd

82. bĭ gĭn′

83. kə mĭt′

84. ĭ fĭsh′ənt

85. sə fĭsh′ənt

86. də fĭsh′ənt

87. prə fĭsh′ənt

88. ŏm nĭsh′ənt

89. kŏn′shəns

90. spē′shēz *or* spē′sēz

91. glā′shər

92. ān′shənt *or* ān′chənt

93. ə nŭf′

94. thro͞o (Aren't you **thro͞o** yet?)

95. ôl thō′

96. thôt

97. trŭb′əl

98. ə bout′

99. kôf

100. dō′nŭt

FIRST QUARTER
General Quiz

1. Write the pronunciation of *m-i-n-u-t-e* as used in the following sentences:

    a. I found a **minute** particle of dirt in your room.

    b. You should clean your room this **minute!**

2. Write the numbers from 1 to 10 in words.

3. Write the following numerals in words:

    a. the year 1990   d. 90

    b. 9th   e. 2

    c. 40   f. 1

4. How are *one*, *once*, and *only* related?

5. Circle the correctly spelled words:

    a. usualy, sincerely, really, probabely

    b. loseing, smiling, writeing, comeing

    c. takeing, making, haveing, giveing

    d. wholely, truly, terribly, fully

6. How might these silly sentences help you to spell the italicized words?

    a. Donna put *mayonnaise* on her broccoli.

    b. Ginny played the piccolo after she ate her *broccoli*.

    c. Emily put the end of her broccoli into the middle of the *cauliflower*.

    d. My daughter caught the *cauliflower* that Barbara threw to her.

    e. Bill grew a flower and some *cauliflower* in his garden.

7. How will exaggerating the pronunciation of *foreign* as **fō′ rān** help you to spell the word?

8. *Neighbor*, *weigh*, *eight*, and *freight* have more than the **ei** to spell correctly. What silent letters must you remember to include in the words?

FIRST QUARTER
General Quiz (Continued)

9. Write the plural for the following:

   a. life

   b. half

   c. roof

   d. belief

   e. wolf

   f. thief

   g. sheriff

10. Choose the one correct spelling in each group:

    a. studing, studiing, studying, studieing

    b. countrys, countries

    c. tries, trys

    d. families, famileys, familys

    e. commitment, committment, commiting, comitted

    f. controlled, bigest, beginer

11. In many words, **ti** gives the **sh** sound—*transportation, education, expectation.*
    What letters give the **sh** sound in *glacier, ancient,* and *efficient*?

12. Use the correct homonym in the sentences below:

    a. We grew _____ many peaches _____ eat in the summer so I

       froze _____ bushels of them. (to, too, two)

    b. I once _____ _____ race. (one, won)

    c. No _____ do I _____ 150 pounds! (way, weigh)

    d. The queen will _____ with a _____ in the _____ .

       (rain, reign, rein)

    e. I _____ _____ sections of the chocolate bar. (ate, eight)

    f. Now I'll _____ for my _____ to go up. (wait, weight)

13. We've all seen the traffic sign "No Thru Traffic." How is "thru" really spelled?

14. In "Dunkin' Donuts," how is "dunkin' " really spelled, and what does it mean? What
    is a more formal spelling of "donut"?

FIRST QUARTER
Spelling Rules Quiz

1. True or false: If a word containing the vowel combination either **ei** or **ie** sounds as a long **a**, then it is always spelled **ei**.

2. There are exceptions to the **c** and **g** rule (mostly short, common words you already know), but the rule applies to each of the words following: *privilege, average, genuine, biscuit, certain, come, receive, sincerely, broccoli, cauliflower, company, cough.* Write the four parts of that rule.

3. What is the rule for words ending in a final silent **e** when you want to add a suffix beginning in a vowel, like **-ed** or **-ing**? Think of words like *take* and *come.*

4. If a word ends in a consonant before the final **y**, what do you do before adding a suffix beginning with a vowel, such as **-er**, **-es**, **-ed**, or **-est**? What do you do before adding the suffix **-ing**?

5. What is the one-one-one rule? What do you do with two-syllable words ending in one final consonant preceded by one vowel if the accent is on the last syllable?

6. If the **c** in an **ie/ei** word sounds **sh**, what combination of vowels do you use?

Answers to First Quarter Quizzes

Sound to Spelling Quiz

1. certain
2. minute
3. spinach
4. genuine
5. privilege
6. average
7. biscuit
8. one
9. only
10. once
11. soldier
12. forty
13. nine
14. ninety
15. nineteenth
16. ninth
17. hundred
18. too
19. to
20. two
21. come
22. coming
23. take
24. taking
25. make
26. making
27. have
28. having
29. give
30. giving
31. receive
32. received
33. write
34. writing
35. smile
36. smiling
37. lose
38. losing
39. real
40. really
41. usual
42. usually
43. sincere
44. sincerely
45. mayonnaise
46. cauliflower
47. broccoli
48. neighbor
49. weigh
50. reign
51. rein
52. foreign
53. eight
54. freight
55. life
56. lives
57. live
58. lives
59. belief
60. beliefs
61. believe
62. believes
63. roof
64. study
65. studies
66. studying
67. studied
68. cries
69. replying
70. flies
71. country
72. countries
73. company
74. county
75. ally
76. allies
77. stories
78. planned
79. planning
80. hopping
81. hopped
82. begin
83. commit
84. efficient
85. sufficient
86. deficient
87. proficient
88. omniscient
89. conscience
90. species
91. glacier
92. ancient
93. enough
94. through
95. although
96. thought
97. trouble
98. about
99. cough
100. doughnut

General Quiz

1. a. mĭ nūt′
   b. mĭn′ĭt
2. one, two, three, four, five, six, seven, eight, nine, ten
3. a. nineteen (hundred) ninety
   b. ninth
   c. forty
   d. ninety
   e. two
   f. one
4. Each word starts with the letters **on**; *once* and *only* are derivatives of *one*.
5. a. sincerely, really
   b. smiling
   c. making
   d. truly, terribly, fully
6. a. *Donna* and *mayonnaise* both have the letters **onna** in them.
   b. Both *piccolo* and *broccoli* have two **c**'s in the middle and one **l** near the end.
   c. The end of *broccoli* is **li**, and *cauliflower* has **li** in the middle of it.
   d. *Daughter, caught,* and *cauliflower* all have the letters **au**.
   e. The letters **flower** are in *cauliflower*.
7. You will hear the long **a** sound in it and spell it **ei**.
8. **gh**
9. a. lives
   b. halves
   c. roofs
   d. beliefs
   e. wolves
   f. thieves
   g. sheriffs
10. a. studying
    b. countries
    c. tries
    d. families
    e. commitment
    f. controlled
11. **ci**
12. a. too, to, two
    b. won, one
    c. way, weigh
    d. reign, rein, rain
    e. ate, eight
    f. wait, weight
13. through
14. dunking; to dip into a liquid; doughnut

Spelling Rules Quiz

1. True

2. a. If a **c** is followed by an **e**, **i**, or **y**, it will be pronounced as an **s**.
   b. If a **c** is followed by an **a**, **o**, **u**, a consonant, or nothing, it will be pronounced as a **k**.
   c. If a **g** is followed by an **e**, **i**, or **y**, it will be pronounced as a **j**.
   d. If a **g** is followed by an **a**, **o**, **u**, a consonant, or nothing, it will be pronounced as a **g** as in *go*.

3. Drop the **e** and add **-ing**.

4. Change the **y** to **i** and add the suffix, but keep the **y** before adding **-ing**.

5. The one-one-one rule states that a one-syllable word ending in one consonant preceded by one vowel doubles that consonant before adding a suffix beginning with a vowel. If a two-syllable word ending in one consonant preceded by one vowel has the accent on the last syllable, you double the consonant, also.

6. **ie**

SECOND QUARTER

LESSON 11

know, knew, known, knowing

You don't hear the **k** in any of those words; you don't hear the **w**, either. Or, you could say that the **ow** gives you the long **o** sound, and the **ew** gives you the long **oo** sound. However you want to look at it, you have to spell the words with the **k** and the **w**.

I *know* the answer today; I *knew* the answer yesterday.

I have *known* the answer all week.

I will still be *knowing* the answer tomorrow.

The tenses are formed like this:

grow, grew, grown
blow, blew, blown
throw, threw, thrown

no

When you have the answer, you *know* something. When you don't want to say yes, you want the word *no:* The answer is **No!**

A. Fill in the blanks with *no* or *know* or *knowing:*

1. I have _____ books to carry home.
2. _____ , I don't _____ everything, but I _____ everything in these books.
3. You have _____ way of _____ everything in these books!

knew, new

Yesterday I *knew* the answer to everything. Today there are *new* things for me to learn.

Knew is the past tense of *know*—to have knowledge.

New is the opposite of old.

A *gnu* (pronounced **nōō**) is an animal. Did you know that?

B. Fill in the blanks with *knew* or *new:*

1. What's _____ ?
2. I _____ you'd ask that.
3. I know a _____ song. Want to hear it?
4. Not if you're going to sing it!

knowledge

Pronunciation: **nŏl′ĭj**

You know the first part: *know.* Although the word doesn't come from *know* and *ledge,* perhaps thinking of those two words could help you spell it—or *know* plus **l** plus *edge.*

I *know* a *ledge* where we can sit and eat our lunch. I *know* I don't want to sit too near the *edge.*

But the second syllable is pronounced **ĭj**—like the ending of *average* and *privilege.* This time it's spelled *-edge.*

acknowledge, acknowledgment

acknowledge—to recognize, give knowledge to
acknowledgment—recognition

Note that the **e** is dropped before the suffix. The **-dg** without the **e** seems to keep the **j** sound as in *judgment* (from *judge*).

These are words I need to look up if I want to be 101% sure whether there is an **e** in them—like *ninety.*

C. Use one of the following words that makes sense in each sentence:

  judgment, acknowledge, acknowledgment, judge

1. I _____ the fact that he was found with a gun.
2. I must _____ from evidence; it is my _____ that he is not guilty.
3. The mayor was given _____ for his good _____ .

LESSON 11 (Continued)

tired

Pronunciation: tīrd

This is the way we feel when we haven't had enough sleep.

The word comes from the verb *tire*:

My grandfather *tires* easily.

Yesterday he *tired* from chopping wood.

He is *tiring* more easily these days.

Tired is the past tense of *tire*, and it is also an adjective made from the verb.

We usually pronounce the word as one syllable, so we may forget the **e**. I have a young friend who purposely pronounces the word in two syllables as tī rĕd; she doesn't misspell the word.

Don't confuse the word *tired* with *tried* by switching the **i** and **r** around. *Tried* comes from *try*. I **try** today; I **tried** yesterday.

Here are some common mixups to keep you on the alert:

>   *fired - fried*   *dairy - diary*
>   *girl - grill*   *tired - tried*

D. Use the above pairs correctly in the sentences below:

1. I _____ the lazy cook who _____ my eggs too slowly.
2. The _____ was cooking hamburgers on the _____ .
3. I kept a daily _____ when I worked in the _____ .
4. I'm _____ today because I _____ to run so hard yesterday.

jewelry

Pronunciation: jōō′əl rē

The word comes from *jewel*. Spell that word first, and the rest is easy: **-ry**. People transpose the **r** and the **l**—maybe because they are used to seeing **-ly** words. Also, they pronounce the word fast and leave out the second syllable: jōō′rē.

E. Use the words *jewel*, *jewels*, or *jewelry* in the following sentences to make sense:

1. We learned how to make _____ from colored seeds and seashells.
2. There are _____ in a fine watch.
3. I own one _____ , a diamond.

judge, judgment

>   *judged, judges, judging*

Pronunciation: jŭj,   jŭj′mĕnt

The second **j** sound comes from the **-dge**. You drop the **e** in *judgment*. If you can't remember, and a lot of people cannot, look the words up in the dictionary, or add them to your special list. *Judgment* is on the top ten misspellings list.

Remember *judicial* with the *judge* words; perhaps it will help you to put the **d** in them.

The **-dge** sound is in *edge, ledge, knowledge, fudge, lodge, badge*.

He *judged* the *fudge* to be the best in the *lodge*.

F. Fill in one of these words that makes sense in each sentence: *jewelry, judge, tired, judgment*.

1. Will you _____ the _____ exhibit?
2. My _____ is that none of the _____ is genuine.

58   *Spelling Demons Week by Week*

LESSON 11
Additional Activities

1. What letter is dropped when you form *judgment* from *judge*? *acknowledgment* from *acknowledge*?

2. Use *no* and *know* in one sentence.

3. Use *new* and *knew* in one sentence.

4. *Grew* is the past tense of *grow*. *Grown* is the past participle. What is the past tense of *know*? the past participle?

5. A past participle can be used as a verb or an adjective. Use the past participle of *grow* or *blow* or *throw* in the following:

   a. She has _____ four inches this year. (as a verb)

   b. He's a _____ man! (as an adjective)

   c. The pitcher was made of _____ glass. (as an adjective)

   d. I've _____ every history test this month. Next month I'll do better. I'll study. (as a verb)

   e. I've never _____ a curve ball. (as a verb)

6. What letter has been added to *grow* to make *grown*? to *blow* to make *blown*? to *throw* to make *thrown*?

7. What letter has been changed in *throw* to make *threw*, the past tense? in *grow* to make *grew*? in *blow* to make *blew*?

8. Use *tired* as an adjective and as a verb. In what ways could you misspell the word?

9. From what word is the word *jewelry* formed?

10. Write *jewelry* in syllables. How many syllables are there?

Answers

LESSON 11

A. 1. no
2. No, know, know
3. no, knowing

B. 1. new
2. knew
3. new

C. 1. acknowledge
2. judge, judgment
3. acknowledgment, judgment

LESSON 11 (Continued)

D. 1. fired, fried
2. girl, grill
3. diary, dairy
4. tired, tried

E. 1. jewelry
2. jewels
3. jewel

F. 1. judge, jewelry
2. judgment, jewelry

LESSON 11: Additional Activities

1. **e**
2. Sample sentence: I **know no** one from Argentina; do you?
3. Sample sentence: I **knew** I would have to buy **new** snow tires this winter.
4. knew, known
5. a. grown
   b. grown
   c. blown
   d. blown
   e. thrown
6. **n**
7. The **o** has been changed to **e**.
8. Sample sentences: My new puppy is **tired**. I **tired** her out with our long walk on the beach. Possible misspellings: tird, tierd, theyrrd, gwyghsn.
9. jewel
10. *jew el ry*; three syllables

LESSON 12

kaleidoscope
Syllables: *ka lei do scope*
   from Greek *kalos*, "beautiful"; and *eidos*, "form"; plus *scope*
Pronunciation: kə lī′də skōp
   EXCEPTION to **ie/ei** rule
Meaning: (1)   a tubelike instrument containing lose bits of colored glass, plastic, etc.
                reflected by mirrors so that various symmetrical patterns appear when
                the tube is held to the eye and rotated
         (2)   anything that constantly changes, as in color or pattern

Ed held the *kaleidoscope* to the window and turned the end to change the patterns he saw.
The sunset was a *kaleidoscope* of colors.

Fahrenheit
Pronunciation: făr′ ən hīt
   German long **i** sound is spelled **ei**: *Einstein, Steinway, Eisenhower*
Meaning: a thermometer scale named after the German Gabriel Fahrenheit.
   On the Fahrenheit scale, 32 degrees is freezing and 212 degrees is boiling. On the
Celsius scale, 0 degrees is freezing and 100 degrees is boiling. The abbreviation for
Fahrenheit is F.

reveille
Pronunciation: rěv′ə lē (Syllables: *rev eil le*)
Meaning: a bugle call telling you, "Wake up!"
   two l's
   an EXCEPTION to the **ie/ei** rule
The word *veil* is in the middle. **Reveille** broke the *veil* of sleep. It's probably easier to
sing it than spell it.

onomatopoeia   ŏn ə mät ə pē′ə
   Meaning: naming a thing by an imitation of the sound associated with it: *hiss,
bang, buzz, crash.*
   Think of *POE*m to help with that string of four vowels. **POE**ts use **onomatoPOEia**.
Pronounce long **a**'s and long **o**'s to help with the spelling: ŏn ō mät ō.
Think: tōmātō, nōmātō.

weird   wîrd
   EXCEPTION to **i** before **e** rule.
These exceptions are *weird*, aren't they? Frankenst**ei**n is *weird*. That counterf**ei**t money is
weird—$5.00 on one side of the bill, and $10.00 on the other side. Seeing shadows on a
rainy day is *weird*.

etc.
   Etc. is the abbreviation for *et cetera*, Latin words meaning "and other things." *Et* is
Latin for "and." Remember **E T**, Call home! It is **etc.**, not **ect.** Pronounce the **t** before the
c. Remember the period.
The art teacher brought pens, pencils, paints, crayons, *etc.*

A.   Answer the following questions:
1.   What song does the bugler blow first thing in the morning?
2.   What is weird about the word *weird*? Name something weird.
3.   What kind of a word is *swish*?
4.   What does a kaleidoscope do?
5.   Celsius zero is freezing. What is freezing for Fahrenheit?
6.   What is the abbreviation for *et cetera*?

LESSON 12 (Continued)

they (them, their)
Pronunciation: *they*: **thā**
The **ey** sounds long **a** as in **obey**, *survey*, *hey*! It is not spelled "thay."
They taught *their* greyhound dog to ob*ey* *them*.

In the above sentence, *they* is a plural subject pronoun, *them* is a pronoun used as an object of the infinitive *to obey*, and *their* is a possessive adjective. Note that *they, them,* and *their* all begin with *the*.

very
Pronunciation: **věr′ē**
Very is most commonly used to intensify an adjective.
The sunset is *very* beautiful.
Its homonym is *vary*, pronounced in the dictionary as **vâr′ē**. In practice, the two words are usually pronounced alike. *Vary* means "to change."

while
Pronunciation: **hwīl**
It is carelessly pronounced as **whŏll**, rhyming with *doll*. Sometimes *I'll* is mispronounced the same way as *Ah'll*. That's okay—as long as you spell it with an **I**.
The initial sound is **hw**—spelled **wh** as in the question words *when, why,* and *where*.
The final silent **e** makes the **i** long.
While is a conjunction, a word that joins. It means "during the time that" or "although."

B. Fill in each blank with one of the following words: *their, theirs, they, vary, very, them, while.*

1. Who won the game? _____ did.

2. Did you give my lemon cake to the losers? Yes, I gave it to _____ .

3. Were they pleased? Yes, they were _____ pleased.

4. What did they say? _____ said, "More, please."

5. How will I know the difference between the cakes? I will _____ the frosting.

6. Whose cake is the lemon one? It is _____ cake.

7. May I have a piece?

8. No, it is _____ .

9. You mean I have to stand here without cake _____

   they eat _____ ?

chihuahua
Pronunciation: **chĭ wä′wä**
A friend of mine, whose last name is Huard, saw this word when she was young and naturally pronounced it **chĭ hōō ə hōō ə**. I would have, too, if my name had been Huard. I laughed, but now when I want to spell the word, I think: **chĭ hōō ə hōō ə**.
It is the name of a very small dog of a breed originating in Mexico. A chihuahua is so small you could put one in your jacket pocket. A large state in Mexico is named Chihuahua. It is the size of our state of Oregon. Its capital city is Chihuahua.
Look in the encyclopedia for a picture of a chihuahua. Find out how large it is, what colors it is, how much it weighs.

LESSON 12
Additional Activities

1. There are many exceptions to the **i** before **e** rule: easy exceptions and hard ones. The following are harder than "after **c**" or "sound long **a**" exceptions. Hard, yes; impossible, no. Let's start with Fahrenheit. It comes from a German word in which the **ei** sounds long **i**—always.

   Einstein, Eisenhower, Fahrenheit. Who were each of these people? Use the three names in one sentence.

2. *Kaleidoscope* has a long **i** sound for the **ei**. What is a kaleidoscope?

3. *Reveille*: How will you remember it? There's a three-letter word—*ill*—in it; a four-letter word—*veil*—also. Write one sentence using *ill*, *veil*, and *reveille*. Use *cheese crackers* in your sentence, too.

4. You can really find a lot of little words in *onomatopoeia*, can't you? How many? What help does that give you in spelling *onomatopoeia*? Not much. Maybe you should try spelling it backwards. Now frontwards. Underline it. Cover it. Write it again without looking at it. I substitute a **t** for the **on** at the beginning of the word; and then it looks like *tomato-poeia*. Think *poem* for the **poe**, and then think that the word ends in **ia**, like *Maria. Tomato, poem,* and *Maria.* Now cross out the letters you don't need and add **on** on to the beginning. Write a sentence using *tomato, onomatopoeia, Maria,* and *poem*. Think you can spell the word now? Try it again.

5. How could thinking of the words *we* and *I* help you to spell *weird*? Use *we, I,* and *weird* in the same sentence. Now use *you* and *weird* in the same sentence. *You* doesn't help you at all, does it? Think *we* and *I* when you think of *weird*.

6. What is the abbreviation for *et cetera*?

7. What is the vowel sound in *they*? How do you spell it?

8. The next time you write a story, don't use the word *very* at all.

9. Have you ever seen a chihuahua? Where might you see one?

10. Use *while* in a sentence.

Answers

LESSON 12

A.
1. reveille
2. It is an exception to the **i** before **e** rule. Example of something weird: Lightning and thunder without rain are weird.
3. onomatopoeic
4. It shows different patterns.
5. 32 degrees
6. etc.

LESSON 12 (Continued)

B.
1. They
2. them
3. very
4. They
5. vary
6. their
8. theirs
9. while; theirs

LESSON 12: Additional Activities

1. Einstein was a mathematician famous for his theory of relativity. Eisenhower was a United States general of World War II who later became president. Fahrenheit was a scientist after whom the Fahrenheit temperature scale was named. Sample sentence: **Einstein** bought a **Fahrenheit** thermometer to give to General **Eisenhower**.

2. A kaleidoscope is a small tube in which patterns of colors are optically produced and viewed for amusement, especially one in which mirrors reflect light transmitted through bits of loose, colored glass contained at one end, causing them to appear as symmetrical designs when viewed at the other. Hence, the word also means a constantly changing set of colors; or a series of changing phases or events.

3. I probably won't remember it unless I write the word and look at it. But I could remember it as an exception to the **i** before **e** rule. I might also think of the *veil* of sleep broken by *reveille* or the word *ill* in *reveille*. Sample sentence: I felt **ill** when **reveille** broke the **veil** of sleep and I remembered all the **cheese crackers** I ate before I went to bed.

4. on, no, ma, mat, at, to, top, atop, Poe, a, topo (slang for topographical map): 11 words

   aieopotamono; onomatopoeia, *onomatopoiea*, onomatopoeia
   tomato, poem, Mafia
   onomatopoeia
   onomatopoeia

5. The first three letters of *weird* are **wei**. Sample sentences: **We** are both **weird**, but **I** am more **weird** than you. **You** are a little **weird**, though. *You* doesn't help. This doesn't make sense: If we are weird, then how come you aren't weird?

6. etc.

7. long **a**; **ey**

8. Okay, I'll try.

9. Yes or no. In Mexico, in a pet store, or at a friend's house in his jacket pocket.

10. Sample sentence: I'll look at this very weird kaleidoscope next to the Fahrenheit thermometer **while** you feed your chihuahua after reveille.

LESSON 13

i before **e**
except after **c**

That's the rule. It works for words with a **c** unless the **c** sounds **sh**. Here are some words for the rule.

ceiling
Pronunciation: sē′lĭng

The vowel combination comes after **c**; therefore it is **ei**.

A. Use the following words to fill in the blanks in the paragraph to make sense: *receive, perceive, conceive, ceiling, deceive.* (You may have to add **-ed** or **-ing** to a word. If so, remember to drop the final **e** first.)

As I watched, a crack appeared in my _____ . It became larger, and a baby dragon crawled out of the crack and walked across the _____ and down the wall. When it reached the floor, it turned to me and said, "Seal that crack in the _____ if you don't want any more dragons in your kitchen."

I thought my eyes must be _____ me. I _____ another surprise, however, as I glanced again at the ever-widening crack in the _____ .

Coming through the _____ crack were eight tiny reindeer followed by a sleigh.

"Hey—you're supposed to come down the chimney!"

receive rĭ sēv′

receipt rĭ sēt′

The vowel combination comes after **c**; therefore it is **ei**.

One trouble with some of these **ei** after **c** words is that they have another **e**, by itself, right before the **c**;

re ceive	**re** c ei v	final silent **e**
re ceipt	**re** c ei pt	(silent **p**)
de ceive	**de** c ei v	final silent **e**
de ceit	**de** c ei t	

The **re-** and **de-** are prefixes.

B. Use a form of the word *receive* in the sentences below: *receive, receives, received, receiving, receipt.*

1. I _____ a letter in the mail. It enclosed a _____ for a bill I had paid.

2. My sister stood in a _____ line at the wedding of her friend. All the guests were introduced to the wedding party.

3. What did you _____ today? An *A* in spelling? Hurray! I _____ a dragon from my ceiling.

deceive	dĭ sēv′	to mislead
deceit	dĭ sēt′	misrepresentation, deception
deceitful	dĭ sēt′fəl	misleading

C. Use a form of *deceive* in each blank:

That little kid tried to _____ me. I asked him if he'd been near my apple tree. He said no. I looked in his bike basket and saw four apples. He was being _____ . He lied. He stole my apples. What _____ !

LESSON 13 (Continued)

conceited

The vowel combination in *conceited*, *perceive* and *conceive* comes after **c**, so it is spelled **ei**.

Pronunciation: **kən sē′tĭd**

Meaning: holding too high an opinion of yourself; stuck up

My turtle is conceited. He said he was *receiving* an award for being the fastest turtle in the world. He said he was not *deceiving* me. I cannot *conceive* of the idea that my turtle is the fastest turtle. I *perceive* him as slow-moving. He talks, though.

perceive

Pronunciation: **pər sēv′**

Meaning: to be aware of, observe

I *perceive* a problem. A barely perceptible crack in my *cei*ling is widening. My perception is that it widens every minute, and something new crawls through the *cei*ling. Anyone perceptive can *perceive* that the crack must be closed. How will I close the crack?

conceive

Pronunciation: **kən sēv′**

Meanings: (1) understand; form an idea (of); (2) to become pregnant

I cannot *conceive* of a zoo without a lion. Our zoo moved the lions to another zoo while workers rebuilt the lion house. We hope that, when the lions return, the female will *conceive* and deliver a baby lion next spring.

D. Choose words from the following list to substitute for the words in parentheses so the paragraph makes sense: (*perceive, deceive, reign, reins, piece, conceited, friend*)

Lion, my (pal) _____ , I (think) _____ you are (stuck up) _____ . You can (rule) _____ over a (part) _____ of this jungle, but do not (fool) _____ yourself that you (control)—hold the _____ to the whole jungle.

E. Go from *believe* to *friend* stepping on correctly spelled words only:

(Start) believe	their	recieve	frend	concieted
freind	receive	piece	cieling	thier
beilive	peice	ceiling	chief	friend (End)

F. Fill in the crossword puzzle with *lei, conceited, Einstein, ceiling, ice, perceive, neither, deceive, receive*:

Across

3. stuck up
5. opposite of floor
8. get
9. not this or that

Down

1. observe
2. mislead
4. _____ cream
6. scientist famous for theory of relativity
7. Hawaiian flower necklace

LESSON 13
Additional Activities

1. Part of the **i** before **e** rule says that it is *not* **i** before **e** after **c**—it's **ei**. There are not many **cei** words, few enough that you can remember them. They are *ceiling*, *conceited*, and the **-ceive** words: *receive, conceive, deceive, perceive,* and the words formed from them such as *receipt* and *deceitful.* (Don't forget that if the **c** sounds **sh**, it will be **cie**, as in *ancient.*) All right, now write the **cei** words. If you couldn't remember them all, look at the list again and then try to write them all.

2. Use each of the **cei** words in a sentence. Or put them all in one sentence.

3. What is the sound of the final **e** in *receive, conceive, deceive,* and *perceive*?

4. How does the word *believe* differ from *receive, conceive, perceive,* and *deceive*? How is it similar?

Answers

LESSON 13

A. 1. ceiling, ceiling, ceiling
2. deceiving, received, ceiling
3. ceiling

B. 1. received, receipt
2. receiving
3. receive, received

C. 1. deceive, deceitful, deceit

LESSON 13 (Continued)

D. friend, perceive, conceited, reign, piece, deceive, reins

E. (Start) ~~believe~~ ~~their~~ recieve frend concieted
freind ~~receive~~ ~~piece~~ cieling thier
beilive peice ~~celling~~ ~~chief~~ ~~friend~~ (End)

F. Crossword Puzzle:

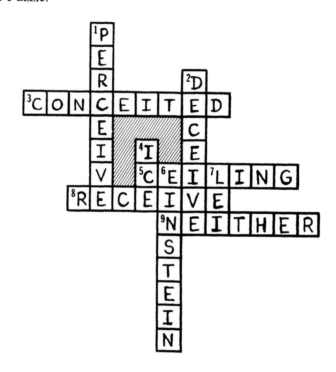

LESSON 13: Additional Activities

1. ceiling, receive, conceive, deceive, perceive, conceited
2. Sample sentence: I **perceived** a **conceited** child who tried to **deceive** me by walking on the **ceiling** after she had **received** an alligator for Christmas—can you **conceive** of that?
3. It is silent.
4. *Believe* is an **i** before **e** word; the others are **cei** words. It is similar to *deceive* and *receive* because it has a two-letter first syllable with a long **e** sound, and it has a second syllable with the ēv sound.

68

LESSON 14

do, does, doing, done, doesn't, don't, did
go, goes, going, gone, went
Verbs have different forms depending on who is doing them and when.

I *do* the dishes, you *do* the dishes, but he *does* the dishes. We've all *done* them many a time.

We *go* to the beach; he *goes* to the beach. We've all *gone* to the beach in August.

Most verbs throw an **s** on the end when it is he or she (or it) who does something: I walk, he walk**s**; you jump, she jump**s**; it happen**s**.

Some verbs, however, add **-es**: *do — does*;   *go — goes*.

(Most *nouns* just add **s** to make the plural: *chair, chairs*. Some add **-es**: *church, churches*.)

With the verbs *do* and *go*, add **-es**, not **-se**, for the third person singular (*he, she, it*).
Pronunciation: *does*: **dŭz**;   *goes*: **gōz**

A. Use a correct form of *do* or *go* in the following sentences. More than one may be correct: *do, does, doing, done, did*;   *go, goes, going, gone, went.*

1. _____ you want to use the computer?
2. _____ she need help in science today?
3. _____ she need help yesterday, too?
4. Dad is _____ the dishes. Why don't you _____ help him?
5. Who is _____ for the ice cream?
6. On Tuesday, Jerry _____ to his piano lesson.
7. He _____ on his bike.
8. Has he _____ yet?
9. Yes, he _____ at three o'clock.

does, does not, doesn't
do, do not, don't
When you write a contraction, you substitute the apostrophe for a letter. In *doesn't* and *don't*, you substitute the apostrophe for the **o** of the *not* part of those words: **n't**.

What mistake do some writers make when they write incorrectly: "dosen't"? They have misspelled *does* as "dose."

Another reason for misspelling *doesn't* as "dosen't" is that you hear **dŭz´ĕnt**. Therefore, you may want to spell that **e** before the **n**. In a contraction of *not*, you will hear what seems to be the vowel **e**, but you don't spell it.

    wasn't; not "wasen't"   *doesn't*; not "dosen't"

If you break the word under the apostrophe when you write it, you are less likely to misspell it. Also, when you write a contraction, stop briefly after the first part of the word. When you write *wasn't* and *doesn't*, you should first see *was*, not "wase", and *does*, not "dose."

B. Use one of the following words in each sentence below: *does, doesn't, do, don't*.

1. I _____ get that homework!
2. She _____ understand it at all.
3. _____ you?
4. No, I _____ .

seize   sēz
    EXCEPTION to **i**-before-**e** rule, like *weird*
Meaning: to grab forcibly
I will *seize* that *wei*rd dandelion in my *lei*sure.

LESSON 14 (Continued)

did, **did not**, **didn't**
was, **was not**, **wasn't**
had, **had not**, **hadn't**
have, **have not**, **haven't**
is, **is not**, **isn't**

Here are some verbs, their negatives (verbs plus *not*), and the contractions of those negatives. In each, the contraction leaves out only one letter: the **o** of *not*.

A problem arises for some people because they hear the pronunciation like this: **dĭd′ənt, wŭz′ənt, hăd′ənt,** and **ĭz′ənt.** They want to spell the schwa they hear as an **e**: "dident," "wasent," "hadent," "isent." No, no, no, no! There is no **e** in those words.

Haven't is made from *have* and *not*, and that *does* have an **e**, but it is *before* the **n**.

can, cannot, can't

The contraction *can't* leaves out not only the **o** of *not* but also the **n** of *not*. *Cannot* has two **n**'s; *can't* has one. *Cannot* is written as one word.

will, will not, won't

Where did *won't* come from? Originally, *will* was written as *woll*; that's where.

C. Circle the correctly spelled contraction in each pair:

1. can't, cann't
2. won't, wonn't
3. haden't, hadn't
4. haven't, havn't
5. didn't, diden't
6. dosen't, doesn't
7. do'nt, don't
8. wasen't, wasn't
9. isn't, isen't

D. Follow the correctly spelled contractions to go from the entrance to the exit:

(Enter)	I'm	doesn't	dont	cann't
	wasen't	don't	isen't	dosen't
	I'am	didn't	haden't	havn't
	diden't	wasn't	won't	haven't	(Exit)

E. Underline the misspellings in the following and write the corrections above them:

Once upon a time I diden't have anything to do, so I walked into the back yard and started digging a hole. It wasen't very long before I heard some sounds. They were sounds of someone else digging.

"Hallo there, I'am digging to reach America," I heard.

I jumped. Then I replied, "I'm digging to get to China. I diden't think I'de meet anyone so soon."

"Why dont we have lunch together? Well meet in a few feet."

LESSON 14
Additional Activities

1. Write the contractions for the following:

   a. does not   f. do not
   b. did not   g. was not
   c. have not   h. had not
   d. is not   i. cannot
   e. will not   j. I am

2. How do you form the third person singular (a verb that he, she, or it does) of a verb like *walk*? How do you form the third person singular of *do* and *go*?

3. The present tense of the verb shows "now" action. (I **go** to school with my lunch.) The past tense shows action before now. (I **went** to school with my lunch yesterday.) The past participle, with a helping verb like *have* or *had*, shows action completed in the past. (I *have gone* to school for many years and eaten my lunch at noon.) Write three of your own sentences using *go*, *went*, and *gone*.

4. Is it incorrect to say "I have went" or "I done it"? The simple past (*went*) does not use a helper verb (like *have*), and the past participle (*done*) *does* use a helper. It *is* correct to say: I went, I have gone, I did it, and I have done it. Write more sentences using *went*, *gone*, *did*, and *done* correctly.

5. Write three sentences using *do*, *did*, and *done*. What is the present tense of the verb *to do*? What is the past tense of *do*? What is the past participle?

6. Write the words that these contractions are made from:

   a. won't   b. can't

   What is different about these two contractions from most other contractions?

7. What's wrong with these words: "wasen't," "dosen't," "diden't," "isen't," and "haden't"? Why do people misspell the words that way? Write the words correctly.

8. Is this correct: *haven't*? Why?

Answers

LESSON 14

A.
1. Do/Did
2. Does/Did
3. Did
4. doing, go
5. going
6. went/goes
7. went/goes
8. gone
9. went

B.
1. don't
2. doesn't
3. Do
4. don't

LESSON 14 (Continued)

C.
1. can't
2. won't
3. hadn't
4. haven't
5. didn't
6. doesn't
7. don't
8. wasn't
9. isn't

D.

(Enter)—~~I'm~~——~~doesn't~~   dont   cann't
wasen't   ~~don't~~   isen't   dosen't
I'am   ~~didn't~~   haden't   havn't
diden't   ~~wasn't~~——~~won't~~——~~haven't~~——(Exit)

E.

diden't   wasen't   Hallo   I'am   Im   diden't   I'de   dont   Well
didn't   wasn't   Hello   I'm   I'm   didn't   I'd   don't   We'll

LESSON 14: Additional Activities

1. a. doesn't
   b. didn't
   c. haven't
   d. isn't
   e. won't
   f. don't
   g. wasn't
   h. hadn't
   i. can't
   j. I'm

2. You just add **s**. You add **-es** to *do* and *go* to make the third person singular: *does, goes.*

3. Sample sentences: I **went** to the corner to wait for the bus. Unfortunately, the bus had already **gone**. Now I will have to **go** to school on my own two feet.

4. Yes. Sample sentences: The next day, I **went** out to the corner earlier. Again, the bus had already **gone**. Again, I **did** what I had **done** before: I walked to school. Tomorrow I'll catch that bus.

5. Sample sentences: I will go to the corner very early and **do** my homework while I am waiting for the bus. I **did** not **do** my homework last night; it is not **done**. **Do** you think I will make the bus?
   Tenses: do, did, done

6. a. will not   b. cannot
   Won't does not seem related to the two words *will not*. In *can't* the apostrophe stands for two letters: **no**.

7. An **e** has been inserted into each word, because the speller heard the **e** pronounced in each word. Correct spellings: *wasn't, doesn't, didn't, isn't, hadn't.*

8. Yes, it is correct because the contraction is made from the two words *have* and *not*, and *have* has a final **e**.

72

LESSON 15

carry, carries, carried, carrying
marry, marries, married, marrying
Rule: A word, noun or verb, ending in **y** preceded by a consonant:
1) changes the **y** to **i** before **-es** or **-ed**;
2) keeps the **y** before the suffix **-ing**.
Pronunciation: **kăr′ē**
   Note that it is spelled with two **r**'s.
   The **y** at the end sounds long **e**. Do you suppose the **y** at the end of multi-syllable words always sounds long **e**? Think about it.

   A. Change the form of the word in parentheses if necessary to make sense in each sentence:

   Today I will (carry) _____ your books home because yesterday you (carry) _____ my books home. Jim always (carry) _____ his little sister's books home. See, he is (carry) _____ them now.
   Someday I am going to (marry) _____ the boy next door, unless he (marry) _____ someone else. I don't want to get (marry) _____ yet, though. I am not (marry) _____ anyone for a long time.

worry, worries, worried, worrying
Rule: A word, noun or verb, ending in **y** preceded by a consonant:
1) changes the **y** to **i** before **-es** or **-ed**;
2) keeps the **y** before the suffix **-ing**.
Pronunciation: **wûr′ē**
   Note that it is spelled with two **r**'s.
   The **y** at the end sounds long **e**.

   B. Change the form of the word in parentheses if necessary to make sense in each sentence:

   Does rain bother the ants? Do they (worry) _____ about it? They certainly look (worry) _____ when you move a stone that had covered their eggs. They are (scurry) _____ around (try) _____ to find a safer place for the eggs. They must be (worry) _____ about what will happen to them. So many (worry) _____ !

library, libraries
Rule: A noun ending in **y** preceded by a consonant changes the **y** to **i** before adding **-es** for the plural.
Pronunciation: **lī′brĕr ē**
   Remember the **r** right after the **b**: *lib*r*ary*.
   The **y** at the end sounds long **e**.

   C. Change the form of the word in parentheses if necessary to make sense in each sentence:
   Carnegie established many (library) _____ in this (country) _____ with money he made in the steel (industry) _____ .
   Although those people in the steel, oil, and railroad (industry) _____ made millions of dollars, they did give a lot of money to (library) _____ , foundations, and (charity) _____ .

   D. Underline the spelling errors in the following paragraph.
   When is the last time you whent to the library? Did you go thier in Feburary, or was it April? Did you read the magazines their, or did you do your sience homework? Have you tried to do your social studyes reports there? Have you carryed books home from the libarry, or are you worryed about losing them? That's a lot of things to think about.

LESSON 15 (Continued)

lb.

 Lb. is the abbreviation for *pound*. It doesn't look much like *pound*, does it? It comes from *libra*, the Latin word for "weight" or "balance." *Lbs.* is the abbreviation for *pounds*.
 I'd like the following groceries:

1 *lb.* spinach
2 *lbs.* broccoli
4 *lbs.* cauliflower

oz.

 Oz. is the abbreviation for *ounce* (ouns). Is that **z** a surprise? Add to my grocery list for the Land of Oz:

4 *oz.* courage
8 *oz.* heart
1 *oz.* way to get home
 Oz. is the abbreviation for both *ounce* and *ounces*, singular and plural.

E. Answer the questions:
1. What is the abbreviation for *pound*?
2. What is the abbreviation for *pounds*?
3. From what Latin word does that abbreviation come?
4. What is the abbreviation for *ounce*?
5. What is the abbreviation for *ounces*?
6. How many ounces are in a pound? Where will you find out?

happy, happier, happiest, happily, happiness
lazy, lazier, laziest, lazily, laziness
easy, easier, easiest, easily, easiness
busy, busier, busiest, busily, business
Rule: An adjective ending in **y** preceded by a consonant:
1) changes the **y** to **i** before **-er** and **-est**;
2) changes the **y** to **i** before suffixes beginning with consonants, like **-ness** and **-ly**;
3) keeps the **y** before the suffix **-ing**.
When you compare two things, you say one is _____ -er than another.
If you compare three or more things, one is the _____ -est of all.
This doll looks *happier* than that doll.
That teddy bear looks the *happiest* of all three teddy bears.

F. Fill in the correct form of the word in parentheses to compare two or more things:
1. (ease) This math problem is _____ than the other one.
2. (ease) This bicycle is the _____ one to ride of all the bicycles.
3. (busy) Jim is _____ than I am.
4. (busy) Jean is the _____ one of all three of us.
5. (happy) I am the _____ that I have ever been.

G. We often make adverbs from adjectives by adding **-ly**. I am a **happy** person; I *do* things **happily**. If the adjective ends in **y**, we change the **y** to **i** before adding **-ly**. Do so in the following sentences:
1. (lazy) She is _____ vacuuming her room.
2. (busy) I am sweeping the kitchen floor _____ .

H. Add **-ness** to the words in parentheses (you have to change the **y** to **i**):
1. (busy) Jean is in charge of the _____ .
2. (happy) Holidays are times of _____ .

LESSON 15
Additional Activities

1. Many words can end in a consonant before the **y**. Here we have verbs (*marry*), nouns (*library*), and adjectives (*happy*) that end in a consonant before **y**. To make the third person singular of verbs that end in a consonant before **y**, you change the **y** to **i** and add **-es** (*marry, marries*):

    a. I carry the tree; she _____ the saw.

    b. I marry the tree surgeon; she _____ the carpenter.

    c. I worry about trees falling; she _____ about saws slipping.

2. When you need the past tense of these verbs ending in a consonant before a **y**, you change the **y** to **i** and then add **-ed**:

    a. I _____ the tree yesterday. (carry)

    b. He _____ the saw carrier yesterday. (marry)

    c. They _____ about the trees and the wood. (worry)

3. Verbs ending in a consonant before a **y** *keep* the **y** before adding **-ing**. That avoids two **i**'s coming together, which is rare in English, and it keeps the pronunciation of the final **y** sounding long **e** before the short **i** in **-ing**:

    a. I have been _____ this tree too long. (carry)

    b. She is _____ the right man for her. (marry)

    c. We are _____ too much about trees and saws and wood. (worry)

4. We make the plural of nouns ending in a consonant before the **y** by changing the **y** to **i** and then adding **-es**.

    a. What is the plural of *library*?

    b. *Worry* is both a noun and a verb. What is the plural of the noun *worry*?

5. What letter do you have to remember in *library*?

6. What is the similar spelling pattern in the words *carry, marry*, and *worry*?

7. We change adjectives ending in a consonant before the **y** to the comparative and superlative forms by making the **y** into **i** and adding **-er** or **-est**. Make the comparative and superlative forms of *lazy, happy, easy*, and *busy*.

8. What is the sound of the **u** in *business*?

9. Write *easy*. What are the sounds of the **s** and the **y**?

10. Write the abbreviation for *pound*; for *pounds*. From what do the abbreviations come?

11. Write the abbreviation for *ounce*; for *ounces*.

Answers

LESSON 15

A. carry, carried, carries, carrying
marry, marries, married, marrying

B. worry, worried, scurrying, trying, worried, worries

C. libraries, country, industry, industries, libraries, charities

D. 12: whent, libary, thier, Feburary, their, sience, studyes, carryed, libarry, worryed, loosing, alot

Correct spellings: went, library, there, February, there, science, studies, carried, library, worried, losing, a lot

LESSON 15 (Continued)

E.
1. lb.
2. lbs.
3. *libra*
4. oz.
5. oz.
6. 16. In a dictionary, math book, cookbook, etc.

F.
1. easier
2. easiest
3. busier
4. busiest
5. happiest

G.
1. lazily
2. busily

H.
1. business
2. happiness

LESSON 15: Additional Activities

1.
a. carries
b. marries
c. worries

2.
a. carried
b. married
c. worried

3.
a. carrying
b. marrying
c. worrying

4.
a. libraries
b. worries

5. the first **r**

6. Each has a consonant, vowel, then **rry**.

7. lazy, lazier, laziest
happy, happier, happiest

easy, easier, easiest
busy, busier, busiest

8. a short **i**

9. *easy*. The **s** sounds **z**, and the **y** sounds long **e**.

10. *lb., lbs.* It comes from *libra*, the Latin word for pound.

11. *oz.* for both *ounce* and *ounces*

LESSON 16

hope, hoping

When a verb ends in a final silent **e**, drop that **e** before adding the suffix **-ing**.

The word is *hope*, with a long **o** sound. The final silent **e** makes it long. It is not *hop*, which is pronounced with a short **o** and is what bunnies are supposed to do.

"I *hope* it rains. I planted rocks in my garden, and they need rain to grow."
"Rocks don't grow!"
"That's because we haven't had enough rain."

A. Write the **-ing** form of each verb in parentheses:
1. (write)   I'm _____ my pen pal a letter.
2. (hope)   Where are you _____ to go for vacation?
3. (smile)   What are you _____ about?
4. (dine)   The _____ room is ready for lunch.
5. (love)   The baby was _____ the kitten so much!
6. (save)   I'm _____ my money for a new mountain bike.
7. (lose)   She is forever _____ her spelling homework.
8. (ride)   He has been _____ his bike for hours.
9. (scare)   This movie is _____ me.
10. (tape)   When will you finish _____ the movie?

hope, hoping; hop, hopping

Hop is a one-one-one word: a word of one syllable, ending in one consonant, preceded by one vowel. You double the final consonant before adding a suffix beginning with a vowel.

Hope has a final silent **e**. You drop the **e** before adding a suffix beginning with a vowel.

Some of these final **e** words are similar to one-one-one words. Keep them straight!

B. Look at these pairs of words. Use each pair in the **-ing** forms in a sentence to show the difference between them (i.e., use *robbing* and *robing* in one sentence, *starring* and *staring* in another sentence, and so on):

1. rob, robbing;   robe, robing
2. star, starring;   stare, staring
3. scar, scarring;   scare, scaring
4. strip, stripping;   stripe, striping
5. grip, gripping;   gripe, griping
6. mop, mopping;   mope, moping
7. tap, tapping;   tape, taping
8. rid, ridding;   ride, riding

Today I *tap* you on the right shoulder. Yesterday I *tapped* you on the left shoulder. I have been *tapping* your shoulder a lot. Is your shoulder all right? Perhaps the doctor can *tape* your shoulder that I *tap*. You say he *taped* it already? I must have *tapped* it too much!

Dining room is sometimes misspelled "dinning." The speller has confused the one-one-one rule with dropping the final **e**. Maybe the speller thought there was too much *din* in the *dining room*!

C. Write the **-ing** form of each of the following:

1. raise, choose, care, shine, please

2. take, love, come, use

3. save, dive, give, have, make

LESSON 16 (Continued)

happen, happened   **benefit, benefited**   **travel, traveled**

happen, happened

Happen is a two-syllable word with one final consonant with one vowel before it. But, because the accent is on the *first* syllable, the **n** is not doubled before a suffix beginning with a vowel.

hap´pen   *happened*

accent *not* on last syllable   not doubled

happen, summon, gallop, utter, parallel, channel, differ, offer, suffer, quarrel

These are words of two or more syllables. They end in one consonant preceded by one vowel. The accent, however, is not on the last syllable, so the final consonant will *not* be doubled before a suffix beginning with a vowel.

One of the reasons these words confuse us is that they *already* have a double consonant in the middle. After we add the suffix, we look at the word and wonder what really should be doubled! Think of the original word and the accent, and it should be easier.

D.   Write the **-ed** and **-ing** form for the following:

differ   _____   _____
parallel   _____   _____
offer   _____   _____
channel   _____   _____
suffer   _____   _____
summon   _____   _____
quarrel   _____   _____
utter   _____   _____
gallop   _____   _____

Happened is the past tense of *happen*. It's a regular verb to which you added **-ed**. You don't hear that **e** before the **d** the way you do in *hunted* and *added* because the **-ed** is not a separate syllable in *happened*. If the word is a regular past tense, you'll still need to spell it **-ed**, as in *awakened*, *frightened*, and *listened*. Be especially alert to words that add **-ed** to a word ending in **-en**. The combination of letters sounds like **end**, but it is spelled **-ened**.

benefit, benefited, benefiting

Benefit is a word of more than one syllable (it has three) with the accent on the first syllable: *ben´* e fit. Since the accent is not on the last syllable, the final consonant will not be doubled before a suffix beginning with a vowel.

travel   label   ravel   cancel   marvel   parcel   rival   quarrel
shovel   enamel   channel   counsel   model   equal   level

These are two-syllable words all ending in one consonant preceded by one vowel. The accent is *not* on the last syllable, so do not double the final consonant before a suffix beginning with a vowel.

For two reasons, mistakes are made with these words. (1) People learn the one-one-one rule and apply it incorrectly to too many words. (2) British spelling doubles the **l**.

The dictionary, for every one of these words, lists the spelling with one **l** first. The only alteration is the word *cancellation*, for which two **l**'s is the preferred spelling; one **l** is also possible.

E.   Write the **-ed** and **-ing** forms of the above words ending in **l**.
Example: *travel, traveled, traveling*.

LESSON 16
Additional Activities

1. From what word is each of the following made?

   hopping   _____

   gripping   _____

   griping   _____

   riding   _____

   robbing   _____

   scaring   _____

   scarring   _____

2. In a two-syllable word ending in one consonant preceded by one vowel, what do you do with that final consonant before adding a suffix beginning with a vowel when the accent of the word is *not* on the last syllable?

3. In the following list, circle the words in which you will *not* double the final consonant before adding **-ed** or **-ing** (the accents are marked for you):

   chan′nel   com mit′   hap′pen   o mit′   trav′el

   of′fer   be gin′   oc cur′   re fer′

4. Circle the correctly spelled words:

   sumonned   sufferred   shovelled   paralelled   suferred

   benefitted offerred   happend   bennefited

5. Why don't you double the **l** before **-ed** and **-ing** in *travel, model, cancel,* and *level?*

6. Add **-ing** to the following; change the spelling as necessary:

benefit	_____	hop	_____
quarrel	_____	give	_____
channel	_____	raise	_____
travel	_____	care	_____
happen	_____	summon	_____
label	_____	take	_____
hope	_____	have	_____
come	_____		

Answers

LESSON 16

A.
1. writing
2. hoping
3. smiling
4. dining
5. loving
6. saving
7. losing
8. riding
9. scaring
10. taping

B. Sample sentences:
1. A burglar was **robbing** the store while Jerry was **robing** a mannequin in the store window.
2. This play is **starring** Justin, who is **staring** into space.
3. The loggers are **scarring** the countryside, which is **scaring** us.
4. Saturday Joe will be **striping** lines on my car while Jacob is **stripping** that table of its old finish.
5. Jim was **griping** about **gripping** the camera for so long.
6. Jeremiah was **mopping** the floor while Jennie was **moping** about all the work that had to be done.
7. Jack was **tapping** on my door while Jacqueline was **taping** the movie.
8. Jean was **ridding** her kitchen of ants as John was **riding** his tricycle in the living room.

C.
1. raising, choosing, caring, shining, pleasing
2. taking, loving, coming, using
3. saving, diving, giving, having, making

LESSON 16 (Continued)

D.

dif´fer	differed	differing
of´fer	offered	offering
suf´fer	suffered	suffering
quar´rel	quarreled	quarreling
gal´lop	galloped	galloping
par´al lel	paralleled	paralleling
chan´nel	channeled	channeling
sum´mon	summoned	summoning
ut´ter	uttered	uttering

E.
1. travel, traveled, traveling
2. label, labeled, labeling
3. ravel, raveled, raveling
4. cancel, canceled, canceling
5. marvel, marveled, marveling
6. parcel, parceled, parceling
7. rival, rivaled, rivaling
8. quarrel, quarreled, quarreling
9. shovel, shoveled, shoveling
10. enamel, enameled, enameling
11. channel, channeled, channeling
12. counsel, counseled, counseling
13. model, modeled, modeling
14. equal, equaled, equaling
15. level, leveled, leveling

LESSON 16: Additional Activities

1. hop, grip, gripe, ride, rob, scare, scar
2. You do not double the final consonant.
3. channel, happen, travel, offer
4. None is correctly spelled.
5. Because the accent is on the first syllable of each word.
6. benefiting, channeling, happening, hoping, hopping, raising, summoning, quarreling, traveling, labeling, coming, giving, caring, taking, having

80

LESSON 17

prefer, **refer**, **transfer**, **confer**

All of these words are two-syllable words. They end in *one* consonant preceded by *one* vowel, and the accent is on the *last* syllable. Therefore, double the consonant before a suffix beginning with a vowel.

prefer´	preferred	preferring
refer´	referred	referring
transfer´	transferred	transferring
confer´	conferred	conferring

With each of these words, however, you can add suffixes beginning with a vowel that move the accent back to the first syllable. In these cases, the final **r** is *not* doubled.

pre fer´	pref´er ence	trans fer´	trans´fer ence
re fer´	ref´er ence	con fer´	con´fer ence

occur, **concur**

These two words are two-syllable words. They end in *one* consonant preceded by *one* vowel, and the accent is on the *last* syllable. Therefore, double the consonant before a suffix beginning with a vowel.

When you add **-ence** to these two words, the accent does *not* revert to the first syllable. It stays on that **r**, and so the **r** *is* doubled.

occur´   occurrence
concur´   concurrence   concurrently

Spelling test booklets love *prefer* and *occur* in all their forms. Practice these, especially.

A. Write the correct form of the word in parentheses in each blank:

1. (prefer) She _____ what kind of salad dressing last night? Her _____ was for blue cheese dressing.

2. (occur) The festival is _____ this October 10. Last year it _____ on October 12. This is the fourth _____ of the festival.

3. (transfer) I _____ my savings account to the new bank yesterday. My brother is _____ his tomorrow.

4. (confer) Is your father attending the _____ ? Yes. He _____ last week with my mother about it.

vacuum

Pronunciation: (1) văk´yo͞o əm   (2) văk´yo͞om

How many words do you know that have two **u**'s? *Continuum*?

If we pronounce the word by its first pronunciation, we might hear the two vowels. Most of us use the second pronunciation, especially when we're in a hurry to clean our room with the **vacuum cleaner**. It's hard writing two **u**'s in a row—easier to type them!

We now use the word *thermos* for any kind of **vacuum** bottle, but that's actually a brand name for the bottle that has a partial **vacuum** between its inner and outer walls to maintain the temperature of the contents.

color

Colorado's license plates say: **Colorful Colora**do. Helpful!

Pronunciation: kŭl´ər

That's the way it's pronounced, but put those **o**'s in when you spell it.

LESSON 17 (Continued)

quit, quite, quiet   kwĭt, kwīt, kwī′ət

First, think of the **qu** together as the **kw** sound in each of the words.

quit: rhymes with *hit*, or *bit*, or *sit*

I just *quit* my bit part in the play after I was *hit* on the head by falling scenery.

quite: **kw** sound again

The final silent **e** makes the **i** long as in *bite*. We don't have too many *-ite* words: *write*, *white*. Our more common ones add a **gh**: *sight*, *right*, *fight*, *might*.

That baby is *quite* active for her age. Look at her crawl across the living room!

quiet: **kw** sound for the **qu**

It is a *two*-syllable word: *qui et*.

The **e** comes *before* the **t**; together they form a separate syllable, as in *diet*.

The baby is finally *quiet* after all that screaming.

let's

Pronunciation: lĕts

This is a contraction for *let us*. You'd rarely write out the two words. The contraction is used in conversation, and so you would be informal in your writing, too:

"*Let's* go to the movies tonight!" I suggested.

It's not related to *lettuce*, which goes in your bacon, *lettuce*, and tomato sandwich. Let's not eat our *lettuce* tonight!

B.   Follow the following directions:

1.   Write the pronunciation for *quit*, *quite*, and *quiet*.

2.   Use one of the above words in the following sentences:

  b.   When the electricity was knocked out, everything in our house became very

    _____ .

  c.   I had to _____ reading my book because I had no light.

  d.   I've eaten _____ enough!

  e.   It's _____ _____ here in the dark.

  f.   Let's _____ this nonsense and go to a movie.

3.   For what two words is *let's* a contraction?

circus, circuses

Pronunciation: sûr′kəs

The word shows the two sounds of the letter **c**:

  1.   *cir* - **sur**   **c** followed by **e, i,** or **y** sounds **s**
  2.   *cus* - **kus**   **c** followed by **a, o, u,** a consonant, or nothing sounds **k**

Think of the rings in a three-ring **circ**us, the **circ**les in which the acts are performed: **circ**le/**circ**us.

To make the plural of *circus*, add **-es**. If you added just an **s** ("circuss"), you wouldn't hear the difference between one circus and two.

If words end in **s, ss, x, z, ch** or **sh**, you add **-es** to make the plural. Write the plurals of: *circus, bus, fox, fuzz, business, bush, gas, mess, stitch, tax, wax, box,* and *buzz.* (The plural of *bus* is *buses*; the plural of *gas* is *gases*. Each word has an alternate plural: *busses, gasses.*)

LESSON 17
Additional Activities

1. Circle the correctly spelled words:

preferred	refer	transferr	occur	concur
prefering	refered	transferred	occurred	concurence
preference	referring	transferring	occurring	concurring
preferrence	reference	transference	occurence	concurred
confer	refference	confer	popcorn	
conferring	refferrence	conferring		
confered		confered		

2. Underline the ones that still trip you up. Use a dictionary or your spelling book to find the correct spelling of these and copy them in your special book.

3. Write the pronunciation of *quit*, *quite*, and *quiet*.

4. Write a sentence using each of those three words.

5. Use *quit*, *quite*, and *quiet* in one sentence.

6. What is odd about the spelling of *vacuum*? Have you ever used a **vacuum cleaner** in your room?

7. For what two words is *let's* a contraction?

8. The two vowels in *color* are the same. What are they? How do they sound?

9. The word *circus* shows the two pronunciations of **c**. What are they? Why is **c** pronounced the way it is each time in *circus*? What are the two vowels in *circus*? What do they sound like?

10. How do you form the plural of *circus*? How is that different from forming the plural of *table*? Why is it different?

Answers

LESSON 17

A. 1. prefers, preference
   2. occurring, occurred, occurrence
   3. transferred, transferring
   4. conference, conferred

LESSON 17 (Continued)

B. 1. quit/kwĭt   quite/kwīt   quiet/kwī′ət

   2. a. quite
      b. quiet
      c. quit
      d. quite
      e. quite quiet
      f. quit

   3. let us

C. circuses, buses (busses), foxes, fuzzes, businesses, bushes, gases (gasses), messes, stitches, taxes, waxes, boxes, buzzes

LESSON 17: Additional Activities

1. preferred, preference, refer, referring, reference, transferred, transferring, transference, confer, conferring, occur, occurred, occurring, concur, concurring, concurred, popcorn

2. No problem. I know them, I think.

3. quit: **kwĭt**

   quite: **kwīt**

   quiet: **kwī′ət**

4. Sample sentences: I **quit** eating popcorn when the bowl was not **quite** empty. I ate so much that my stomach is not very **quiet**. In fact, it is **quite** noisy. I guess I should **quit** eating **quite** so much at one time.

5. Sample sentence: I will **quit** eating so much if it is **quite quiet** in here.

6. It has two **u**'s in it. Yes, I have.

7. *let's* = *let us*

8. They are both **o**'s. The first **o** sounds like a short **u**, and the second **o** sounds as a schwa.

9. The first **c** sounds as an s because it is followed by an **i**. The second **c** sounds as a **k** because it is followed by a **u**. The two vowels are **i** and **u**. The **i** sounds like a **u**; the **u** sounds as a schwa.

10. You add **-es** to form the plural. You add just **-s** to form the plural of *table*. You couldn't hear the difference in pronunciation between the singular and the plural if you added just **-s** to *circus* for the plural. When you add **-es**, you hear the plural form.

84

LESSON 18

clothes

Pronunciation: **klōz, klōthz**   (**th** as in *then*)

clôth   -   **klôth**   (**th** as in *thin*); noun, meaning "fabric"

clōthe   -   **klōth**   (**th** as in *then*); verb, meaning "to put into clothes"

Clothes is a plural noun; there is no singular. You can speak of *an* article of clothing, but clothes are always clothes. The word comes from the verb *to clothe*, with a long **o** sound.

    Notice the two pronunciations:

      klōz   (without a **th** sound)

      klōthz   (with a **th** sound)

The first pronunciation causes confusion with the word *close*.

close, closes, closed, closing

Pronunciation: **klōz**

    Here, **c** sounds like a **k**, the **s** sounds like a **z**, and the final silent **e** makes the **o** long.

    One of the pronunciations of *clothes* is **klōz**, and so these two words are sometimes confused.

    The meaning of this word is "to shut" or "to end."

I think I'll *close* the door, take off my **clothes**, and jump into the shower. This August weather is awful.

close Pronounced **clōs**, this is an adjective meaning "near." You're **close** (**clōs**) to the door. **Close** (**clōz**) it, please.

often

Pronunciation: **ôf′ ən**, so it should be spelled "offen," right? Yes, but it isn't. The **t** is silent. An older English word is *oft*, in which the **t** *is* pronounced. *Oft* have I misspelled **often**.

    So, pronounce the word incorrectly when you spell it. Say *often*.

    Next spell *soften*. When you pronounce *soft*, you say the **t**. When you say *soften*, you *don't* pronounce the **t**, nor do you in *listen* or *fasten*.

    Often, you *soften* butter for toast or radishes. You've never tried butter on a radish? It removes some of the sharpness.

A. Complete the puzzle with real spelling for these words spelled according to the dictionary markings: *often, oft, bottom, right, stopped, clothes, close, soften, purpose, seem, guessed.*

Across

3. **klōz** (to shut)
6. **ôf′ ən**
7. **bŏt′ əm**
8. **pûr′ pəs**
10. **gĕst** (made a guess)
11. **sôf′ ən**

Down

1. **klōz** (what you wear)
2. **sēm** (appear)
4. **ôft**
5. **stŏpt**
9. **rīt** (opposite of left)

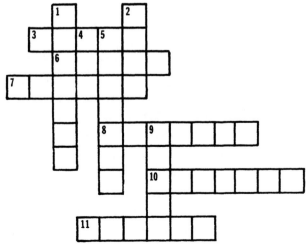

          Spelling Demons Week by Week

LESSON 18 (Continued)

rhyme
Pronunciation: rīm
    The final silent **e** gives the **y** a long **i** sound. There's something funny looking about that word: ah yes, a silent **h**. We have a few words in English beginning in **rh** where the **h** is silent. *Rhyme, rhythm, rhinoceros,* and *rhododendron* are the most common.
    If you have trouble finding words in the dictionary that begin with the **r** sound, try looking under **rh**.
Most of the time
I cannot *rhyme.*

rhythm
Pronunciation: rĭth´əm
    In this word, the **y** sounds like a short **i**. It also begins **rh**, like *rhyme;* you don't hear the **h**. It has an unaccented vowel sound before the **m**. Actually, there isn't any vowel there. Tricky! Don't write a vowel in there even though you hear one.
Mr. Bartosiewicz has a good sense of *rhythm.*

principal, principle
principal   **prĭn´sə pəl**
    As an adjective, it means "first in importance."
    As a noun, it means "the head of a school." It also means, in finance, "the main body of an estate," as opposed to the interest.

principle   **prĭn´sə pəl**
    It is *only* a noun, and it refers to basic truths, rules of human conduct, fundamental laws.
    The pronunciation of both words is the same. In both the **s** sound is spelled by a **c**. (The **i** following the **c** gives the **c** the **s** sound.)
    In *principal,* the ending is spelled **-pal**; it sounds **pəl.**
    In *principle,* the ending is spelled **-ple**; it sounds **pəl.**

B. Answer the questions and fill in the blanks:

1. What sound does the **y** have in *rhyme*? What makes the **y** long?
2. What sound does the **y** have in *rhythm*?
3. What sound does the **c** have in *principal* and *principle*?
4. If you think of the head of a school building as being a "pal," how does that help you spell the word?
5. The **principal** of a school is the most important person there. That word is a noun. The adjective meaning the most important thing is spelled the same way. How do you spell it?
6. If we talk about basic truths and laws—no matter how important—that word is spelled _____ .
7. Our _____'s name is Mr. Hudson.
8. The _____ reason I work overtime is that I need the money.
9. The _____ of coexistence is discussed in this paper.
10. He is a man of strong _____ (s).
11. I don't understand that new _____ we talked about in physics.
12. What is his _____ source of income?
13. How much interest does he earn on the _____ ?

C. Draw lines connecting the rhyming words:

      rhinoceros, preposterous, jelly, banana

      through, rough, blue, shoe, though, too, you

LESSON 18
Additional Activities

1. What is the sound of the **y** in *rhyme*? What final letter on the word would make you think the vowel would be a long sound?

2. What are the two silent letters in *rhyme*?

3. Waht is the sound of the **y** in rhyme?

4. What silent letter does *rhythm* have? Is it the same as the silent consonant in *rhyme*? Use the dictionary to find all the **rh-** words. Copy five correctly that you might use.

5. In the second syllable of *rhythm* there is no vowel. How it that possible?

6. If you think of the head of your school as a "pal," how may it help you to spell that word? What gives the *s* sound in that word? What are the first two vowels?

7. What is the meaning of the homonym for *principal*? How do you spell it? Use it in a sentence.

8. If I give you a pair of jeans, a shirt, a sweater, and a pair of sneakers, what would you call all of these things? Do you pronounce the word as **klōz** or **klōthz**?

9. If I shut the door, what do I do to it?

10. To add **-es**, **-ed**, or **-ing** to a word ending in final **e**, what do you do with that final **e**?

11. What letter is silent in *often*? in *soften*? Does *often* have two **f**'s? Do you hear the **t** in *soft*? Is *oft* a word? How might that help you spell *often*?

Answers

LESSON 18

A. Crossword Puzzle:

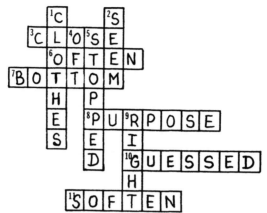

LESSON 18 (Continued)

B.
1. long **i**; the final silent **e**
2. short **i**
3. **s**
4. The last three letters of *principal* are *pal*.
5. principal
6. principles
7. principal
8. principal
9. principle
10. principle
11. principle
12. principal
13. principal

C. rhinoceros/preposterous
through, blue, shoe, too, you

LESSON 18: Additional Activities

1. long **i**; the final silent **e**
2. **h** and **e**
3. ~~short i~~ *long*
4. the first **h**; yes
   rhapsody, rhea, Syngman Rhee, rheostat, rhesus monkey, rhetoric, rheumatic fever, rheumatism, Rhine, rhinestone, rhinoceros, rhizome, Rhode Island, Rhodes, Rhodesia, rhododendron, rhombus, Rhone, rhubarb, rhyme, rhythm
5. I guess it shouldn't be, but it is. We put a schwa sound before the **m**.
6. The word referring to the head of a school—*principal*—ends in the letters **pal**. The **c** gives the **s** sound. The first two vowels are both **i**.
7. Meaning: a basic truth, law, or assumption
   Spelling: *principle*
   Sample sentence: I believe in the **principle** of honesty.
8. clothes; both ways
9. You close it.
10. You drop that final **e**.
11. The **t** is silent in both *often* and *soften*. *Often* has one **f**. You hear the **t** in *soft*. *Oft* is a word, an adverb meaning *often*. It is a poetic form, usually used in combinations such as *oft-repeated*. It might help you to spell *often* because you hear the **t** in *oft*.

LESSON 19

lose
Pronunciation: lo͞oz (a verb)
Meaning: cannot find; not win

I *lose* every game I pitch. I *lost* again yesterday

My father is *losing* his hair. He *loses* some each year.

People write *loose* instead, thinking it rhymes with *choose*. But if you want a verb that means you didn't win or you can't find something, *lose* is what you want.

loose
Pronunciation: lo͞os (an adjective)
Meaning: not tight

Loose is pronounced lo͞os with an **s**, not a **z**.

If your shoes are too *loose*, you may *lose* them if you run.

He is *losing* battles to *lose* pounds. His clothes aren't *loose*.

until
Syllables: *un til*
Pronunciation: ŭn tĭl´
Spelling: *until* (one **l**)
Meaning: up to the time that

I slept *until* noon!

Like the word *full*, which as a suffix becomes **-ful** (with one **l**), *till* becomes **-til** with one **l** in the word *until*.

surprise
Pronunciation: sər prīz´

I think of surprises as being nice; therefore, I think of a prize with *surprise*. But *surprise* has nothing to do with *prize*. That is not the meaning. It means "to take unawares." The word comes from:

     sur   -   "over"
     prendre   -   "to take"

Other people have trouble remembering the **r** before the **p** because they pronounce the word as sŭ prīz´. Pronounce that **r** at the end of the first syllable (*sur*) to spell the word correctly.

Rise up and spell sur*prise* correctly.

build, built
Pronunciation: bĭld, bĭlt

Buy and *build* have a silent **u** before the vowel **i**. I can't see any reason for it, but there it is.

I *build* many houses each year. Last year I *built* a dozen.

Homonym for *build*: *billed*, which is the past tense of *bill*.

He *billed* me for *building* my house.

A. Answer the questions and fill in the blanks:
1. Two letters can cause problems in *surprise*. Which are they?
2. How many **l**'s in *until*? How many **l**'s in *beautiful, awful,* and *careful*?
3. What is the silent letter in *built*? *build*? *buy*?
4. Use the correct homonyms (*build, billed*):
    I _____ you for the lumber. Now I will _____ your house.
5. Choose the correct spelling: *lose* or *loose.*
    My socks are too _____ .
    Don't _____ your keys through the hole in your pocket.
    Is the goose _____ ? Bring her in and shut the gate. I don't want to _____ her.

LESSON 19 (Continued)

guess

Pronunciation: **gĕs**

What do you do when your teacher marks a word as "misspelled," "WRONG," or "look up the spelling" Do you **guess**? No, no.

If it's a word that begins with **g** and it is followed by a vowel sound, look up **gu** and then the vowel sound.

When you have nothing better to do, look through the **gu**-section of your dictionary and just see how many of your familiar words have a **u** between the **g** and the next vowel. Here are a few: *guess, guest, guide, guild, guilty, guard, guarantee, guy, guitar*.

What does that **u** do? First of all, it may cause you to misspell the word. Second, it keeps the **g** sounding like a **g**, not a **j**. **Guess** you never thought about that, did you? Not very often, anyway.

guest

Pronunciation: **gĕst**

If the word were spelled "gest," you would probably have to pronounce it **jĕst** because an **e** after the **g** usually gives the **j** sound to the **g**. With the **u** after the **g**, the **g** is pronounced as a **g**.

Guessed (pronounced **gĕst**) is the past tense of **guess** and a homonym for **guest**. (I *guessed* my *guest* needed a nickel.)

nickel

Pronunciation: **nĭk′əl**

This is one of the words that ends **-el** rather than the more frequent **-le**. Here are some others: *camel, travel, model, towel, channel, level, angel, sequel.*

B. Can you use those in one sentence? Can you write another sentence with all the **gu**-words listed above with *guess*?

C. Fill in the correct spelling for *guest, guess,* and *nickel*:

"Please put the g _____ st towels in the bathroom for the g _____ sts."

"Why can't they use ours?"

"They're too dirty."

The g _____ sts?"

"No, our towels."

G _____ ss what we had for lunch? G _____ ss which g _____ st ate the most biscuits.

How many nick _____ s in a quarter? How many nick _____ s in two dollars?

choir

Pronunciation: **kwīr**

Do you sing in a **kwīr**? How about **kôr′əs**? **glē** club?

kwīr is spelled *choir*; **kôr′əs** is spelled *chorus*.

They are similar. Both start with **cho**.

In *choir*, the **ch** sounds **k**, a **w** sound drops into the word from nowhere, and then you hear the **ir**. I hope your **choir** sounds as fancy as the word is spelled. If you can't spell it, maybe you could get out your guitar and sing. Can you spell *guitar*? Without looking?

ocean

Pronunciation: **ō′shən**

The first and the last letters (**o** and **n**) cause no problems. It's the middle of the word. Since it's the ocean, you would think the word could at least spell the middle letters as "sea," but no! It had to be **cea**. What you're getting out of the **c** is the **sh** sound. The **ea** gives the schwa sound, the unaccented vowel sound.

sea, ocean, beach   Each of these words has an **ea**.

LESSON 19
Additional Activities

1. If you can't find something, did you **lose** or **loose** it?

2. If your tooth is finally going to fall out, what is it?

3. Write *lose* and its pronunciation; write *loose* and its pronunciation.

4. What letter follows the **g** in *guess* and *guest*? Why is it there? Use the dictionary to find other **gu-** words in which the **u** is silent before a succeeding vowel. What is the sound of the **u** in *build* and *built*? What other word has a silent **u** after the **b**? Use a dictionary to find out.

5. How many **s**'s in *guess*? in *guest*?

6. What is half of a dime? five pennies?

7. *Nickel* rhymes with *pickle*. How, other than the initial letter, does the spelling differ? What is the most usual spelling of the final **l** sound?

8. How would associating *sea beach* with *ocean* help you spell *ocean*?

9. What is the sound of the **c** in *ocean*?

10. The **ch** in *choir* is pronounced **k**. How is the **ch** in *school* pronounced? Do you sing in your **school choir**? It's easier to spell "play in the band," isn't it? How might you mispronounce *choir* in order to help you spell it?

11. Divide *surprise* into syllables. How do you spell the first syllable? What other words do you know that start with this syllable? What is the sound of the second **s** in the word? How might you remember that there is a second **s** in the word?

12. Spell *until*. How do you know it is correct? Look it up in the dictionary. How might you spell it incorrectly? Don't.

Answers

LESSON 19

  A. 1. the **r** before the **p** and the second **s**
      2. one; one, one, one
      3. **u, u, u**
      4. billed; build
      5. loose
          lose
          loose, lose

LESSON 19 (Continued)

  B. Sample Sentences: In the **sequel**, the **camel** was an **angel** as the **model traveled** by the **level channel** with only a **towel**.
        Our **guilty guest guided** the **guard** with the **guitar** to the **guild** with a **guarantee** to **guess** the song or pay the **guy**.

  C. **ue, ue**
      ue
      ue, ue, ue
      el, el

LESSON 19: Additional Activities

  1. lose
  2. loose
  3. lose, lo͞oz; loose, lo͞os
  4. The **u** after the **g** keeps the **g** hard, sounding like a **g**, not a **j**.

      guarantee, guard, Guernsey, guerilla, guess, guest, Guiana, guidance, guide, guild, guile, guillotine, guilt, Guinea, guinea pig, guise, guitar, guy

    The **u** in *build* and *built* is silent.

    buy

  5. There are two **s**'s in *guess* and one in *guest*.
  6. a nickel; a nickel
  7. *Nickel* has the **e** before the **l**. The most usual spelling is **-le**.
  8. Each word has the vowel combination **ea**.
  9. **sh**
 10. **k**. I would say **ch-o-i-r**.
 11. *sur prise*; **sur**

      surcharge, surface, surfeit, surgeon, surmise, surmount, surname, surpass, surplice, surplus, surreal, surrender, surreptitious, surrey, surrogate, surround, surtax, surveillance, survey, survive

    The second **s** sounds **z**.

      It's hard for me to remember it. Maybe I can think that the word has two **s**'s in it. Or, **surprise**: no **prize**; it's an **s**.

 12. *until*; I've learned it; I did; "untill"; okay, cross it out and make it *until*.

LESSON 20

pretty
Pronunciation: **prĭt′ē**
   It sounds as if it should be spelled with an **i** rather than an **e**, doesn't it? It has two **t**'s and a **y** after that **e**.
Betty is *pretty*. I walked on the *jetty* with *pretty* Betty. She's *pretty*, she's beautiful, she's gorgeous! *Ugly* is easier to spell than any of those.

been
Pronunciation: **bĭn.** The two **e**'s sound short **i**.
It's part of the verb *to be*.
I *am* pretty today. I *was* pretty yesterday. I have *been* pretty every day of my life.
   To be, this most common verb of ours, is a wild one. You can expect any spelling from that irregular one: *am, is, are, was, were, been.*

woman, women
   Woman and *women* are easy words to spell if you forget about their pronunciation. The singular ends in **man**, which you can spell; the plural ends in **men**, which you can also spell. Write **wo** for the beginnings, and you have *woman* and *women.*
   But the pronunciation has probably been throwing you off:

woman: **wŏŏm′ən**   *women:* **wĭm′ĭn**

The **o** in the singular sounds like a double short **o**. The **o** in the plural sounds like a short **i**.

manila
Pronunciation: **mə nĭl′ə**
Manila is a large city in the Philippine Islands. *Manila hemp* is the fiber from the tropical plant abaca grown in the Philippines. *Manila paper* is thin cardboard with a smooth finish made originally from *Manila hemp*, or wood fibers similar to it. It is usually a buff color. The *manila folder* that holds your science report is made of *manila paper*.
   I always thought the teacher was talking about "vanilla" folders. I didn't think they smelled at all like vanilla, but I kept hoping they might some day.
   Vanilla, as in vanilla ice cream, has two **l**'s. *Manila*, which is not in ice cream, has only one **l**. So does *Philippines*.

A.   Fill in the blanks with these words: *pretty, manila, women, been, woman.*

1.   A rose is a _____ flower.

2.   I have _____ living in the Philippines.

3.   You can pay the _____ at the counter for those _____ folders.

4.   How many _____ are in the U.S. Senate?

B.   Answer these questions:

1.   What is the sound of the **e** in *pretty*?

2.   What is the sound of the **ee** in *been*?

3.   What is the sound of the **o** in *women*?

4.   What is the sound of the **o** in *woman*?

5.   What is the sound you make when you're called for dinner?

C.   Write a sentence using *been, pretty, woman,* and *women* without calling the woman or women pretty.

LESSON 20 (Continued)

any, many

Any and many sound as if the first vowel is spelled with a short **e**, because that's the sound of the **a** in both words. (There is a short **e** sound in says, said, again, and against, too.)

The **y** at the end of the word sounds like a long **e**.

Do you have any broccoli plants?

No, I didn't grow many broccoli plants. Any I did grow, the woodchuck ate. I have some cauliflower, though.

says, said

These are parts of the verb to say.

I say, she says; we are saying; they said.

Say and saying have the long **a** sound.

Says and said have the short **e** sound. (They are not spelled "sez" and "sed"!)

"Who says we can't have any ice cream?"

"Mom said so, that's who."

"Oh."

again, against

Again and against are two words that begin with an unaccented vowel sound, a schwa spelled with an **a**. There are a lot of those words (a lot is two words): again, against, around, about, along, afraid.

When you spell these words, say the **a** as a short or a long **a** to remind you of their spelling.

The **ai** is pronounced short **e**—the same as in any, many, says, and said. British speakers tend to pronounce these two words with a long **a** as ə gān′ and ə gānst′. This pronunciation has merit in helping you to spell the words.

D. Answer these questions:

1. What is the pronunciation of the **a** in any, many, and says?

2. What is the pronunciation of the **ai** in said, again, and against?

E. Complete the crossword puzzle with one of the following words according to the pronunciation in the sentences: any, many; says, said; again, against.

Across

2. Isn't there (ĕn′ē) ice cream left?

3. She (sĕz) we can't buy any more.

6. She says she is (ə gĕnst′) buying any more ice cream.

Down

1. Summer has too (mĕn′ē) days to go without ice cream.

4. We need to buy ice cream (ə gĕn′).

5. I hear what she (sĕd). I disagree with her.

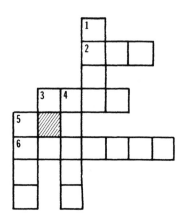

LESSON 20
Additional Activities

1.   Draw a picture showing the meaning of *against*.

2.   Show me a manila folder.

3.   Draw a picture of a pretty frog. If you cannot draw one, tell me how many **t**'s are in *pretty* and what the sound of the **e** is.

4.   What two letters are added to *again* to spell *against*?

5.   *Been* is the past participle of the verb *to be*. There are a few verbs that form the past participle with **-en**: *beaten, bitten, broken, chosen, driven, eaten, fallen, frozen, given, ridden, risen, shaken, spoken, stolen, striven, written,* and *woven*. Think: I have _____ en, I have "be-en." How will pronouncing the word as **bēn** or **bē-ĕn** help you to spell it?

6.   What is the sound of the **o** in *woman*? in *women*?

7.   What is the sound of the **a** in *any* and *many*? What is the sound of the **y**?

8.   What is the sound of the **ay** and the **ai** in *says, said, again,* and *against*? How might you pronounce those words to help you spell them?

9   *Said* is the past tense of *say*. How is it spelled rather than with the usual **-ed** ending for the past tense? What is the past tense of *pay*?

Answers

LESSON 20

A.
1. pretty
2. been
3. woman, manila
4. women

B.
1. short **i**
2. short **i**
3. short **i**
4. short double **o** (o͞o)
5. a happy sound

C. Sample sentence: I've **been pretty** tired of spelling **woman** and **women**.

LESSON 20 (Continued)

D.
1. short **e**
2. short **e**

E. Crossword Puzzle:

LESSON 20: Additional Activities

1. Sample drawing:

(He is sitting *against* the tree.)
2. You must have a manila folder someplace.
3. There are two **t**'s in *pretty*, and the **e** sounds short **i**.
4. **st**
5. Pronouncing it with a long **e** may help you to remember the double **e**. Pronouncing it as "be-en" may help you to remember both **e**'s.
6. short double **o** in *woman*; short **i** in *women*
7. short **e**; long **e**
8. short **e**; pronounce them with a long **a** sound
9. It is spelled **-id** rather than **-ed**. The past tense of *pay* is *paid*.

96

Second Quarter Quizzes

This section starts with a choice of oral quizzes to dictate to your students for this quarter of the work: 10 words, 20, 50, or 100. Choose the one or ones best suited to the individual needs of your students, the time you have, and how many words you feel are important for each quarter. If the word is a homonym, I have provided a sentence.

The oral quizzes are followed by three reproducible written quizzes: Sound to Spelling, Spelling Rules, and General.

Oral Quizzes

Test I: 10 Words

1. judgment
2. weird
3. receive
4. doesn't
5. library
6. benefited
7. preferred
8. rhythm
9. surprise
10. says

Test II: 20 Words

1. judgment
2. known
3. weird
4. while
5. receive
6. ceiling
7. doesn't
8. don't
9. library
10. carried
11. benefited
12. happened
13. preferred
14. reference
15. rhythm
16. principal (of a school)
17. surprise
18. until
19. says
20. many

Test III: 50 Words

1. judgment
2. known
3. tired
4. jewelry
5. know (I know the answer.)
6. no (I have no freckles on my feet.)
7. weird
8. while
9. very
10. receive
11. ceiling
12. deceive
13. conceited
14. doesn't
15. don't
16. wasn't
17. haven't
18. can't
19. won't
20. didn't
21. isn't
22. library
23. carried
24. worrying
25. happiness
26. benefited
27. happened
28. hoping
29. hopping
30. traveled
31. preferred
32. reference
33. quite
34. quiet
35. circuses
36. rhythm
37. principal (The principal awarded the degrees.)
38. principle (It's the principle of the thing I dislike.)
39. clothes (I will wear my oldest clothes to paint the kitchen.)
40. close (I will close the paint can after I am finished.)
41. surprise
42. until
43. built
44. guess
45. nickel
46. ocean
47. says
48. many
49. woman
50. women

Oral Quizzes (Continued)

IV: 100 Words

1. know (I know the difference between a cardinal and a robin.)
2. no (I have no birds in my yard.)
3. new (I have a new birdhouse.)
4. knew (I knew no birds before this year.)
5. known
6. knowing
7. knowledge
8. acknowledge
9. acknowledgment
10. tired
11. jewelry
12. judgment
13. they
14. very
15. while
16. chihuahua
17. kaleidoscope
18. Fahrenheit
19. reveille
20. onomatopoeia
21. weird
22. etc. (abbreviation for *etcetera*)
23. ceiling
24. receive
25. receipt
26. deceive
27. conceited
28. does
29. done
30. doesn't
31. don't
32. goes
33. gone
34. went
35. didn't
36. was
37. wasn't
38. hadn't
39. have not
40. haven't
41. isn't
42. cannot
43. can't
44. won't
45. carried
46. marries
47. worrying
48. libraries
49. lb. (abbreviation for *pound*)
50. lbs. (abbreviation for *pounds*)
51. oz. (abbreviation for *ounce* or *ounces*)
52. happier
53. laziness
54. easiest
55. busily
56. hoping
57. hopping
58. happened
59. channeled
60. benefited
61. benefiting
62. traveled
63. canceled
64. cancellation
65. modeled
66. preferred
67. reference
68. transferring
69. conference
70. occurred
71. concurrently
72. vacuum
73. color
74. quite
75. quiet
76. let's
77. circuses
78. clothes (I like old clothes.)
79. close (Close the door!)
80. often
81. rhyme
82. rhythm
83. principal (The principal officer of the bank talked with me.)
84. principle (We talked about the principles of sound banking.)
85. lose
86. until
87. surprise
88. built
89. guess
90. nickel
91. choir
92. ocean
93. pretty
94. been
95. woman
96. women
97. manila (folder)
98. many
99. says
100. against

SECOND QUARTER
Sound to Spelling Quiz

In the following test, spell the word correctly from the sound of the word given by the dictionary markings.

1. nō (I don't nō the answer.)
2. nō (I have nō questions.)
3. nōō (I nōō you'd say that.)
4. nōō (I have nōō shoes.)
5. nōn
6. nō´ĭng
7. nŏl´ĭj
8. ăk nŏl´ĭj mĕnt
9. tīrd
10. jōō´əl rē
11. jŭj
12. jŭj´ mĕnt
13. kə lī´də skōp
14. făr´ən hīt
15. rĕv´ə lē
16. ŏn ə mät ə pē´ə
17. ĕt sĕt´ə rə (You pronounce the whole word but write just the abbreviation.)
18. thā
19. vĕr´e
20. hwīl
21. chĭ wä´ wä
22. sē´lĭng
23. rĭ sēv´
24. dĭ sēv´
25. kən sē´tĭd
26. pər sēv´
27. kən sēv´
28. dōō
29. dŭz
30. dōō´ĭng
31. dŭn
32. dŭz´ ənt
33. dōnt
34. gōz
35. gôn
36. wĕnt
37. dĭd´ ənt
38. wŭz
39. wŭz´ ənt
40. hăd´ ənt
41. hăv
42. hăv´ ənt
43. ĭz
44. ĭz´ ənt
45. kăn nŏt (accent on either syllable)
46. kănt
47. wōnt
48. kăr´ē
49. wûr´ē
50. lī´brĕr ē

© 1986, 1997 J. Weston Walch, Publisher

Spelling Demons Week by Week

SECOND QUARTER
Sound to Spelling Quiz (Continued)

51. ē′zē

52. bĭz′ē

53. hōp′ĭng

54. hŏp′ĭng

55. skär′ĭng

56. skâr′ĭng

57. hăp′ĕnd

58. trăv′əld

59. prĭ fûr′

60. prĕf′ər ĕns

61. rĭ fûr′

62. rĕf′ər ĕns

63. trăns fûr′

64. ə kûr′

65. văk′yōō əm *or* văk′yōōm

66. kŭl′ər

67. kwĭt

68. kwīt

69. kwī′ət

70. lĕts

71. sûr′kəs

72. klōz *or* klōthz (what you wear)

73. klōz (the door)

74. ôf′ən

75. rīm

76. rĭth′əm

77. prĭn′sə pəl (of a school)

78. prĭn′sə pəl (ideas)

79. lōoz

80. lōos

81. ŭn tĭl′

82. sər prīz′

83. bĭld

84. bĭlt

85. gĕs

86. gĕst

87. nĭk′əl

88. kwīr

89. ō′shən

90. prĭt′ē

91. bĭn

92. wŏom′ən

93. wĭm′ən

94. mənil′ə (folder)

95. ĕn′ē

96. mĕn′ē

97. sĕz

98. sĕd

99. ə gĕn′

100. ə gĕnst′

SECOND QUARTER
General Quiz

1. How could you exaggerate the pronunciation of or mispronounce the following words to help you spell them?

   tired _____   been _____

   chihuahua _____   cannot _____

   vacuum _____   receipt _____

   said _____

2. Contractions:

   a. After the word, write the negative and then the contraction for the negative. Example: *do, do not, don't*

      i. does   v. have

      ii. did   vi. is

      iii. was   vii. can

      iv. had   viii. will

   b. *Let's* and *I'm* are also contractions. What two words are each made from?

   c. What common error is made in forming the contractions of negatives?

   d. What does the pronunciation spelling of *don't* and *won't* leave out of those words?

   e. Just to be silly: We have *does, does not,* and *doesn't.* What about *goes, goes not . . .*? How would you form the contraction of *goes not*—if it were a word?

3. Tell the difference between adding **-ing** to *hope* and to *hop.*

SECOND QUARTER
General Quiz (Continued)

4. What words do each of the following come from?

   Example: *hoping* comes from *hope*.

   a. hopping   e. griping

   b. starring   f. tapping

   c. staring   g. taping

   d. gripping

5. Choose the correct spelling for derivatives of each word in parentheses.

   a. loveing, loving, lovving (love)

   b. dineing, dining, dinning (dine)

   c. riding, rideing, ridding (ride)

   d. raissing, raising, raiseing (raise)

   e. useing, using, ussing (use)

6. Choose the correct homonym:

   a. I _____ _____ one here. (no, know)

   b. He _____ I had _____ skis. (new, knew)

   c. I will _____ the _____ closet door. (close, clothes)

   d. My _____ explained the _____ of relativity to our class.

      (principal, principle)

7. Choose the correct spelling:

   a. judgment   acknowledgement   nickle   meny

   b. vacum   traveled   rhythym   referrence

   c. occured   surprize   untill   won't

   d. cieling   whent   marrys   cannot

   e. benefited   oshean   loze   agenst

   f. lazyness   recieve   they   rhym

SECOND QUARTER
Spelling Rules Quiz

Answer the questions and give an example for each rule.

1. What is the **ie/ei** rule for the vowel combination after the letter **c** when it sounds **s**, not **sh**?

2. If an **ie/ei** word has a German derivation and it has the long **i** sound, how will it be spelled?

3. For words ending in **y** preceded by a consonant:

    a. What do you do to form the plural of a noun?

    b. How do you form the third person singular of the verb?

    c. How do you form the past tense?

    d. What do you do before adding **-ing**?

    e. What do you do before adding any suffix to an adjective?

4. For words ending in a final silent **e**, what do you do before adding the suffix **-ing**?

5. For words of more than one syllable ending in one consonant preceded by one vowel with the accent *not* on the last syllable, what do you do before adding a suffix beginning with a vowel? What if one of these words ends in l? What if it has a double consonant in the middle of the word?

6. For words of more than one syllable ending in one consonant preceded by one vowel with the accent on the last syllable, what do you do before adding a suffix beginning with a vowel?

    For these words, when you add the suffix **-ence** and the accent reverts to a syllable other than the last syllable, what happens to the spelling?

7. How do you form plurals of words ending in **s**, **ss**, **x**, **z**, **ch**, or **sh**?

Answers to Second Quarter Quizzes

Sound to Spelling Quiz

1.	know	35.	gone	68.	quite
2.	no	36.	went	69.	quiet
3.	knew	37.	didn't	70.	let's
4.	new	38.	was	71.	circus
5.	known	39.	wasn't	72.	clothes
6.	knowing	40.	hadn't	73.	close
7.	knowledge	41.	have	74.	often
8.	acknowledgment	42.	haven't	75.	rhyme
9.	tired	43.	is	76.	rhythm
10.	jewelry	44.	isn't	77.	principal
11.	judge	45.	cannot	78.	principle
12.	judgment	46.	can't	79.	lose
13.	they	47.	won't	80.	loose
14.	very	48.	carry	81.	until
15.	while	49.	worry	82.	surprise
16.	chihuahua	50.	library	83.	build
17.	kaleidoscope	51.	easy	84.	built
18.	Fahrenheit	52.	busy	85.	guess
19.	reveille	53.	hoping	86.	guest
20.	onomatopoeia	54.	hopping	87.	nickel
21.	etc.	55.	scarring	88.	choir
22.	ceiling	56.	scaring	89.	ocean
23.	receive	57.	happened	90.	pretty
24.	deceive	58.	traveled	91.	been
25.	conceited	59.	prefer	92.	woman
26.	perceive	60.	preference	93.	women
27.	conceive	61.	refer	94.	manila
28.	do	62.	reference	95.	any
29.	does	63.	transfer	96.	many
30.	doing	64.	occur	97.	says
31.	done	65.	vacuum	98.	said
32.	doesn't	66.	color	99.	again
33.	don't	67.	quit	100.	against
34.	goes				

Answers to General Quiz

1. tī′rĕd; chĭ h (letter **u**) ä h (letter **u**) ä; vắk (spelled **c**), 2 **u**'s, **m**; sắ ĭd; bĕ′ ĕn; two words (*can not*) written as one; rē letter **c** ei (after **c**) p t

2. a. i.   does, does not, doesn't
        ii.   did, did not, didn't
        iii. was, was not, wasn't
        iv.   had, had not, hadn't
        v.   have, have not, haven't
        vi.   is, is not, isn't
        vii. can, cannot, can't
        viii. will, will not, won't

    b. let's—let us;   I'm—I am

    c. Spellers insert an **e** before the **n** because they hear a schwa pronounced: **dĭd′ent.**

    d. the apostrophe

    e. goesn't

3. *Hope*, with a final, silent **e**, drops the **e** before adding **-ing** (*hoping*). *Hop*, a one-one-one word (one syllable, one final consonant preceded by one vowel) doubles that consonant before adding **-ing** (*hopping*).

4. a. hopping/hop
    b. starring/star
    c. staring/stare
    d. gripping/grip
    e. griping/gripe
    f. tapping/tap
    g. taping/tape

5. a. loving
    b. dining
    c. riding
    d. raising
    e. using

6. a. know, no
    b. knew, new
    c. close, clothes
    d. principal, principle

7. a. judgment
    b. traveled
    c. won't
    d. cannot
    e. benefited
    f. they

Spelling Rules Quiz

1. When **c** sounds **s**, spell the vowel combination **ei**. (*ceiling*)

2. Words of German derivation sounding long **i** spell the vowel combination **ei**. (*Fahrenheit*)

3. a. Nouns change the **y** to **i** and add **-es** for the plural. (*library/libraries*)

    b. Verbs change the **y** to **i** and add **-es** for the third person singular. (*marry/marries*)

    c. Verbs change the **y** to **i** and add **-ed** to make the past tense. (*married*)

    d. Verbs keep the **y** before adding **-ing**. (*marrying*)

    e. Adjectives change the **y** to **i** before adding any suffix. (*lazy/lazier/laziest/laziness*)

4. Words ending in final silent **e** drop that **e** before adding **-ing**. (*come/coming*)

5. Words of more than one syllable ending in one consonant preceded by one vowel with the accent *not* on the last syllable do not change anything before adding a suffix beginning with a vowel. They do **not** double the last consonant. It doesn't make any difference whether there is a double consonant in the middle of the word or if the word ends in **l**—you still don't double the final consonant. British spelling *does* double the **l**. The dictionaries list the double **l** as the second spelling. (*model/modeled; channel/channeled*)

6. Words of more than one syllable ending in one consonant preceded by one vowel with the accent on the last syllable *do* double that consonant before adding a suffix beginning with a vowel. When you add **-ence** and the accent does not stay on the original last syllable, you do *not* double the consonant. (*refer/referred/reference; occur/occurring/occurrence*)

7. To form the plural of words ending in **s**, **ss**, **x**, **z**, **ch**, or **sh**, add **-es**. (*circus/circuses*)

THIRD QUARTER

LESSON 21

Wednesday
Pronunciation: **wĕnz′dā**
Abbreviation: *Wed.*

It's amazing how many people can spell the abbreviation correctly and then misspell the first three letters of *Wednesday*, which are the same as the abbreviation. Maybe they didn't know that. Now they do.

We're told that the word comes from "Woden's Day." Woden was a Teutonic god of the old days. Does that help? Maybe, maybe not. You know the last part is *day*. It's the middle part that doesn't make much sense: **nes**.

The best way I know to learn the parts is to mispronounce the word as you spell it: **wĕd nĕs dā**. Pronounce the silent **d** and the **nĕs**.

I will be *wed* on *Wednesday*.

*Nes*tor fell out of the *nes*t on *Wednesday*.

There are nine letters in *Wednesday*:

Wed	1, 2, 3
nes	4, 5, 6
day	7, 8, 9

Tuesday
Pronunciation: **to͞oz′dā**
Abbreviation: *Tues.*

You know the last part: *day*. The vowel combination in the first part is what you have to remember: **ue**.

Tuesday is the only word in my dictionary that starts **Tues**. In fact, it's the only word that is spelled *Tuesday*. Imagine that!

S*ue* will be married on *Tuesday*; R*ed* will be *wed* on *Wednesday*.

How many S*ues* pay their d*ues* on *Tuesday*?

A. Fill in the blanks, *por favor*:

1. Abbreviation for *Tuesday*: _____ .
2. Abbreviation for *Wednesday*: _____ .
3. *Wed.* is the abbreviation for _____ .
4. *Tues.* is the abbreviation for _____ .
5. Both words end in the letters _____ .
6. All the days of the week end in the letters _____ .
7. The first syllable of *Tuesday* is spelled _____ .
8. The whole word *Tuesday* is spelled _____ .
9. The first syllable of *Wednesday* is spelled _____ .
10. The second syllable of *Wednesday* is spelled _____ .
11. The whole word *Wednesday* is spelled _____ .

B. Writing across, fill in the missing letters:

1. T _ _ _ _ _ _   W _ _ _ _ _ _ _ _
2. _ u _ _ _ _ _   _ e _ _ _ _ _ _ _
3. _ _ e _ _ _ _   _ _ d _ _ _ _ _ _
4. _ _ _ s _ _ _   _ _ _ n _ _ _ _ _
5. _ _ _ _ d _ _   _ _ _ _ e _ _ _ _
6. _ _ _ _ _ a _   _ _ _ _ _ s _ _ _
7. _ _ _ _ _ _ y   _ _ _ _ _ _ d _ _
8.   _ _ _ _ _ _ _ a _
9.   _ _ _ _ _ _ _ _ y

Do you think you know how to spell those words now? Want to write them just one more time?

LESSON 21 (Continued)

ache

Pronunciation: āk

You can see that the final silent **e** makes the **a** long. That's true for a lot of words.

It's the **ch** sounding **k** that surprises you. But **ch** sounds **k** in *school, Christmas, echo,* and *stomach,* to name a few words.

How about remembering **stomachache** to help you spell ache? Who wants to remember a stomachache?

stomach

Pronunciation: stŭm′ǝk

There's the **o** sounding like a short **u** as in *some, brother,* and *come.*

The **ch** sounds **k** as in *ache* and *school.* Remember **stomachache**. I don't want to remember a **stomachache**! I'd rather remember chocolate ice cream.

The **a** is unaccented and sounds a little like a short **i. Ick!** I had a **stomachache**. I got it in school, and my brother had to come take me home.

August

Pronunciation: ô′gŭst

au   -   **o** sound as in *caught* and *daughter* (Remember both the **a** and the **u**.)

gust   -   If you pronounce this part of it rapidly, you may hear an **i** for the vowel instead of a **u**. Spell it with a **u**.

August comes after July and before September. If it's very hot, it seems to go slowly. As school approaches in September, however, *August* appears to go by more rapidly. I'd like to take *August* off and enjoy the weather at the ocean.

school

Pronunciation: skōōl

The **ch** sounds **k**.

Ch often sounds **k**: *ache, stomach, technical, chemistry, chorus, Christmas.*

Sch starts some words besides *school*. You probably know these: *schedule, scholar, scheme.*

The double **o** has the long double **o** sound as in *Boo!*

My *school sch*edule in *Sch*enectady Junior High *School* includes social studies, art, and *ch*orus. I'll learn some *ch*emistry in science.

C. Answer the questions:

1. What starts in September?

2. What month comes before September?

3. What happens if you eat too many green apples? You get a _____
_____ .

4. What is the sound of the **ch** in *stomach, ache,* and *school*?

5. What words are misspelled in the following? Underline them and write the correct spelling above them.

Its Agust allready and I half to get reddy for skool.

I have a headake thinking abot sckool. Tomorow Ill have a stummickach.

6. Think of *school* and *schedule* together.

What letters in *school* give you the **sk** sound?

What letters in *schedule* give you the **sk** sound?

LESSON 21
Additional Activities

1. What day comes after Monday?

2. What day comes before Thursday?

3. How do you spell the middle syllable of *Wednesday*?

4. How do you spell the vowels in the first syllable of *Tuesday*?

5. What are the first three letters of *school*?

6. How do we mark the double **o** vowel sound in *school*?

7. What are the first two letters of the month before September? What letter is on either side of the **g** in *August*?

8. What is the sound of the **ch** in *school*, *ache*, and *stomach*?

9. What is the sound of the **o** in *stomach*? the **a** in *stomach*? Write that word the way you would pronounce it. Now spell it correctly.

10. Try writing all six words in one sentence: *Wednesday*, *Tuesday*, *ache*, *stomach*, *August*, *school*.

Answers

LESSON 21

A.
1. Tues.
2. Wed.
3. Wednesday
4. Tuesday
5. day
6. day
7. Tues
8. Tuesday
9. Wed
10. nes
11. Wednesday

B.
1. **T** u e s d a y
2. T **u** e s d a y
3. T u **e** s d a y
4. T u e **s** d a y
5. T u e s **d** a y
6. T u e s d **a** y
7. T u e s d a **y**
8.
9.

W e d n e s d a y
W **e** d n e s d a y
W e **d** n e s d a y
W e d **n** e s d a y
W e d n **e** s d a y
W e d n e **s** d a y
W e d n e s **d** a y
W e d n e s d **a** y
W e d n e s d a **y**

Yes. Tuesday, Wednesday.

LESSON 21 (Continued)

C.
1. school
2. August
3. **stomachache**
4. **k**
5. Corrected words are in dark type: **It's August already**, and I **have** to get **ready** for **school**.

   I have a **headache** thinking **about school. Tomorrow I'll** have a **stomachache.**
6. sch; **sch**

LESSON 21: Additional Activities

1. Tuesday
2. Wednesday
3. **nes**
4. **ue**
5. **sch**
6. double o long ($\overline{oo}$)
7. **au; u**
8. **k**
9. The o sounds short **u**; the **a** sounds as the unaccented vowel sound schwa. Written as pronounced: "stumik" (I hear almost a short **i** in the word). Correct: *stomach*.
10. Sample sentence: Last **August**, on **Tuesday**(s) and **Wednesday**(s), our **school** let everyone who had a **stomachache** go home.

114

LESSON 22

potato, potatoes

You hear every letter in *potato*; spell the word as it sounds: **pō tā′tō**.

The plural of *potato* is *potatoes*. I remember the **e** for **e**at.

People make two mistakes with these words:

(1) They spell *potatoes* correctly with an **-es**. Then they go back to spell *potato* and they write "potatoe" because they took off just the **s** from the plural. The two letters **es** were used to form the plural.

(2) Sometimes people writing price signs in the grocery stores write an apostrophe and an **s** for their plurals. This is wrong. The only time you need an apostrophe for a plural is for a single letter or number or words used merely as words that would cause problems if pluralized by **s** or **-es**. Examples:

three **i**'s in *invisible*

the three **R**'s

two **and**'s in that sentence (*And* is used twice in the sentence, not *ands*.)

tomato, tomatoes

You hear every letter in *tomato*; spell the word as it sounds: **tō mā′tō**. The plural of *tomato* is *tomatoes*. Think of the **e** in **e**at.

An alternative pronunciation of *tomato* is **tō mä′tō**. It's still ripe when it's red.

Once you learn to spell *tomatoes* correctly (**-es**), don't spell *tomato* incorrectly by putting an **e** on the singular. And don't spell it with an apostrophe the way some grocery store clerks do.

mosquito, mosquitoes

Pronunciation: **mə skē′tō**

When people pronounce this word fast, it sounds like "mis"*quito*, but that first syllable is spelled with an **o**.

The **qu** gives the **k** sound.

The **i** after the **qu** gives the long **e** sound.

Mosquito is not an easy word to spell, and mosquitoes are not easy to live with.

The plural is **-es**; **e** for they **e**at you and for the **net** that will keep them away from you.

A. Spell the correct singular or plural form of the words in parentheses:

1. I like French fried (potato) _____ , mashed (potato) _____ , home fried (potato) _____ , (potato) _____ chips, and (potato) _____ salad.

2. I like sliced (tomato) _____ ; (tomato) _____ in a salad; bacon, lettuce, and (tomato) _____ sandwiches; and cheese dreams: open-face sandwiches with melted cheese and a slice each of (tomato) _____ and bacon.

3. When I went to the garden to pick (tomato) _____ and dig (potato) _____ , the (mosquito) _____ found me. I told the (mosquito) _____ to go chew on the (buffalo) _____ instead, but they said the (buffalo) _____ were all gone!

4. In the grocery store I looked for (tomato) _____ , (potato) _____ , and onions. The clerk was printing signs for the vegetables and fruits. He had written: potato's   tomatos   onion's

Can you help out the clerk with the correct spelling?

Can you tell him **why** he shouldn't use an apostrophe?

LESSON 22 (Continued)

radio, **radios**
auto, **autos**

If a word ending in **o** has a vowel before the **o**, just add **s** for the plural. I'll say that again: If a word ending in **o** has a vowel before the **o**, just add **s** for the plural (*radios*, *ratios*, *zoos*, *studios*). That makes sense—you don't want another vowel ("radioes")—not if you can help it!

On words that have been clipped, or shortened from their full words, just add **s** for the plural.

auto,	from *automobile*:	*autos*
memo,	from *memorandum*:	*memos*
photo,	from *photograph*:	*photos*

For foreign words, like *taco*, *poncho*, and *gaucho*, just add **s**: *tacos*, *ponchos*, *gauchos*.

For Italian musical terms, just add **s**: *cello*, *cellos*; *piano*, *pianos*; *soprano*, *sopranos*; *alto*, *altos*.

Webster's Ninth Edition says:

tomato, tomatoes	echo, echoes
potato, potatoes	torpedo, torpedoes
hero, heroes	veto, vetoes

For the other **o** words with a consonant before the **o**, *Webster's* gives you a choice. But *every* time, the **-es** ending is stated first.

As long as you don't spell the plural as **'s** or transfer the **e** from the **-es** back to the singular, I don't care whether you add **-es** or **s**. But it seems simpler to me to use **-es** every time.

Look at this chart of the **o** words.

Vowel before **o**	*Consonant before* **o**				
	foreign	Italian music	clipped	all the rest	
(s)	**(s)**	**(s)**	**(s)**	(always **-es**)	(choice of **-es** or **s**)
ratio studio radio rodeo zoo	taco poncho gaucho	cello alto soprano piano	memo auto photo	tomato potato echo hero torpedo veto	cargo mosquito volcano motto no buffalo

B. Check the words you'll probably use. Add them to your special list. Take the ones you'll use and put them into one sentence, no matter how silly, like this:

I wrote **memos** about the **sopranos** and **altos** singing with the **cellos** and **pianos** over the **radios** after eating **tacos**, **potatoes**, and **tomatoes** by **volcanoes** while fighting **mosquitoes**.

C. Take the singular chart above and make a plural one, adding **s** or **-es** as you are directed by the chart.

LESSON 22
Additional Activities

1. *Tomato* and *potato* are frequently used words. Write the plural of each.

2. What mistake is commonly made in writing these plurals?

3. What is the singular form of *tomatoes* and *potatoes*?

4. If a word ending in **o** has a vowel before the **o**, how do you form the plural?

5. Write the plurals for these words: *taco* _____ , *cello* _____ ,
   studio _____ , *auto* _____ , *radio* _____ ,
   zoo _____ , *poncho* _____ , *memo* _____ ,
   piano _____ , *photo* _____ , *rodeo* _____ ,
   alto _____ .

6. Some plurals of words ending in **o** preceded by a consonant always are spelled with
   -es. Write the plurals of *hero* _____ , *echo* _____ ,
   torpedo _____ , and *veto* _____ .

7. For some plurals of words ending in **o** preceded by a consonant, you have a choice of
   -es or **s**. Write the plurals of *mosquito* _____ , *volcano* _____ ,
   motto _____ , *no* _____ , *buffalo* _____ , and
   cargo _____ .

Answers

LESSON 22

A.
1. potatoes, potatoes, potatoes, potato, potato
2. tomatoes, tomatoes, tomato, tomato
3. tomatoes, potatoes, mosquitoes, mosquitoes, buffaloes (buffalos, buffalo), buffaloes (buffalos, buffalo)
4. tomatoes, potatoes
   potatoes, tomatoes, onions

An apostrophe is used to indicate something left out, as a letter in a contraction. It is also used to indicate possession, as in "Bill's car." Here the expression means "the car of Bill." The only time you use an apostrophe for a plural is when adding just an **s** will make the word into something else, for example:

I used four *and*'s in that sentence. (I used *and* four times, not *ands*.)

LESSON 22 (Continued)

B. Sample words that will be used: *studio, zoo, taco, cello, alto, piano, auto, tomato, potato, mosquito, volcano.*

Sample sentence: In our **studios** at the **zoos**, we ate **tacos** made of **tomatoes** and **potatoes** before playing the **cellos** while **altos** sang at the **pianos** and **mosquitoes** drove their **autos** to the **volcanoes**.

C.

Vowel before **o**	Consonant before **o**				
	foreign	Italian music	clipped	all the rest	
				(always -es)	(choice of -es or s)
ratios studios radios rodeos zoos	tacos ponchos gauchos	cellos altos sopranos pianos	memos autos photos	tomatoes potatoes echoes heroes torpedoes vetoes	cargoes* mosquitoes* volcanoes* mottoes* noes* buffaloes*+

*also can be spelled with just **s**
+also can be spelled *buffalo*

LESSON 22:   Additional Activities

1. tomatoes; potatoes
2. They are written mistakenly as *tomato's* and *potato's*.
3. tomato, potato
4. Just add **s**.
5. tacos, cellos, studios, autos, radios, zoos, ponchos, memos, pianos, photos, rodeos, altos
6. heroes, echoes, torpedoes, vetoes
7. mosquitoes, mosquitos; volcanoes, volcanos; mottoes, mottos; noes, nos; buffaloes, buffalos (buffalo); cargoes, cargos

LESSON 23

colonel
Pronunciation: **kŭr′ nəl**
Meaning: a military officer; an honorary title in some southern and western states
    Earlier spelling included the **r**.

    It has a homonym: *kernel*, the seed; central part of something, most important part.

A.   Write *colonel* or *kernel* in the following sentences:

1.   _____ Sanders' picture is on the Kentucky Fried Chicken restaurant signs.

2.   My uncle was a lieutenant _____ in the army.

3.   There's a _____ of truth in that story.

4.   It's fun when the popcorn _____(s) pop.

picnic
Pronunciation: **pĭk′ nĭk**
    Each syllable of the word ends in a **c**. When **c** is followed by a consonant or nothing (as well as by **a**, **o**, or **u**), it sounds like a **k**. Here you see **c** followed by a consonant once and by nothing at the end.

    If you want to say *picnicking*, you add the **k** so you don't lose the **k** sound of the **c** when you add the **-ing**. But when you go back to spelling *picnic*, leave off the **k**. It is like going back to *potato* from *potatoes*, when you leave off the **e**.

    We'll have music at our *picnic*.
    We will be *picnicking* at the beach.

B.   Many words end in **-ic**, especially adjectives.

    Here are a few of them. Can you use them all in one sentence? *public, electric, athletic, arctic, magic, garlic, metric, republic, panic*

silhouette   sĭl ōō ĕt′
    Named after a Frenchman of that name, a **silhouette** is an outline drawing, usually a profile portrait filled in with a solid color. A silhouette is often cut from black paper and placed on a light background. The word has come to mean any dark shape seen against a light background.

    Break the word into parts:
        sil
        hou   -   Did you expect the **h**? the **ou**?
        ette

C.   Make a silhouette. To make a silhouette of your best friend, have him or her sit in front of a piece of paper taped to the wall. Ask someone to shine a bright light toward him or her. Trace his or her profile on the white paper. Tape a black piece of paper to the back of the white paper and cut the shape out of both pieces. Discard the white paper. Paste the black silhouette on light-colored paper.

somersault
Pronunciation: **sŭm′ ər sôlt**
    Originally from *supra* ("over") and *saltus* ("leap").
    The **o** sounds short **u** as in *some*.
    The **au** sounds the same as it does in *daughter* and *August*.

    Can you do a *somersault*? Give me a pillow for my head and I'll do a *somersault* for you.

D.   Can you use *somersault*, *August*, and *daughter* in one sentence?

LESSON 23 (Continued)

I

I is always capitalized, when it stands alone as *I* or when it is part of a contraction:
I'll is the contraction for *I will* or *I shall.*
I've is the contraction for *I have.*
I'd is the contraction for *I had* or *I would.*
I'm is the contraction for *I am.*

One of the more common mistakes in spelling is to write "I'am" for *I'm.* The person doing that forgets that he or she is writing a contraction and includes both the apostrophe and the whole word *am.*

because   bĭ kôz′

Many people pronounce it **bē cŭz′**. The trouble is, they spell it that way, too. When you use the word *because,* you are saying that one thing is the *cause* of another thing. Would you say that something was the "cuz" of something else? Of course not. *Because* is made up of *be* plus *cause.*

Because it is raining, I'll open my umbrella.

I'll run to the bus stop *because* I'm so late.

used to   yo͞ozd′ to͞o

You know what it means to *use* something.

I *use* chocolate morsels to make a cake frosting.

If you *used* something, it means you did so in the past.

I *used* four squares of chocolate to make that cake.

When you add *to* to *used,* you indicate a former (before now) fact:

I *used to* make that cake with cocoa, but now I think chocolate is better. I *used to* use cocoa.

When you say, "I am **used to** doing it that way," you mean you are accustomed to doing it that way.

How is it misspelled? As "use to" without the **d** on *use,* probably because people find it difficult to pronounce the **d** before the **t.**

E.   Use the following words in the crossword puzzle: *I'll, I've, which, because, cause, used to, don't, doesn't, whether, while.* Be sure to put in necessary apostrophes. Spaces were left for them.

Across

2. contraction for *I have*
4. time word meaning "during the time that"
6. reason for something
8. contraction for *does not*
9. contraction for *do not*

Down

1. question word wanting to know what one
2. contraction for *I will*
3. word introducing the reason for something
4. word asking if
5. contraction for *I am*
7. two words meaning "accustomed to doing something"

LESSON 23
Additional Activities

1. In *picnic*, why are the two **c**'s pronounced the way they are?

2. In order to keep the **k** sound of the final **c**, what must you do before adding **-ing** to the word?

3. Can you do a somersault? If you can, you don't have to spell the word—right now.

4. Explain how you make a silhouette.

5. What is the homonym for *colonel*? What is a colonel? What colonel(s) do you know?

6. Without looking, spell correctly *silhouette*, *somersault*, and *colonel*.

7. What word is always capitalized? Write it. Write it in some contractions: with *am*, *had*, *have*, and *will*.

8. What is the second syllable of *because*? What is the final letter of *because*? What are the two vowels after **c**? Are they the same vowels that are in *August* or *hawk*?

9. Write *used to* in a sentence.

10. What are the three syllables in *silhouette*?

Answers

LESSON 23

A.
1. Colonel
2. colonel
3. kernel
4. kernel

B. Sample sentence: The **arctic metric republic** went into a **panic** when it lost its **electric** power, but as if by **magic**, **garlic** produced the electricity needed for the **public athletic** events.

C. A silhouette:

D. Sample sentence: Last September, my **daughter August** won the **somersault** championship of the arctic metric republic's public athletic events and won a magic garlic bulb.

LESSON 23 (Continued)

E. Crossword Puzzle:

LESSON 23:   Additional Activities

1. They both sound **k** because the first one is followed by a consonant and the second one is followed by nothing; those two situations both give the **k** sound.
2. You add the letter **k** so the word is spelled *picnicking*. (But don't put a **k** in the middle of the word after **pic-**.)
3. I'll spell it: *somersault*.
4. Put a piece of white paper on the wall behind the subject. Have someone shine a light at the person (toward the wall), and draw around the outline of the person that shows on the paper. Back your white paper with black paper and cut out the outline in both pieces. Use the black one for the silhouette.
5. Homonym: *kernel. Colonel* is generally a military title. I know several retired colonels. I also know of Colonel Sanders' Fried Chicken.
6. silhouette, somersault, colonel
7. I, I'm, I'd, I've, I'll
8. cause, **e, au**, August
9. Sample sentence: I **used to** play soccer.
10. *sil hou ette*

122

LESSON 24

of

This is the first day **of** school.

Pronunciation: **ŭv**

The **o** sounds **ŭ** (short **u**) as in *come, mother, cover, done, once.*

The **f** sounds **v** — unique!

So what's hard about spelling *of*? Nothing! *Of* isn't hard. But don't throw it in where it shouldn't be after *should, would,* or *could.* Don't write "should of" for *should've* because the **'ve** sounds like the *of* you know. *Should've* is the contraction for *should have.*

could, would, should

Pronunciation: **cŏŏd, wŏŏd, shŏŏd**

The **l** is silent; the vowel sound is spelled **ou.**

could have, would have, should have

The contractions for these words are *could've, would've,* and *should've.* Don't write "could of," "would of," and "should of" just because the **'ve** sounds like *of.*

could have been:	*could've been*
would have been:	*would've been*
should have been:	*should've been*

A. Correct the misspellings: We could of been there by now if you would of been ready. You should of bin ready a lot earlier.

which hwĭch

Which is a question word that starts with **wh.** Say these words: *which, when, where, whether, while, why,* and *what.*

The **wh** sounds **h/w** when you say the beginning slowly but a blend of **hw** when you say it rapidly. It is spelled **wh,** just the opposite of its sound.

You don't think you say **hw?** Then try saying **w/h.** It doesn't sound right, does it? Although the **h/w** becomes blended into one sound, it is still **h/w.**

Some people pronounce the word just as **wĭch.** That's one reason the word may be misspelled.

When the **ch** sound ends a word, it usually is spelled **tch.** Yet a few of our most commonly used words end just in **-ch:** *which, much, such,* and *rich*—plus a very few others. Remember these words, and perhaps it will help you to spell *which.*

So, you have two problems in spelling this word: the beginning (**wh**) and the end (**ch**). I don't think the **i** in the middle will cause any trouble.

Don't confuse *which* with the Halloween *witch. Witch* is not a question word, and it does not start with **wh.** Think of the **t** in the middle as the witch's broom.

B. Answer the questions:

1. What is the sound (not spelling) at the beginning of *which*?
2. How is that sound spelled?
3. What is the vowel sound in the middle of *which*?
4. How is that sound spelled?
5. What is the sound of the two consonants at the end of *which*?
6. How do you spell the word *which*?
7. What other question words start like *which*?
8. I forgot. How do you spell *which*?

LESSON 24 (Continued)

beautiful

Syllables: *beau ti ful*

Pronunciation: **byoo′ tə fəl**

There are several hard parts to this word:

beau   –   originally meant "beautiful" (The French word *beau* is sometimes used in English as the word for a girl's boyfriend.)

ti   –   In *beauty*, this sound is **ty**. The **y** changes to **i** in *beautiful*, like *busy* to *business*.

ful   –   one **l** when *full* becomes a suffix

I believe I will probably take my doll Bab to a *beauty* parlor for a *beautician* to make her *beautiful*. Although she has a certain amount of natural *beauty*, her doll's hair needs to be separated from some gum that her Teddy Bear friend Swer put there.

busy

Busy doesn't sound the way it's spelled. It's pronounced **biz′ ē**.

The **u** sounds **i**.   The **y** sounds **e**.

The **s** sounds **z**.   (The **b** sounds **b**, though!)

Busying keeps the **y** before the suffix **-ing**, like *carry*, *carrying* and *worry*, *worrying*.

C. Use one of these forms of *busy* correctly in each of the following sentences: *busy, busies, business, busily, busying, busiest, busier, busied*

1. My older brother is in the _____ of designing beautiful T-shirts.
2. My little sister was _____ cleaning out her playhouse.
3. My mother is _____ herself getting ready to open a beauty parlor.
4. She _____ herself preparing the broccoli casserole.
5. February is _____ than January at the ski schools.
6. Their _____ season is, however, in March.
7. Yesterday I _____ myself making mayonnaise.

Two compound words with *busy* keep the **y**: *busybody* and *busywork*.

That *busybody* in the bus stop queue listened to everything we said.

Now that I can say my multiplication facts accurately and rapidly, these exercises are just *busywork* for me.

Busy signal is two words. I do not expect to get a *busy signal* when I call long distance.

D. Answer the questions:

1. How do you change *busy* to *business* and *beauty* to *beautiful*?
2. How is the ending on *awful* and *beautiful* spelled?
3. What are the three vowels after the **b** in *beauty* and *beautiful*?
4. What vowel in *busy* sounds like a short **i**?

E. Go from Start to Finish, using only correctly spelled words:

Start	beautiful	buisness	brocolli	alot
beautyful	business	separate	probaly	pepol
hunderd	seperate	probably	people	answer
untill	liberry	libary	anser	February
mayonaisse	awfull	surprize	Febuary	Finish

F. What are the three syllables of *beautiful*? Underline the vowels in each syllable. Spell the vowels in the first syllable.

LESSON 24
Additional Activities

1. In the word *of*, what is the sound of the **o**? the **f**?

2. In the words *could*, *should*, and *would*, how is the short double **oo** (as in *foot*) spelled? What letter is silent?

3. Write *would have*. _____   Write the contraction for it. _____

    Write *could have*. _____   Write the contraction for it. _____

    Write *should have*. _____   Write the contraction for it. _____

    Write *could have been*. _____   Write the contraction for it. _____

    Write *should have been*. _____   Write the contraction for it. _____

    Write *would have been*. _____   Write the contraction for it. _____

4. Write *which* five times, all correctly. What different ways can you spell it incorrectly? Now spell it correctly again, ten times.

5. When the sound **ch** ends a word, it is usually spelled **-tch**. *Which* is spelled with just a **-ch**. What other commonly used words are spelled with just a **-ch** ending?

6. What word does *beautiful* come from?

7. What happened to the **y** when the word was changed to *beautiful*?

8. *Beautiful* has every vowel but one. Which one is missing?

9. How are you going to remember the order of the vowels in the first part of *beautiful*?

10. In *busy*, what letters give you the short **i** sound, the **z** sound, and the long **e** sound?

11. Write *business, busily, busying, busied, busy, busiest, busier,* and *busied*. Which two have the **y**?

Answers

LESSON 24

A. We **could have** (could of) been there by now if you **would have** (would of) been ready. You **should have been** (should of bin) ready a lot earlier.

B.
1. **hw**
2. **wh**
3. short **i**
4. **i**
5. **ch**
6. which
7. what, when, where, why
8. which

LESSON 24 (Continued)

C.
1. business
2. busy
3. busying/busy
4. busies
5. busier
6. busiest/busy
7. busied

D.
1. Change the **y** to **i** and add **-ness** to **busi-** and **-ful** to **beauti-**.
2. **-ful** (one **l**)
3. **eau**
4. **u**

E.

Start —————— beautiful	buisness	brocolli	alot
beautyful	business ——— separate	probaly	pepol
hunderd	seperate	probably ——— people ——— answer
untill	liberry	libary	anser
mayonaisse	awfull	surprize	Febuary Finish

F. beau ti ful; **eau**

LESSON 24: Additional Activities

1. short **u**, **v**
2. **ou**, **l**
3. would have, would've
   could have, could've
   should have, should've

   could have been, could've been
   should have been, should've been
   would have been, would've been

4. *which, which, which, which, which.* Sample misspellings: wich, witch, whitch, hwich, hwitch. *Which* (ten times).
5. such, much, rich
6. beauty
7. The **y** was changed to **i**.
8. **o**
9. I'll write the first syllable to see what looks right: *baeu, buea, beua*—those all look wrong. *Beau* may look odd, also, but it looks right. I'll also try to remember that *beau* is a French word meaning "beautiful."
10. The short **i** comes from the **u**, the **z** comes from the **s**, and the long **e** comes from the **y**.
11. business, busily, busying, busied, busy, busiest, busier, busied; *busying* and *busy*

LESSON 25

a lot

A lot is two words.

    a lot
    a little
    a whole bunch

"Would you like *a lot* of broccoli or a little?"
"I would like a little bit of broccoli with *a lot* of mayonnaise."

    Don't write *a lot* like *again*. *Again* is one word; *a lot* is two words.

polka dot, **polka dotted**

Polka is pronounced **pō′kə**.

Meaning: 1) One of a number of dots forming a pattern on cloth
           2) a pattern or fabric with such dots

    The origin of the word is unclear. The *American Heritage Dictionary* suggests that perhaps it is a respelling of "poke a dot."
    It has nothing to do with the polka dance, although the word is spelled the same way.

Her skirt has white *polka dots* on a blue background. That red and white *polka dotted* material makes my eyes swim!

February **fĕb′ rōo ĕr ē**

    Divide the word into parts so you can see them:

      Feb -   The abbreviation for *February* is *Feb*.
      ru   -   Say: **rōo**. (People forget the **r** in **ru**.)
      ar
      y

    Do you know anyone born on the 29th of *February*?

library **lī′ brĕr ē**

    Divide it into parts: *li*   *brar*   *y*

    Both *February* and *library* end in **-ary**. Both have an **r** after the **b**. People tend to forget the **r** after the **b**. Say that **r**: *br* just as you say the **r** in *February*.

The *library* is open from nine to four Wednesday through Saturday.
The *library* had an open house in *February*. One hundred people came.

  A. Answer the questions:

   1. There are usually *only* 28 days in which month?

   2. In a leap year, what is the last day of February?

   3. What letter comes after the **b** in *February*?

   4. What letter comes after the **b** in *library*?

   5. How many words is *a lot*?

   6. How many words is *polka dotted*?

   7. Can you draw a piece of polka dotted material? Put in a lot of dots.

   8. What letter must you make sure to include in *February* and *library*?

   9. What three letters end both *library* and *February*?

  10. Which of these words is always capitalized: *library, February, a lot*?

  11. What is the first word of *a lot*?

  12. What is the second word of *a lot?*

LESSON 25 (Continued)

all right

Meaning: all correct; very well, yes; without doubt

It is two words: the first word is *all*; the second is *right*.

If it is spelled as one word with one or two **l**'s,
   it is ALL WRONG.

You got the spelling words *all right*! Hurray!
All right, go ahead. See if I care!

all ready	-	Meaning: everyone (is) ready
		Are we *all ready* to go swimming?
already	-	Meaning: by this time, previously
		We had *already* been swimming on Tuesday.
all ways	-	Meaning: in every way
		All ways to the seashore start here.
always	-	Meaning: at every time
		I've *always* liked chocolate—ever since I can remember.

B. Fill in the blanks correctly with one of these words: *already, all ready; always, all ways; all right.*

1. On Tuesday, I had my science homework _____ _____ to take to school.
2. I got the problems on the science test _____ _____ .
3. I looked at _____ the _____ to do the problem.
4. I have _____ liked science.
5. My older brother had _____ taken science last year.

al- words

   already, almost, although, almighty, always, also, altogether

   These words all begin **al-**. Those two letters may give the sense of "all," but not necessarily.

   Confusion arises because:

Always and *all ways* are homonyms. *Already* and *all ready* are homonyms. *All right* is correct only as two words.

   already—by this time; previously
I have *already* traveled the Alaska Highway through the forty-ninth state.
   almost—not quite
I have *almost* finished my Wednesday chores.
   although—regardless of the fact that
Although it is Saturday, I believe I'll do my algebra.
   almighty—all powerful
We speak of God as being *almighty*.
   always—forever; at every time
A toasted cheese sandwich *always* tastes good.
   also—too; in addition
A cheese sandwich with bacon *also* tastes good.
   altogether—entirely; all told
Altogether, there were forty of us at the Albuquerque park.

C. Can you send Uncle Alfred and Aunt Alexandria on a trip? Write a story on a separate page, using as many of the following **al-** words as you can:

Albany	alphabet	Alfred	algae	alcohol	almost	although
Alexandria	Alberta	always	almighty	Alabama	altogether	also
algebra	already	alarm	alfalfa	albatross	albescent	alcove
alas!	alabaster	Alamo	Albania	albino	album	Alcatraz
alder	Algeria	alibi	alpine	altitude	Altoona	

LESSON 25
Additional Activities

1. *A lot*: How many words?

2. What is the silent letter in *polka dot*? Write the two words.

3. Draw a picture of one part of a library. What's the vowel in the word between the two **r**'s? What letter comes after the **b**?

4. *All right*: How many words?

5. Write a sentence or sentences using *all ready* and *already*; *all ways* and *always*.

6. Spell: *almost, although, almighty, always, also,* and *altogether.*

Answers

LESSON 25

A.
1. February
2. the 29th
3. **r**
4. **r**
5. two
6. two
7. Picture of polka dotted material:

8. the **r** after the **b**
9. **ary**
10. February
11. a
12. lot

LESSON 25 (Continued)

B.
1. all ready
2. all right
3. all ways
4. always
5. already

C. Sample Story: Uncle **Alfred** and Aunt **Alexandria** started on a trip from **Albany**, **Algeria** to **Altoona**, **Albania**. They never learned their **alphabet** past the letter **A**, so their trip was a strange one. First they saw the **algae** in the **alcohol** at an **alcove** in the city of **Alabama**. They sounded an **alarm**, but by then, the **albatross** had stopped harvesting the **alfalfa** and **alder** that had caused the **algae** in the **alcohol**. **Always** looking for high **altitude**, they searched for **alabaster** in the **alpine** areas of **Alcatraz**, but all they saw was an **albino** elephant. **Almighty** as they thought the elephant was, they had **already** seen enough elephants **almost** to fill a zoo. **Although** they were slowing down, on they went, using their **algebra** and **also** an **alibi** to find an **album** of the latest hits by the **Albescent Alamo**. **Altogether**, the trip was a success, from **A** to **A**.

LESSON 25: Additional Activities:

1. *A lot* is two words.
2. **l**; polka dot
3. Sample picture:

The vowel between the two **r**'s is an **a**. An **r** comes after the **b**.
4. *All right* is two words.
5. Sample sentences: We are *all ready* to go. The others have *already* gone. *All ways* of shoveling snow work. I have *always* used a snow shovel.
6. almost, although, almighty, always, also, altogether. (Each has just one **l**.)

130

LESSON 26

success

Pronunciation: sək sĕs′

    Two syllables: *suc cess*; two **c**'s in the middle

    Pronunciation of **c** rule:

        Before **i**, **e**, or **y**, **c** is pronounced **s**: *cess*

        Before another consonant, **c** is pronounced **k**: *suc(c)*

    Two **s**'s are at the end as in *mess*, *less*, and *Bess*.

  A. Fill in the blanks correctly with one of these words: *success, succeed, succeeded, successful, successfully.*

        Our visit to the city was a _____ . We were determined to _____ in getting around the mess of construction. We had _____ shopping trips. We _____ negotiated the subway and the buses. We _____ in not getting lost. It was a very _____ trip for Bess and me. We _____ in doing everything that you suggested we do.

seem

Pronunciation: sēm

Meaning: appear

    It *seems* to me these apples are ripe. These plums *seem* too ripe.

    Seem has a homonym: *seam.* When you sew two pieces of material together, you form a *seam.* Coal may be found in a *seam*—a layer. It *seems* to me that most of the time you would use the word *seem*, not *seam*, unless you were sewing or mining.

true

Pronunciation: trōō

    If someone is **true** blue, that one is really loyal, **true** to you. *True* and *blue* are both spelled with the same vowels, so it's a handy saying for spelling.

  B. Can you use *true, clue, due, Sue,* and *Tuesday* in one sentence?

truly

Pronunciation: trōō′lē

    Usually, **-ly** is just added to words without changing the spelling. There are some exceptions, however, and *truly* is one of them. You drop the final **e** before adding the **-ly**: *true—truly.*

    Another like *truly*: *whole, wholly*

    You often sign a letter: *Yours truly,*

toward

Pronunciation: tôrd, tōrd, tə wôrd′

    The word is made up of **to** plus **ward**; **-ward** is a suffix meaning "direction." **To** plus **-ward** is "in the direction of"; *forward*—"to the fore or front"; *backward*—"to the back." Those last two are easier to spell because you hear the **w** in **ward** in them. Most people do not pronounce *toward* as tə wôrd′; they say the word in one syllable: tôrd.

  C. Underline the errors in this letter and write the corrections above them.

    Dear Sheila,

        I wish you sucess in you're knew job. I think your headed tord better luck. It seams to me your doing the write thing.

               You'rs truely,

               Trudy

LESSON 26 (Continued)

awful

Pronunciation: ô′fəl

It means "full of awe," but look what dropped off both *awe* and *full*:

awe - to *aw*

full - to *ful*

When *full* becomes a suffix, it uses only one **l**, as in *beautiful, awful, careful*.

Dropping the **e** off *awe* before adding the suffix **-ful** is an exception to the rule—it's **awful**. Maybe it'll help you to remember the word because you're taking *both* the **e** off *awe* and an **l** off *full*.

D.   Write *awful* or *awfully* in the blanks:

I have an _____ stomachache. This one is_____ painful.

speak, speech

Pronunciation: spēk, spēch

This pair can cause trouble because when you speak, the vowel is **ea**; when you give a speech, the vowel is **ee**. List these words under the heading "unfair."

There are a lot of **ea** words. There are also a lot of **ee** words. There are no rules to help you know which to use. Your choices are to memorize the words or to check in the dictionary if you're not sure.

I knew my *speech* so well I could give it in my sl**ee**p.
Then when I got up to *speak*, all I could do was squ**ea**k.

E.   Use the correct word (*speak* or *speech*) in each sentence:

1.   _____ louder, please.

2.   Her _____ was five minutes long.

blue

Pronunciation: blo͞o

There are many wrong ways to spell this word. How many can your class come up with?

What's the right way? *Blue*, like *Sue, due, clue, Tuesday, true.*

Sometimes *blew* and *blue* are mixed up. *Blew* is the past tense of *blow*: The wind *blew* yesterday. Today we have a *blue* sky. She was feeling *blue* because she *blew* the test.

F.   Use one of these words ending in **-ue** to make sense in each sentence: *value, argue, due, blue, true, barbecue, avenue, Sue, Tuesday.*

1.   Shall we _____ the chicken on the grill?

2.   _____ of the Americas is a long name for a street.

3.   The color is _____ .

4.   My sister _____ is _____ home on _____ .

5.   I can't _____ over the _____ _____ of the piece.

whole, hole; wholly, holy

Whole is "the total of something." You know what a *hole* is.

You dig a *hole*.
You eat the *whole* pizza.

Wholly is "totally"; *holy* has to do with religion.

The garden was wrecked *wholly* by the woodchuck.
Passover is a *holy* time of year for Jews.
I ate the *whole* pizza *wholly* by myself, sitting in a *hole*.

LESSON 26
Additional Activities

1. What are the sounds of the first and the second **c** in *success*?

2. Choose the correct word:
   These bananas (seem/seam) overripe.

3. Use *true blue* in a sentence.

4. What is the silent letter in *whole* (meaning the total)?

5. What is the homonym for *whole*?

6. *Wholly* and *truly* do not follow the rule for keeping the **e** before adding **-ly**. Write *whole/wholly* and *true/truly*.

7. The word *awful* is made from *awe* and *full*. What letters have been dropped to form the one word *awful*?

8. How would knowing *backward* help you to spell *toward*?

9. Use *speech* and *speak* in a sentence.

10. Use *wholly* and *holy* in sentences.

Answers

A. success, succeed, successful, successfully, succeeded, successful, succeeded

B. Sample sentence: My **true** blue dog **Sue** found a **clue** on **Tuesday** about the book that was **due** at the library.

C. Dear Sheila,

I wish you **success** (sucess) in **your new** (you're knew) job. I think **you're** (your) headed **toward** (tord) better luck. It **seems** (seams) to me **you're** (your) doing the **right** (write) thing.

Yours truly, (You's truely,)
Trudy

LESSON 26 (Continued)

D. awful; awfully

E. 1. Speak
2. speech

F. 1. barbecue
2. Avenue
3. blue
4. Sue, due, Tuesday
5. argue, true, value

LESSON 26: Additional Activities

1. The first **c** sounds **k**; the second sounds **s**.

2. *seem*

3. Sample sentence: My friend is **true blue**.

4. **w**

5. hole

6. whole/wholly; true/truly

7. The **e** has been dropped from *awe*, and the last **l** has been dropped from *full*.

8. You hear the **-ward** part of the word pronounced in *backward*, but you don't hear it in *toward*. If you relate the two words, you may remember to spell *toward* with the **-ward** ending.

9. Sample sentence: When I rose to give my **speech**, I could not **speak**.

10. Sample sentences: The snow is almost **wholly** gone. An altar is a **holy** place.

LESSON 27

excitement
Pronunciation: ĕk sīt′mənt
    The **x** sounds **ks**. We still have a **c** after that (sounding **s**). That helps to make the **x** sound like **ks**, not **gz**.
    Look at the word without the **c**: *exitement*. The beginning looks almost like *exit*.
    Pronounce it ĕk/sīt to hear the beginning of the second syllable. *Excellent* has that **c** also.
Meaning: stimulation

Trailing 21–0 did not generate much *excitement* for the fans.

except
Pronunciation: ĕk sĕpt′
Meaning: with the exclusion of, other than, but
    This is another word in which the **x** sounds **ks**, and an additional **s** sound is gained from the **c** (followed by an **e**).

Everyone had a chocolate doughnut *except* me.

    The word is confused with *accept* (pronounced ăk sĕpt′), meaning "to receive with consent."

I will *accept* a chocolate doughnut, yes.
    Know thy prefixes and roots:

            ac-   -   an assimilation of the prefix **ad-**, meaning "to"
         capere   -   "to take"
           ex-   -   "out"
accept: take *to* oneself, as opposed to take *out* in *except*

excel
Pronunciation: ĕk sĕl′
    The **x** sounds **ks**.
    Although you don't need the **c** (**s** sound) in *excel* to give you the **s** sound because the **x** contains both the **k** and **s** sounds, that consonant **c** reinforces the idea that **x** will be pronounced **ks**, not **gz**.

         ex   -   **ks** sound
        cel   -   more **s** sound; remember *one* l

excel, excels, excelled, excelling
    Excel is a two-syllable word ending in one consonant preceded by one vowel with the accent on the last syllable, so the final consonant is doubled before a suffix beginning with a vowel: *excelled, excelling*.

excellent ĕk′sə lənt
    Even though the accent in *excellent* has reverted to the first syllable, you keep the two l's to keep the short **e** sound in the middle of the word.
    The word has three **e**'s: *excellent*.

A. Follow the directions and answer the questions:

1. Add the following endings to *excel*; don't forget to double the **l** when you need to: *s*, **-ed, -ing, -ence, -ent**.
2. How are each of the following words misspelled: *exitement, excitment, exsitement*?
3. What is the difference in pronunciation between *except* and *accept*?
4. What is the difference in meaning between *except* and *accept*?

LESSON 27 (Continued)

sure, **surely**

Pronunciation: shŏŏr

Two common words—*sure* and *sugar*—have the initial **sh** sound spelled **s**.
The vowel sound is a double short **oo** (ŏŏ) spelled **u** with a final silent **e**.

B. Underline the spelling errors in this paragraph and write the corrections above them:

I'm not shur I want to go to the oshun. I think it will be warmer at the lake.

Shurely we could go to the ochen another time, couldn't we?

Be shure, when you buy doughnuts, to get the fat-free kind without shuger on them.

sugar

Pronunciation: shŏŏg′ər

Two problems with this word:

1) The **sh** sound is spelled **s** (**s** for *sweet*?).
   Sugar and *sure* are both spelled with an **s**, not an **sh**.
2) The unaccented vowel before the **r** is spelled with an
   a, not an **e**—as in *grammar, liar, scholar*.

I like brown *sugar* on sour grapefruit, I like powdered *sugar* on strawberries, but I like salt on my cantaloupe. Yes, I am *sure* that is what I like.

weather

Pronunciation: wĕth′ər

The short **e** sound is spelled **ea** here—as it is in *sweater, bread, head, feather, heather, leather*.

Note that the beginning consonant is pronounced **w**—just the way it is spelled. Its first vowel sound (short **e**) is spelled **ea**.

This August *weather* is so cold that I think I'll need warm clothes at the ocean. I believe I'll take a sw*ea*ter along and my l*ea*ther gloves. Perhaps I'll find a f*ea*ther from a sea gull.

whether

Pronunciation: hwĕth′ər

Students often drive spelling teachers crazy by asking "which witch?" as if the two words had the same pronunciation. Then they say "whether the weather is good" as if those two words were pronounced the same. They aren't.

Whether starts with the two letters **wh** that are pronounced **hw**. *Weather* starts with the **w** sound pronounced **w**.

In *whether*, you have the short **e** sound spelled with an **e**. In *weather*, the short **e** sound is spelled with **ea**.

Whether is a question word involving alternatives. Many of our question words begin with **wh**: *when, why, where, which*.

C. Fill in the blanks with the correct word: *whether* or *weather*.

1. I don't know _____ to go to the ocean or the lake in this _____ .
2. I can't decide _____ to eat one chocolate doughnut or two.
3. I am unable to tell _____ the _____ will be sunny or rainy tomorrow.
4. Do you know _____ she's coming to the library?
5. What do you think about the _____ ?

LESSON 27
Additional Activities

1. What do the three words *excitement*, *except*, and *excel* have in common?

2. Why is the **c** in each of them pronounced **s**?

3. Why do we double the **l** to make *excellent* from *excel*?

4. What is the sound of the **s** in *sure*, *surely*, and *sugar*?

5. Do you keep the final **e** in *sure* to make *surely*?

6. How do you spell the woman's name that sounds like *surely*?

7. How is the schwa/**r** sound spelled in *sugar*?

8. Use *leather*, *cold*, and *weather* in one sentence.

9. Use *when* and *whether* in one sentence.

10. What does *except* mean? *accept*? Use them in sentences.

Answers

LESSON 27

A. 1. excels, excelled, excelling, excellence, excellent
2. exitement: no **c** after **x**
   excitment: no **e** after the first **t**
   exsitement: **s** instead of **c**
3. *Except* begins with a short **e** sound; *accept* begins with a short **a** sound. If you pronounce those beginning sounds as a schwa, you won't hear the difference between the words.
4. *except*: with the exclusion of, other than, but
   accept: take, receive

LESSON 27 (Continued)

B. I'm not **sure** (shur) I want to go to the **ocean** (oshun). I think it will be warmer at the lake. **Surely** (Shurely) we could go to the **ocean** (ochen) another time, couldn't we? Be **sure** (shure), when you buy doughnuts, to get the kind with **sugar** (shuger) on them.

C. 1. whether, weather
2. whether
3. whether, weather
4. whether
5. weather

LESSON 27: Additional Activities

1. Each word has a **c** after the **x**; each starts **exc**.
2. Because the **c** is followed by an **e** or **i**.
3. *Excel* is a one-one word with the accent on the last syllable.
4. **sh**
5. yes
6. Shirley
7. **-ar**
8. Sample sentence: I will use my new **leather** boots in this **cold weather**.
9. Sample sentence: I don't know **when** or even **whether** we can go skating.
10. *Except* means "but" or "excluding"; *accept* means "to take or receive."

Sample sentences: Everyone **except** Susan rode the raft down the Colorado River. Susan left the camping trip early to **accept** a job in Phoenix.

LESSON 28

children

One child, two children

Pronunciation: **chĭl′drən**

Most people know that *children* is the plural of *child.* They don't say "two childs," but sometimes they reverse the **e** and the **r** and spell the word "childern" rather than *children.*

A. 1. How are *children* and *hundred* misspelled in the sentence below? How are *library* and *February* misspelled? Write the sentence with correct spellings:
The childern go to the libary in Febuary by the hunderds.
2. Write the numeral 100 in words.
3. How many students are in your class? Use the word *children* in your answer.

straight

Pronunciation: **strāt**

This word has a few superfluous letters, doesn't it? Do you know what *superfluous* means? It's a long word for "extra."

You've seen **ai** in *rain* for the long **a** sound. And you've seen plenty of words with **gh** thrown into them but not pronounced: *thought, though, daughter, neighbor.*

Actually, I think this is the only **aigh** word I've come across, so this is one of a kind: unique. If you know of another one, let me know, please.

I'll write it five times, and maybe I'll get it **straight**:

straight, straight, straight, straight, straight.

Nothing looks right after you've written it five times!

Here's another word for you: *strait.*

A *strait* is a narrow passageway, such as the Bering *Strait* between Asia and Alaska. If you are in dire *straits* or desperate *straits,* you're having a rough time.

B. Fill in the correct word: *strait(s)* or *straight.*
1. I am in dire _____ trying to keep _____ and _____
_____ .
2. I thought my neighbor's daughter had _____ hair.
3. Can you draw a _____ line? With a ruler?
4. The _____ of Gibraltar is between Spain and Africa.

practice

Pronunciation: **prăk′tĭs**

The word has two **c**'s.

prac - pronounced **k**, because if **c** is followed by an **a, o, u,** a consonant, or nothing, it is pronounced **k.** This **c** is followed by a **t.**

tice - pronounced **s**, because if **c** is followed by **e, i,** or **y,** it is pronounced **s.** This **c** is followed by an **e.**

It's related to the word *practical.*

If there is a final silent **e,** why isn't the **i** long? Because it's an unaccented syllable, as in definite.

C. Write the correct spelling for the italicized misspelled words:

I *beleive* _____ I'll *practise* _____ my figure 8's on the ice

today. I'd rather skate down the river, but I think I'll be *practikal* _____

and stay in one spot and *praktice* _____ . Wouldn't it be fun if the *oshens*

_____ froze and we *cood* _____ skate all the way to *Ingland*

_____ ?

LESSON 28 (Continued)

off

Pronunciation: ôf

There is nothing terribly difficult about the word *off*, but people confuse it with *of*.

of   -   **ŭv**   I have done a lot **of** practicing today.

off   -   **ôf**   I'd like to take tomorrow **off**.

Double **f** is used at the end of some familiar words—*off, Jeff, stuff*—and in the middle of some words—*different, difficult, effort, daffodils, raffle*.

The ô sound is the sound you hear in *often, soft*, and *moss*.

I have such an awful stomach ache that I think I'll take my clothes *off*, put on my pajamas, and go back to bed. I'll put *off* thinking about anything else for a while.

some

It's pronounced **sŭm**, but it is spelled *some*, like *come*. It's one of those many **o** words pronounced with a short **u**:

     one, come, some, stomach, tongue, done, Monday, monkey, of

Some other time I'll go with you to see the monkeys. Now I have **some** other things to do.

The final silent **e** doesn't make the **o** long. Look at *done, once, one, glove, none*. All of them have a short **u** sound for the **o**.

Some has a homonym: *sum*. It means "the total."

The *sum* of one and one is two.

something

Pronunciation: sŭm′thĭng

This is a compound word made up of *some* and *thing*. You have to spell *some* correctly first: *S O M E*. Don't leave the **e** out. And just because you sometimes say the word fast as "sumpin" does not mean you can spell it that way. Well, you can, but it will be wrong.

Some, no, any, and *every* combine with other words to make a lot of compound words; for example: *anybody, everywhere, nothing, somewhere, sometimes*.

Occasionally they are not compounds, depending on the meaning you want. Compare:

Put *some time* in on the garden, please.

Sometime weed the garden, will you, please?

D.   Answer the questions when you have time.

1.   Write the correct spelling for these "dictionary-spelled" words.
   a.   **ôf**
   b.   **ŭv**
   c.   **sŭm**
   d.   **sŭm′thĭng**

2.   Use a compound of *some* (*somebody, someone, something, sometimes*) in the following sentences:

       _____ I wonder about you. Whenever I call you to help, you already

have _____ to do. "Get _____ else," you say. Well, today that

_____ is you.

3.   What is the pronunciation of the **o** in *some* and *something*?

4.   What is the pronunciation of the **o** in *off*? in *of*?

5.   How is the following misspelled: "somthing"?

6.   I spent _____ time on my _____(s) in mathematics.

              Spelling Demons Week by Week

LESSON 28
Additional Activities

1. What is the sound of the first **c** in *practice*? the second **c**? Why?

2. Draw a straight line. Label it "Straight Line" with your name.

3. Draw a map with a strait on it.

4. Draw a picture of three children. Label the picture "Three Children." Put someone else's name on the picture.

5. Draw a picture showing the meaning of *off*.

6. How does the spelling of *off* differ from the spelling of *of*?

7. What is the hononym for *sum*?

8. Spell *some*. Spell *thing*. Put them together into one word. Spell *somewhere, somebody, sometimes*.

9. In what way are the spellings of *hundred, library,* and *February* similar?

Answers

LESSON 28

A. 1. "Childern" and "hunderds" have the **e** and the **r** reversed. "Libary" and "Febuary" have the **r** after the **b** omitted. The children go to the library in February by the hundreds.
2. one hundred
3. Sample answer: There are 45 children in my class.

B. 1. straits, *strait*, *straight*, straight (second and third words can be reversed)
2. straight
3. straight
4. strait

C. believe, practice, practical, oceans, could, England

LESSON 28 (Continued)

D. 1. off, of, some or sum, something
2. Sometimes, something, someone, someone
3. short **u**
4. The **o** in *off* is marked ô. It is the same sound you have in *cough, soft, daughter, ball, moss,* and *awful.* The **o** in *of* is a short **u** sound.
5. The **e** has been left out after the **m**.
6. some, sum

LESSON 28: Additional Activities

1. The sound of the first **c** is a **k**, because the **c** is followed by a consonant. The sound of the second **c** is an **s**, because that **c** is followed by the vowel **e**.

2.

Straight line, by Elizabeth Hagner

3.

The Hagner Strait

4. Three children

J. M. Browning

5. Sample picture: The ball rolled **off** the table.

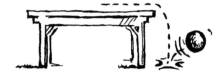

6. *Off* has two f's; *of* has only one **f**.
7. some
8. some, thing, something; somewhere, somebody, sometimes
9. Each has an **r** in the middle of the word that is often either not pronounced or pronounced in the wrong place.

LESSON 29

mean/meant; hear/heard

Meant and *heard* are often misspelled. People spell the vowel combination the way they hear the words: "ment" and "hurd." Think what word each comes from, and the spelling will be easier.

Meant is the past tense of *mean*.

I *mean* to clean the kitchen today, Wednesday.
I *meant* to do it yesterday, Tuesday, but I put it off.
Heard is the past tense of *hear*.

I *hear* you practicing; I *heard* you early this morning, also.
You *hEAR* with your EAR; you also *hEARd* with your EAR.
There is a homonym for *heard*: *herd*.

Herd is a group, usually of animals. It can be people, too.
That *herd* of cows moved across the pasture.

read

Pronunciation: rēd   Today I shall **read** a book.
                rĕd   Yesterday I **read** a book.

The spelling is the same, but there is a different pronunciation according to the tense (time) you want. If it is now or in the future, you **rēd**. If you've already done it, you've **rĕd** it.

Ah, but don't mix up the color *red* with *read* pronounced **rĕd**.

In Monopoly, you may land on the **Rĕd´ĭng** Railroad, which goes from Philadelphia to Reading (**Rĕd´ĭng**), Pennsylvania.

please

Pronunciation: plēz   The **z** sound is spelled **s**.

You will *ease* your way in life by saying *please*.

pleasant

Pronunciation: plĕz´ənt

The **z** sound is spelled *s*. The short **e** sound is spelled **ea**. If you can remember that *pleasant* comes from *please*, that should help you remember the **ea**—if you remember that *please* is spelled with an **ea**!

In the **-ant** ending, you don't hear that **a**. Exaggerate it when you pronounce it for spelling: **plĕz´ănt**.

It's *pleasant* to see a ph*easant* in the woods.
I mean to *please*; I meant to be *pleasant*.

A number of words spelled with **ea** sound long **e** in the present tense and short **e** in the past tense or in another form of the word:

heal, healthy, healthful   please, pleasant, pleasure
    read, read   clean, cleanser   mean, meant

early

Pronunciation: ûr´lē (pronounced ûr, but spelled **ear**)

The *early* bird catches the word. The *early* bird will catch a mosquito in his *ear* if he's in the woods too **early**.

A. Use the following words to replace the dictionary-spelled words in the sentences: *read, meant, heard, herd, red, please, pleasant.*

1. Yesterday I **rĕd** _____ a book; tomorrow I will **rēd** _____ another book.
2. That **rĕd** _____ cushion is a **plēz´ĭng** _____ color.
3. **Plēz** _____ forgive me. I **mĕnt** _____ no harm.
4. That's a **plĕz´ənt** _____ scene: a **hûrd** _____ of cows out **ûr´lē** _____ in the field.

LESSON 29 (Continued)

break

Pronunciation: **brāk**

If you can't remember how to spell *break*, you might choose to use, instead, one of the following words: *crack, fracture, rupture, burst, split, splinter, shatter, shiver, smash,* or *crush.* Actually, one of them might be more exact.

If you do use *break*, remember that it's **ea**—as in *great, steak,* and *yea!* Those are about the only **ea** words that sound long **a**, so try to think of them together.

Y*ea*! What a *break*! We have a gr*ea*t st*ea*k tonight.

The tenses of *break*: *break, broke, broken.*

I *break* for lunch at 11:30 today. Yesterday I *broke* at 12:00. All this week I've *broken* at a different time each day.

Break has a homonym: *brake*.

Braking has to do with slowing a motion or stopping it.

breakfast

Fasting means "not eating." When you break a fast, you interrupt it. In the morning when you eat **breakfast** you interrupt the fasting you've been doing since the night before when you finished supper—or maybe you had popcorn during the evening?

Pronunciation: **brĕk′fəst** The long **a** in *break* becomes a short **e**.

B. Choose the correct word: *break, broke, broken, breakfast, brake(s).*

1. Did you _____ that glass today?

2. Who, me? No. I just came downstairs for _____ .

3. Next time, put your _____ on before you come into the kitchen.

4. I _____ a glass yesterday, though. I've _____ three glasses this week, but none this morning.

caught, taught, daughter, naughty

"See the fish I *caught*?"

"Will you look at the size of that fish?" my *daughter* exclaimed.

The dictionary marks the vowel spelling as the ô. It is spelled **augh** or **au** with a silent **gh**—however you view it.

Here are two more **-aught** words: *slaughter* and *haughty.*

C. Can you write a sentence using all six **au** words? Do you know any other **au** words?

D. Fill in each blank with one of these **-aught** words correctly spelled: *haughty, slaughter, caught, taught, daughter, naughty.*

1. The farmer will_____ the pigs on Wednesday.

2. My father _____ me to milk the cows.

3. My puppy chewed my slipper. She is _____ .

4. I _____ her with the slipper in her mouth.

5. My _____ would rather make the salad than set the table.

6. That fashion model certainly has a _____ look on her face.

tonight

Pronunciation: **tə nīt′**

Don't forget to write the **gh** in the word, as in *night* and *light.*

Tonight we'll make the cake.

tomorrow tə môr′ ō—the day following today

Two **r**'s, ends in **ow**

Tomorrow we'll eat the cake.

LESSON 29
Additional Activities

1. What are the homonyms for *grate, stake, brake*?

2. Write one sentence or more with *break, great, steak,* and *yea*.

3. How do you pronounce the **ea** in *breakfast*?

4. How does the dictionary mark the vowel sound in *caught* and *taught*? How do you spell the sound?

5. *Tonight* is made from what two words?

6. Draw a picture of a steak. Label the kind of steak it is.

7. A number of words have the long **e** sound spelled **ea** in the basic verb form. What is the sound of the **ea** in the past tense or in another form of the word? (Examples: *please, pleasant; mean, meant.*)

8. From what word is *pleasant* made? *meant*? *heard*?

9. How do you spell the present tense of *read* (as in "to read a book")? the past tense?

10. What two letters does *tomorrow* end in? Are there two **m**'s or two **r**'s in *tomorrow*?

Answers

A. 1. read; read
   2. red, pleasing
   3. Please, meant
   4. pleasant, herd, early

B. 1. break
   2. breakfast
   3. brakes
   4. broke, broken

C. Sample sentence: My **naughty, haughty daughter taught** me to **slaughter** the pig that I **caught**. Ugh!

Other **au** words: August, autumn, autistic, automatic, automobile, Audrey, auction, auburn, audience, audacity, audio, audit, auditorium, Audubon, augment, augur, auk, auld lang syne, aunt (not pronounced ô, but spelled **au**), aurora borealis

D. 1. slaughter
   2. taught
   3. naughty
   4. caught
   5. daughter
   6. haughty

LESSON 29: Additional Activities

1. grate/great; stake/steak; brake/break
2. Sample sentence: **Yea!** What a **break!** We will have a **great steak** tonight.
3. short **e**
4. ô; **au**
5. to, night
6. Sample:

   T-bone Steak
7. short **e**
8. pleasant/please; meant/mean; heard/hear
9. read, read
10. **ow**, two **r**'s

NAME _____   DATE _____

LESSON 30

probably
Syllables: *prob a bly*
Pronunciation: **prŏb′ə blē**
    The word is not "probly" or "probely." When you mispronounce the word those ways, you cause yourself trouble.
    I had a doll named *Bab. Bab* was *probably* my favorite doll. If you turned her upside down, she said, *"bab, bab, bab, bab."*
    These words are related to *probably: pro**bab**le; pro**bab**ility.*

answer
Syllables: *an swer*
Pronunciation: **ăn′sər**
    You don't hear the **w**, so you probly forget to write it. ("*Probly*? That's not a word!"
"I know. I just wanted to see if you were awake. It's *probably.*")
My little brother has a teddy bear he named *Swer.*
"What kind of a name is '*Swer*'?" I asked him.
"Just as good a name as 'Bab,'" he *answered.*

people (pē′pəl)
    This is a ridiculous word. Somebody's pen must have slipped when writing *populace,* or *popular,* or *population,* and that somebody wrote an **e** before the **o** by mistake. Now we pronounce the **e** and not the **o**.
    The **-ple** ending you have seen: *dimple, steeple.*
    You hear the **e**. Think of the **o** as an open mouth. A lot of **people** have their mouths **o**pen a lot of the time! *pe* **O** *ple*

separate
Syllables: *sep a rate*
Pronunciations: as a verb: **sĕp′ə rāt**
              as an adjective: **sĕp′ə rət**
    It is the **a** after the **p** that gives people trouble. *Separate* is the one English word I learned from Latin class, because the teacher said, "Remember *separo* and you won't misspell *separate.*" I *did* remember that. She'd be pleased to know it. Too bad she didn't tell me to remember some other things!
    Some students think of *part* and *separate* together. To **separate** is to divide into parts.
"Let's have a *separate par*ty at my a*par*tment. We'll *par*cel out the *par*sley on the *par*snips and sing "*Par*tridge in a Pear Tree," said my friend *Par.*
"*Par*don me. You call that a *par*ty?" Swer asked.
"It's a *par*ticular kind of *par*ty," Par answered.
"Why are we talking in all these *par* words?"
"Because se*par*ate has *par* in it."

A. Answer the questions:
1. Each of these words—*separate, people, answer, probably*—has a problem letter or spot to remember. What are they?
2. *Answer* has a silent letter. What is it?
3. Which is the one correct spelling in each of the following groups? Circle it:
    a. peple, peeple, peepul, pepol, people
    b. probaly, probly, probely, probably, probabley
    c. separate, seperate, seprate, separite
    d. ansser, answer, ansewr, annser

LESSON 30 (Continued)

interesting

Pronunciation: 1. ĭn´trĭs tĭng
                 2. ĭn´tə rĕst ĭng

The first pronunciation doesn't give you much help with those **e**'s, does it? Pronounce it the second way to help you spell it.

in ter est	three syllables
in ter est ed	four syllables
in ter est ing	four syllables

Please be careful with the scissors. We need them for an *interesting* art project.

picture

Pronunciation: pĭk´chər

Things to remember:

1. The **k** sound is spelled **c**.
2. The **ch** sound is spelled **tu** as it is in *nature, lecture,* and *mixture.*
3. Picture is confused with *pitcher* (pĭch´ər). The *pitcher* throws the ball to the batter, or it's what you put milk in for your cereal.
    Pictures are what you have on the wall.

Do you have a *picture* of your favorite *pitcher*?

with

The *th* is like the *th* in *then.*

This is spelled just the way it sounds. DON'T put another **h** in it. It's not "whith." Maybe people who put that extra **h** in are confusing *with* with *which.* But **you** spell it correctly, don't you?

different

Pronunciation: 1. dĭf´ə rənt
                 2. dĭf´rənt

If you pronounce the word the second way, you may forget an **e**. There are two of them in *different,* just as there are in *interesting.*

Just because that pizza is *interesting* and *different* doesn't mean that it is good.

B.   Someone was asleep when writing the following. Can you underline and correct the six errors in it?

That pitchur above the desk is intresting. It certainly is a diffrent pikture. What makes it diferent is the color. It's green whith blue.

C.   Answer the questions, *bitte* (please).
1.   How is the **ch** sound spelled in *nature, lecture,* and *picture?*
2.   Fill in the missing letters:

int ___ r ___ sting

diff ___ r ___ nt

pi ___ ture

___ ith

pic ___ re

3.   What is a picture? What are two meanings for *pitcher*?
4.   Which is the correct spelling: *whith, wihth, with, hwith, wif?*
5.   Can you think of a word that rhymes with *with*?
6.   If you add **-ered** to *with,* you'll get a word describing the plant you forgot to water. What is the word?

LESSON 30
Additional Activities

1. Draw a picture of a pitcher.

2. Draw a picture showing the meaning of **with**.

3. Spell **answer**.

4. Why did my little brother An name his teddy bear Swer?

5. Write the syllables for **probably**. How many are there? Write the word. Ask your neighbor if you've spelled it correctly. If you haven't, look at the correct spelling of it, and then write it again.

6. What common ending is on **people**? What uncommon vowel combination is in the first syllable?

7. Write the syllables of **interesting**. How many syllables are there? How will pronouncing them all help to spell the word?

8. Write the syllables of **different**. How many syllables are there? How will pronouncing them all help to spell the word?

9. What letter causes trouble for people in **separate**?

Answers

LESSON 30

A. 1. The first **a** in *separate*, the **o** in *people*, the **w** in *answer*, and the **a** in *probably*.
2. **w**
3. people, probably, separate, answer

LESSON 30 (Continued)

B. 1. That **picture** (pitchure) above the desk is **interesting** (intresting). It certainly is a **different** (diffrent) **picture** (pikture). What makes it **different** (diferent) is the color. It's green **with** (whith) blue.

C. 1. **tu**
2. **e, e; e, e; c; w; tu**
3. A picture is a visual representation on a flat surface. ("I really enjoy that visual representation on a flat surface that you painted of me.") The two meanings of *pitcher* are (1) a vessel for liquids, with a handle and a lip or spout for pouring, and (2) in baseball, the player who throws the ball from the mound for action by the batter. ("Say, player who throws the ball from the mound for action by the batter, would you please pass the vessel for liquids with a handle and a lip or spout for pouring the syrup for my pancakes?")
4. with
5. No, and I couldn't find one in my rhyming dictionary, either.
6. withered

LESSON 30: Additional Activities

1. Sample Drawing:

pitchers

2. Sample Drawing:

I have my bicycle **with** me.

3. answer
4. to remember the spelling of the end of the word: *ans*wer
5. *prob a bly*; three; *probably*
   I spelled it correctly.
6. **-le; eo**
7. *in ter est ing*; four; it will help you to include the first **e**, between the **t** and the **r**.
8. *dif fer ent*; three; again, it will help you to include the first **e**, here between the second **f** and the **r**
9. the **a** after the **p**. Think of **a** *rat* in that word.

Third Quarter Quizzes

This section starts with a choice of oral quizzes to dictate to your students for this quarter of the work: 10 words, 20, 50, or 100. Choose the one or ones best suited to the individual needs of your students, the time you have, and how many words you feel are important for each quarter. If the word is a homonym, I have provided a sentence.

The oral quizzes are followed by two reproducible written quizzes: Sound to Spelling and General.

Oral Quizzes

Test I: 10 Words

1. Wednesday
2. Tuesday
3. because
4. used to
5. beautiful
6. all right
7. February
8. weather
9. probably
10. separate

Test II: 20 Words

1. Wednesday
2. August
3. Tuesday
4. stomach
5. because
6. used to
7. which
8. could've been
9. beautiful
10. a lot
11. all right
12. February
13. awful
14. except
15. weather
16. meant
17. probably
18. different
19. separate
20. answer

Test III: 50 Words

1. Wednesday
2. August
3. Tuesday
4. stomach
5. because
6. used to
7. which
8. could've been
9. beautiful
10. a lot
11. all right
12. February
13. awful
14. except (All except Susan went to the show.)
15. weather
16. meant
17. probably
18. different
19. separate
20. answer
21. school
22. ache
23. potato
24. business
25. mosquitoes
26. radios
27. already (They have already gone.)
28. tomatoes
29. colonel (I like Colonel Sanders.)
30. success
31. truly
32. toward
33. wholly (I did it wholly by myself.)
34. excitement
35. all ready (The group is all ready to go.)
36. sure
37. surely
38. sugar
39. whether
40. true
41. speech
42. children
43. practice
44. something
45. heard (We heard the music.)
46. pleasant
47. early
48. people
49. picture
50. different

Oral Quizzes (Continued)

Test IV: 100 Words

1. Wednesday
2. August
3. Tuesday
4. stomach
5. because
6. used to
7. which
8. could've been
9. beautiful
10. a lot
11. all right
12. February
13. awful
14. except (All except Susan went to the show.)
15. weather
16. meant
17. probably
18. different
19. separate
20. answer
21. school
22. ache
23. potato
24. business
25. mosquitoes
26. radios
27. already (They have already gone.)
28. tomatoes
29. colonel (I like Colonel Sanders.)
30. success
31. truly
32. toward
33. wholly (I did it wholly by myself.)
34. excitement
35. all ready (The group is all ready to go.)
36. sure
37. surely
38. sugar
39. whether
40. true
41. speech
42. children
43. practice
44. something
45. heard (We heard the music.)
46. pleasant
47. early
48. people
49. picture
50. different
51. potatoes
52. tomato
53. autos
54. heroes
55. silhouette
56. picnic
57. picnicking
58. somersault
59. I'm
60. of
61. would have been
62. should've been
63. beauty
64. busy
65. polka dot
66. always (He has always walked to school.)
67. rich
68. much
69. such
70. library
71. almost
72. all ways (All ways are partially correct.)
73. altogether (This is an altogether different problem.)
74. libraries
75. I'll (I'll see you at school.)
76. seem (That doesn't seem right.)
77. speak
78. blue
79. whole (I ate the whole pizza.)
80. hole (I dug a deep hole.)
81. excel
82. excellent
83. excelled
84. awfully
85. straight (Walk a straight line.)
86. strait (We sailed the Bering Strait.)
87. off
88. some (I have some candy to share with you.)
89. someone
90. mean (I mean to clean my room tomorrow.)
91. hear (I hear with my ears.)
92. read (I will read the newspaper tonight.)
93. read (Yesterday I read a magazine.)
94. please
95. daughter
96. tonight
97. taught
98. interesting
99. with
100. caught

THIRD QUARTER
Sound to Spelling Quiz

In the following test, spell the word correctly from the sound of the word given by the dictionary markings.

1. wĕnz′dā

2. tōoz′dā

3. āk

4. stŭm′ək

5. ô′gŭst

6. skōol

7. pə tā′tō

8. pə tā′tōz

9. tə mā′tō

10. tə mā′tōz

11. mə skē′tō

12. rā′dē ō

13. ô′tō

14. kûr′nəl (My father was a kûr′nəl in the army.)

15. pĭk′nĭk

16. pĭk′nĭk ĭng

17. sĭl ōo ĕt′

18. sŭm′ər sôlt

19. ī

20. īm

21. īl

22. īv

23. bĭ kôz′

24. yōozd′ tōo

25. ŭv

26. cŏod

27. wŏod

28. shŏod

29. cŏod′əv

30. wŏod′əv

31. shŏod′əv

32. cŏod′əv bĭn

33. hwĭch

34. byōo′tə fəl

35. bĭz′ē

36. ə lŏt′

37. pō′kə dŏt

38. fĕb′rōo ĕr ē

39. lī′brĕr ē

40. ôl′rīt′

41. ôl′rĕd′ē (We are ôl′rĕd′ē.)

42. ôl rĕd′ē (She has ôl rĕd′ē left for work.)

43. ôl′wāz′ (ôl′wāz′ lead to rome.)

44. ôl′wāz (I have ôl′wāz carried an umbrella in the rain.)

45. ôl thō′

46. ôl mōst′

47. sək sĕs′

48. sēm (I sēm to have lost my umbrella.)

49. sēm (The sēm in my skirt is coming apart.)

50. trōo

THIRD QUARTER
Sound to Spelling Quiz (Continued)

51. tro͞o′lē

52. tôrd, *or* tōrd, *or* tə wôrd′

53. ô′fəl

54. ô′fəl lē

55. spēk

56. spēch

57. blo͞o (color)

58. hōl (The hōl pie is gone.)

59. hōl (The prairie dog came out of its hōl.)

60. hō′lē (The pie is hō′lē gone.)

61. hō′lē (We sang the hymn "Hō′lē, hō′lē, hō′lē.")

62. ĕk sīt′mənt

63. ĕk sĕpt′

64. ăk sĕpt′

65. ĕk sĕl′

66. ĕk′sĕ lənt

67. sho͝or

68. sho͝or′lē

69. sho͝og′ər

70. wĕth′ər

71. hwĕth′ər

72. chĭl′drən

73. strāt (Can you draw a strāt line?)

74. strāt (We sailed through the strāt of Gibraltar.)

75. prăk′tĭs

76. ôf

77. sŭm (Want sŭm ice cream?)

78. sŭm′thĭng

79. mēn (I mēn to do the right thing.)

80. mĕnt

81. hîr (I hîr a noise.)

82. hûrd (I hûrd a noise.)

83. rēd (I will rēd a book today.)

84. rĕd (I rĕd a book yesterday, too.)

85. plēz

86. plĕz′ənt

87. ûr′lē

88. brāk (I don't want to brāk a dish.)

89. brĕk′fəst

90. côt

91. tôt

92. tə nīt′

93. prŏb′ə blē

94. an′sər

95. pē′pəl

96. sĕp′ə rāt (verb) *or* sĕp′ə rət (adjective)

97. ĭn′trĭs tĭng *or* ĭn′tə rĕst ĭng

98. pĭk′chər

99. wĭth

100. dĭf′ə rənt *or* dĭf′rənt

Spelling Demons Week by Week

THIRD QUARTER
General Quiz

1. How will you remember the plural of words ending in **o**? Choose one option.

   a. I just will. They're no problem.

   b. By learning the rules, which are:

   c. By making a list of the words I'll use or the ones that will trouble me.

   d. By looking them up in the dictionary when I need to.

   e. By keeping the chart in my own special spelling notebook.

   f. A combination of the above choices (list the choices you'll combine):

2. How well do you understand the rule? Choose the correct ending to each sentence:

   a. For words ending in a vowel before the final **o**, such as *radio*, (add **s**, add **-es**).

   b. For Italian or musical words ending in a consonant before the **o**, such as *piano*, (add **s**, add **-es**).

   c. For clipped words ending in a consonant before the **o** such as *photo*, (add **s**, add **-es**).

   d. For foreign words ending in a consonant before the **o**, such as *taco*, (add **s**, add **-es**).

   e. For all the rest ending in a consonant before the **o**,
      (1) such as *tomato*, (add **s**, add **-es**).
      (2) such as *mosquito*, and *volcano*, (add **s**, add **-es**, add either **s** or **-es**).

3. Lessons 21–30 cover a number of words with problem areas. Circle the letter or letters in the following that may cause you hesitation in spelling.

a. Wednesday	o. separate
b. Tuesday	p. interesting
c. February	q. different
d. library	r. because
e. polka dot	s. could've
f. truly	t. would've been
g. toward	u. which
h. awful	v. beautiful
i. excitement	w. busy
j. meant	x. whole
k. breakfast	y. weather
l. probably	z. whether
m. answer	zz. children
n. people	

4. Circle the correct words.

   always   already   all ways   all ready   all right   alright

THIRD QUARTER
General Quiz (Continued)

5. Circle the correct spelling in each line:

   a. useto   use to   used to

   b. alot   a lot

   c. alright   all right   allright

6. Choose the correct homonym:

   a. She thought (eye, I) was angry.

   b. They had (all ready, already) gone.

   c. We have (all ways, always) had strawberries with ice cream.

   d. That (seems, seams) crazy.

   e. I (blue, blew) up the (blue, blew) balloon.

   f. The (whole, hole) chocolate cake is gone!

   g. Everyone had a piece (accept, except) me.

   h. That's the (strait, straight) story.

   i. Couldn't you have saved me (some, sum)?

   j. You're (mean, mien) to eat it all.

   k. I (hear, here) the news as I sit (hear, here).

   l. I've already (heard, herd) it.

   m. I (read, red) the message: "The cake is gone."

7. What is the sound of—

   a. the **ea** in *mean*?

   b. the **ea** in *meant*?

   c. the **s** in *sure*?

   d. the **ch** in *stomach*?

   e. the **u** in *busy*?

   f. the **ce** in *practice*?

   g. the **w** in *answer*?

   h. the **t** in *picture*?

8. Circle the incorrect spelling:

   a. Tuesday, Wednesday, potatos, August

   b. probly, picture, a lot, all right

   c. different, intresting, wholly, February

   d. alright, already, altogether, also

   e. off, of, some, whitch

   f. somersault, silhouette, colonel, seperate

Answers to Third Quarter Quizzes

Sound To Spelling Quiz

1. Wednesday
2. Tuesday
3. ache
4. stomach
5. August
6. school
7. potato
8. potatoes
9. tomato
10. tomatoes
11. mosquito
12. radio
13. auto
14. colonel
15. picnic
16. picnicking
17. silhouette
18. somersault
19. I
20. I'm
21. I'll
22. I've
23. because
24. used to
25. of
26. could
27. would
28. should
29. could've
30. would've
31. should've
32. could've been
33. which
34. beautiful
35. busy
36. a lot
37. polka dot
38. February
39. library
40. all right
41. all ready
42. already
43. all ways
44. always
45. although
46. almost
47. success
48. seem
49. seam
50. true
51. truly
52. toward
53. awful
54. awfully
55. speak
56. speech
57. blue
58. whole
59. hole
60. wholly
61. holy
62. excitement
63. except
64. accept
65. excel
66. excellent
67. sure
68. surely
69. sugar
70. weather
71. whether
72. children
73. straight
74. strait
75. practice
76. off
77. some
78. something
79. mean
80. meant
81. hear
82. heard
83. read
84. read
85. please
86. pleasant
87. early
88. break
89. breakfast
90. caught
91. taught
92. tonight
93. probably
94. answer
95. people
96. separate
97. interesting
98. picture
99. with
100. different

General Quiz

1. The choice should be f, a combination of d and e.
2. a. add **s**
   b. add **s**
   c. add **s**
   d. add **s**
   e. (1) add **es**
      (2) add **s** or **es**
3. a. Wednesday
   b. Tuesday
   c. February
   d. library
   e. polka dot
   f. truly
   g. toward
   h. awful
   i. excitement
   j. meant
   k. breakfast
   l. probably
   m. answer
   n. people
   o. separate
   p. interesting
   q. different
   r. because
   s. could've
   t. would've been
   u. which
   v. beautiful
   w. busy
   x. whole
   y. weather
   z. whether
   zz. children
   (or any spots that cause you trouble)
4. always   already   all ways   all ready   all right
5. a. used to
   b. a lot
   c. all right
6. a. I
   b. already
   c. always
   d. seems
   e. blew, blue
   f. whole
   g. except
   h. straight
   i. some
   j. mean
   k. hear, here
   l. heard
   m. read
7. a. long **e**
   b. short **e**
   c. **sh**
   d. **k**
   e. short **i**
   f. **s**
   g. silent
   h. **ch**
8. a. potatos
   b. probly
   c. intresting
   d. alright
   e. whitch
   f. seperate

159

FOURTH QUARTER

LESSON 31

Special Days I
Abraham Lincoln's Birthday
Pronunciation of Lincoln: lĭng′kən
    The first **n** sounds like **ng**.
    The second **l** is silent.
    The **o** is an unaccented schwa sound.
    Abraham Lincoln was born on February 12; George Washington, on February 22.
The birthdays of both presidents are celebrated in one holiday in late February.

Leap Year Day — February 29
    If you were born on February 29, do you celebrate only on that day, on February 28, or on March 1?
    Does that make you one quarter as old as everyone else?
    Leap Year — both **ea**

ides
Pronunciation: īdz
Meaning: the 15th day of March, May, July, or October or the 13th day of any other month in the ancient Roman calendar. Caesar was warned to "Beware the **ides** of March." He didn't. No 16th of March for Caesar.
    While we think of the **ides** particularly in March, they occur in every month.

April Fools' Day — April 1
    This calls for an apostrophe after the **s** (a day for many fools!).
    It takes a special person to endure being born on this day of jokes and jokers. Happy Birthday, John!

April 6 — National Birthday Day
    When we were children, we made a cake every year on April 6. Our mother objected, but we showed her the date (April 6) stamped on the side of our stove, and we told her we had to have a birthday cake for the stove. Perhaps you can think of a birthday to celebrate with a cake. Remember, it's **birthday**, not **brithday**.

April 31 — National Spelling Day
    Every year that you have Leap Year, you also have National Spelling Day. On that day you can have whatever you want to eat: free ice cream, popcorn, chocolate dough-nuts, French fries, oranges, and spinach. All you can eat. You just have to spell correctly what you eat. (Just kidding—there's never any April 31; April always only has 30 days.)

Memorial Day   mə môr′ē əl
    Memorial Day is May 30. It honors those who died for our country in its wars. On this day, people also remember others who have died, and they visit cemeteries to decorate graves. The day used to be called Decoration Day. It's now observed as a legal holiday (no school!) on the last Monday of May in most states.

A.   Answer the questions:

1.   What month does not normally have a 29th?

2.   What month do you associate with the ides?

3.   What date in April would you think about fools?

4.   In what month is Memorial Day?

LESSON 31 (Continued)

Special Days II
Independence Day—July 4

Four **e**'s for July 4: Independence Day

Do you go to the cemetery on **Independence Day**? No, cemetery has only three **e**'s. Let's go to the parade on **Independence Day**.

Bastille Day—July 14

The Bastille was a fortress in Paris used as a prison until it was captured on July 14, 1789, at the beginning of the French Revolution. The French celebrate **Bastille Day** as we celebrate July 4.

Pronunciation: **Băs tēl′** (French: **Bàs′ tē y'**)

Friday the 13th

There can be any number of these days in a year. A word to think about on **Friday the 13th** is **triskadekaphobia**. It means a fear of the number 13.

I have no triskadekaphobia. Thirteen doesn't scare me. Does being born on **Friday the 13th** give you special good luck?

Columbus Day

Columbus Day is October 12, when Columbus sailed up the Mississippi River to Denver, right? No? Down the St. Lawrence to Albuquerque? No? Up the Columbia River to Columbus, Ohio? You tell me. **Columbus Day** is now observed as a legal holiday on the second Monday in October in many states.

Halloween hăl ō ēn′

November 1 is All Saints' Day, a *hallowed,* or holy, day. The evening before is All Hallow Evening, abbreviated to E'en. Sometimes **Halloween** is spelled *Hallowe'en.*

When you think of **Halloween**, you think of witches and ghosts. Think of the ghosts going E-e-e-e-e-e-e! in the cemetery—all **e**'s in *cemetery.*

Veterans Day

no apostrophe

Formerly, this was called Armistice Day, and was observed on November 11, commemorating the end of World War I. Now it's called **Veterans Day** to honor the veterans of all wars, and it's a legal holiday on the fourth Monday of October.

Indian summer

Pronunciation: **ĭn′dē ən**

The word has three syllables. Don't transpose the **i** and the **a** for "Indain." It doesn't end like *mountain.*

Indian summer is a period of mild weather in late autumn, frequently after the first frost. Can you spell *autumn*? **(ô′təm)**

au   -   ô sound as in *daughter*
tum   -   no problem
n   -   silent **n** at the end (When you say *autumnal,* you pronounce the **n**.)

B.   Answer the questions, *s'il vous plaît* (if you please):

1.   On what date of a month might you think about triskadekaphobia?

2.   On what date of what month might you think about the French Revolution?

3.   On what date of what month is Halloween? (The *real* Halloween, not the date some towns have the children celebrate it)

LESSON 31
Additional Activities

1. Spell the names of all the months of the year and the days of the week. I know they weren't part of this lesson, but you should know them by now.

2. Which special day has an apostrophe/**s**? Which day has an **s**/apostrophe? Which does not have an apostrophe before or after the **s**?

3. From what word does *memorial* come?

4. On what day do you trick or treat?

5. Which holiday honors the dead?

6. Which holiday honors the members of our country's armed forces?

7. What letter is silent in Lincoln's name?

8. In what month does Leap Year Day occur?

9. What is Indian summer?

Answers

LESSON 31

A. 1. February
    2. March
    3. April 1 (April Fools' Day)
    4. May

LESSON 31 (Continued)

B. 1. the 13th
    2. July 14
    3. October 31

LESSON 31: Additional Activities

1. January, February, March, April, May, June, July, August, September, October, November, December; Monday, Tuesday, Wednesday, Thursday, Friday, Saturday, Sunday
2. Lincoln's Birthday; April Fools' Day; Veterans Day
3. *memory*
4. Halloween
5. Memorial Day
6. Veterans Day
7. the second l
8. February
9. a period of mild weather occurring in late autumn or early winter, usually after a frost

LESSON 32

think, thought
Pronunciation: **thôt**

The **-ought** words have the ô vowel sound, and the **gh** is silent:
ought   bought   brought   fought   nought   sought   thought   wrought
I **thought** I knew the correct answer, but I was wrong. I **think** I now know it, though.
Nought means "nothing." *Wrought* means "made or worked." *Wrought iron* is iron hammered with tools.
Ought implies an obligation: I **ought** to fix that **wrought** iron railing for **nought** since I broke it.

bring, brought
Pronunciation: **brôt**

Today I **bring** the mail into the house. Yesterday I **brought** the mail in. Every day of this week I have gone out into the rain and **brought** the mail in. (There are no such words as "brang" or "brung." You say *sing, sang,* and *sung;* but it is *bring, brought,* and *brought.*)
Look at the verb forms of the following:

bring	brought	brought
buy	bought	bought
think	thought	thought
fight	fought	fought
seek	sought	sought

buy, bought, bought
Pronunciation: **bī, bôt**

Two words (and their derivatives) beginning with **b** have a silent **u** before the following vowel: *buy* and *build.*
I will **buy** a new car today; I **bought** one yesterday; I have **bought** one every day for five years now. I'm lying.
That guy is going to **buy** my car, I think. Yesterday I **bought** a newer car, so I **ought** to sell this one.

A. Follow the directions:

1. Can you write a sentence (or two) using *brought, bought, thought, fought,* and *sought?*

2. Circle the correct past tense of the verb to go with the present tense:

bring	brang	brung	brought
buy	buyed	buid	bought
think	thank	thunk	thought
fight	fighted	feet	fought
seek	seeked	seekt	sought
sing	sang	singed	singded

3. Now write a story using wrong spellings instead of the correct **-ought** ones, such as "Yesterday i thinkded I would buy a coat. I boughted one. . . ." See how wrong you can make the spelling. See if your neighbor can correct the mistakes.

4. What is wrong with the following? "I brang my lunch to school."

    Buy has two homonyms: *by,* meaning "near or past"; and *bye,* short for "good-bye" or a sports term meaning "passed over."
    Our team received a **bye** in the first tournament round. **Bye!** See you later. I'll come **by** your house after the game.

LESSON 32 (Continued)

say, **pay**, **lay**

A few vowel/**y** words change the **y** to **i** and then add the **d** without the **e**:
say/said   *pay/paid*   *lay/laid*

A few add **n**:   *lay/lain*   *slay/slain*

A few add **-ly**:   *gay/gaily*   *day/daily*

There are no such words as "payed" or "sayed" or "layed"!

lay, **laid**, **laid**, **laying**

When you have something in your hand and you want to put it down, you use the word *lay*.

I **lay** it down today, or I am **laying** it down. I will **lay** it down tomorrow. I **laid** it down yesterday. Yesterday I was **laying** it down. I have **laid** it down, or I had **laid** it down, every day of my life.

lie, **lay**, **lain**, **lying**

If you're just tired or lazy, and you don't want to stand up or sit anymore, you use the word *lie*.

I think I'll **lie** down on the beach. Yesterday I **lay** on the beach. I think I have **lain** on the beach for five hours by now! I have been **lying** here too long. I'm sunburned.

The confusion comes from the fact that *lay* is a form for both verbs.

1. *lay*—present tense for putting something down.
    See me **lay** the book down. (Someone wrote a song with the words: **Lay** that pistol down, Babe. . . .)

2. *lay*—past tense of *lie*. With this verb, you didn't put anything down—you just relaxed.
    Earlier this morning I *lay* in the sun.

lie, **lied**, **lied**, **lying**

When you don't tell the truth, you **lie**. Maybe you **lied** yesterday, too. Have you been **lying** all this week?

The word *lying* is another source of confusion: If you've told a lie or were just tired, it is spelled the same: *lying*. Add the word *down*, and you're innocent!

I was *lying*.

I was *lying* down.

B. Choose the correct form of the verb for each sentence:

lay	laid	laid	laying
lie	lay	lain	lying
lie	lies	lied	lying

1. I shall _____ this book on the bed.

2. I will _____ down beside the book.

3. Yesterday I _____ down on the bed.

4. Today I will _____ the pillows on the bed.

5. Have you been _____ down long?

6. I _____ four dollars on this desk. Where is the money now?

7. I have _____ in the sun too long, I think.

8. The dead skunk was _____ in the road.

9. How long has it _____ there?

10. She didn't tell the truth. She _____ !

11. She does _____ . She always does!

12. Why don't you _____ the skunk in her desk, then?

LESSON 32
Additional Activities

1. Can you use "brang" in a sentence? Now cross it out and write *brought*.

2. What do the words *thought, brought,* and *bought* have in common?

3. How is *buy* like *build*?

4. Does *caught* rhyme with *thought*? How are they spelled differently?

5. Choose the correct word in the sentence:
   a. Yesterday I (lay, laid) on the floor mat doing my exercises.
   b. Yesterday, I (lay, laid) my book bag on the iceberg outside the gym door.
   c. Those penguins have (laid, lain) on the iceberg for six weeks now.
   d. They are (laying, lying) eggs.
   e. You are the one who is (lieing, lying).

Answers

LESSON 32

A. 1. Sample sentence: I **bought** some cats and **brought** them to the city, where they **fought** the dogs so I **sought** a solution and **thought** of the pound.

2. brought, bought, thought, fought, sought, sang

3. Sample story: Yesterday I **brang** my lunch to school. I've **brung** it every day. I **buid** milk to go with my lunch. I **buyed** cake, too, but I couldn't eat it because I **fighted** my neighbor and the principal took away my cake. I **sekt** another piece of cake, so I **singded** a song hoping someone would buy me some more cake. No luck!

4. You're supposed to say: I **brought** my lunch to school.

LESSON 32 (Continued)

B. 1. lay
2. lie
3. lay
4. lay
5. lying
6. laid
7. lain
8. lying
9. lain
10. lied
11. lie
12. lay

LESSON 32: Additional Activities

1. I can, but it's wrong. I brang my lunch to school. I **brought** my lunch to school.
2. They all sound ôt; they all end in the letters **-ought**.
3. Each has a silent **u** between the **b** and the **i**.
4. Yes; *caught* is spelled with **-aught**, and *thought* is spelled with **-ought**.
5. a. lay
   b. laid
   c. lain
   d. laying
   e. lying

LESSON 33

stop, stopped

I *stop* at the library today. I *stopped* at the library yesterday.

Stop is a one-one-one word (one-syllable word ending in one consonant preceded by one vowel). When you add **-ed** or **-ing** to a one-one-one word, you double the final consonant first to keep the short vowel sound. You want **stŏpped**, not "stōped."

After final **p**, the **-ed** sounds like a **t**. Look at the pronunciation of *stopped*: **stŏpt**. It may *sound* like a **t**, but you spell it **ed**. It *is* the past tense of *stop*.

fish, fished

Pronunciation: **fĭsh, fĭsht**

The final **-ed** sounds like a **t** also.

I *fished* for minnows yesterday; today I *fish* for trout.

laugh, laughed

Pronunciation: **lăf, lăft**

The final **-ed** sounds like a **t**; **-ed** is the past tense ending.

I *laugh* at the weather today. I *laughed* at it yesterday.

The **gh** is pronounced **f** as in *cough, enough, rough*.

The **au** is pronounced short **a** (**ă**). Laugh and *aunt* are the only **au** words I know that are pronounced as short **a**.

l	-	no problem
au	-	short **a**
gh	-	**f**
ed	-	**t**

What a lot of work for one word! But *laugh* is a happy word; it deserves some work, I think.

ask, asked

Pronounciation: **ăsk, ăskt**

Ask refers to today; *asked* is past tense. *Ask* is a regular verb, so you add **-ed** to make the past, regardless of how you pronounce it.

Today I shall *ask* for mint chocolate chip ice cream.

Yesterday I *asked* for butter pecan.

The final **-ed** on *asked* sounds like **t**, not **d**. It's a little hard to pronounce both the **k** and the **t**. You tend to leave out either the **k** or the **t** sound.

A. Use the past tense of the words in parentheses to complete the sentences:

1. (ask) I _____ if I could read the newspaper after breakfast.
2. (stop) We started at the beginning; we _____ at the end.
3. (laugh) I _____ and _____ looking at the monkeys in the zoo.
4. (fish) Yesterday I _____ in my soup for onions and potatoes.

B. Remember: After the sounds of **f, k, p, s, th, sh,** and **ch,** the final **-ed** will sound **t**, not **d**. How will you spell these words? They are all past tense forms of the verbs.

Example: **fisht** - *fished*

Respell each dictionary-spelled word correctly:

1. **măpt** I **măpt** the route to the lake.
2. **wôcht** I **wôcht** the loons splash in the water.
3. **băsht** He **băsht** his toe on the dock.
4. **mĭst** He **mĭst** his landing.
5. **kôft** They **kôft** when they had their colds.
6. **tăkt** I **tăkt** a notice on the bulletin board.

LESSON 33 (Continued)

choose, chose, chosen

I will *choose* to go swimming today. I *chose* to go swimming yesterday. Every time I have *chosen* to go swimming.

There is no such word as "choosed."

Pronunciation:

choose: **chō̄z** double long **o**

chose: **chōz** long **o**

chosen: **chōz'ən** long **o**

The **s** has a **z** sound each time.

The verb *freeze* has similar past tenses: *freeze, froze, frozen.*

before   **bǐ fôr'**

Don't forget the **e** on the end. Some people think the word is spelled by combining *be* and *for*. Instead, it is related to *fore*, which refers to "in front of" or "beforehand."

America

Pronunciation: **ə mĕr'ĭ kə**

The first syllable is spelled with an **a**, but because it is unaccented, you hear the schwa sound, almost a short **u** sound.

There are two schwa sounds in that word. Exaggerate the real vowels when you pronounce the word for spelling: **ā mēr ī kā**, or **ā mĕr ĭ kă**, or something similar to sort out the vowels. You have to remember an **e** before the **r** also. It's not "Amarica"; we just sometimes pronounce it that way.

So you know why our country is called **America**? Of course. Ever since you learned that Columbus came in 1492, you were told that the country was named for Amerigo Vespucci.

tongue

Pronunciation: **tŭng**

To begin with, the **o** is pronounced **u** as in *some, done, Monday*. Then the **ue** on the end of the word is silent. It's like *league* (Little League), *vague, fatigue, plague*. Try saying **g u e** when you spell it.

Tongue and groove is the name for a wood joint made by fitting a **tongue** (projection) on the edge of a board into a groove on another board. Most hardwood flooring is made this way.

A number of idiomatic expressions are made from *tongue:*

on the tip of one's tongue—You can almost remember something, but not quite.

tongue-in-cheek—If you say something **tongue**-in-cheek, you are fooling.

tongue-tied—As if your **tongue** were physically shortened, you find it difficult to speak because of shyness or embarrassment.

tongue twister—words difficult to say because of a succession of similar consonants ("Peter Piper picked a peck of pickled peppers").

C.   Underline the misspellings in these sentences and write the correct spellings above them:

1.   If you could chose another name for Amerika, what would you chooze?

2.   I chooseded Columbia.

3.   Did you know that you had sweet and sour taste buds on your tung?

4.   I have choosen vanilla ice cream all week; today I chosed chocolate.

LESSON 33
Additional Activities

1. Spell the past tense of *stop, fish, laugh, ask,* and *choose.* Which verbs are regular (just add **-ed**)? In which one must you double the final consonant before adding **-ed**? How do you form the past tense of the other one?

2. Why do people misspell words like *stopped* and *fished* as "stopt" and "fisht"?

3. Write the correct word for each sentence:
   a. I will (choose, chooz) the red one.
   b. Yesterday I (choosed, chose) the green one.
   c. I've always (choosen, choosed, chosen) the red or green lollipop.

4. What is the final letter of *before*?

5. What is the vowel before the **r** in *America*?

6. Can you sing the first verse of "America"? the last verse?

7. What vowel gives the short **u** sound in *tongue*? What letters are silent?

         Spelling Demons Week by Week

Answers

LESSON 33

A.
1. asked
2. stopped
3. laughed, laughed
4. fished

B.
1. mapped
2. watched
3. bashed
4. missed
5. coughed
6. tacked

LESSON 33 (Continued)

C.
1. If you could **choose** (chose) another name for **America** (Amerika), what would you **choose** (chooze)?
2. I **chose** or **choose** (chooseded) Columbia.
3. Did you know that you had sweet and sour taste buds on your **tongue** (tung)?
4. I have **chosen** (choosen) vanilla ice cream all week; today I **chose** or **choose** (chosed) chocolate.

LESSON 33: Additional Activities

1. stopped, fished, laughed, asked, chose
   regular verbs: fish, laugh, ask
   regular with spelling change: stop
   irregular: choose
2. They hear the final sound as a **t** and forget that the words are formed by adding **-ed** to form the past tense.
3. a. choose
   b. chose
   c. chosen
4. **e**
5. **e**
6. Yes, with the words in front of me.
7. **o; ue**

LESSON 34

since

Since and *science* don't have anything to do with each other except that they are both often misspelled as a combination of the two words. *Since* is a one-syllable word pronounced **sĭns**. *Science* is a two-syllable word pronounced **sī´ĕns**.
Meaning: from a time in the past until now.
I haven't eaten a quince *since* I left California Wednesday.
Since you left home Tuesday, I sincerely miss you very much.

science

Pronunciation: **sī´ĕns**

1. Pronounce it with two syllables. Don't mispronounce it as **sĭns**. That's what makes you misspell it as "since" or "sinse." There are two vowel sounds: long **i** and short **e**.
2. The first **c** is silent—as in *scissors* and *scenery*.
3. The second **c** sounds like an **s**. The **e** after this **c** makes the **c** soft.

Scientists study *scientifically*. They study *sciences*.
My baby sister took Mother's *sci*ssors and cut my *science* paper into shreds. I created quite a *sce*ne over that, *since* I need the paper to study my *science*.

A. Fill in either *since* or *science*, or answer the questions:

1. _____ has two syllables; _____ has one syllable.
2. Both *science* and *since* end in what three letters?
3. Can you underline the letters that are silent in *science*?
4. Ever _____ you came home, the house has been a mess.
5. How can you study _____ in such a messy room?
6. It's been noisy ever _____ you came into my room.

our, are

Pronunciation: *are* - **är** *our* - **our** (*hour* - **our**)

Our and *hour* are homonyms, both sounding **our**. *Are* is not a homonym for *our*, but many people mix up the two words.

Our is a possessive pronoun meaning "belonging to us."
Are is a verb—a form of *to be* used with *you, we,* and *they.*

B. Fill in the correct word: *our, are, hour.*

1. _____ family is going away Saturday. What _____ you going to do?
2. _____ relatives _____ coming. They should be here any _____ .

pass, passed

Passed is pronounced **păst**, and that is how its homonym, *past*, is also pronounced. If you **pass** something, you go by it or you hand it to someone.

Present tense: I **pass** the library every day on my way to school.
Past tense: I **passed** the library yesterday on my way to school.

past

As a preposition, it means "beyond—in time or position."
I walked *past* the library.

As an adjective or adverb—it means "time earlier than the present." The *past* tense of *pass* is *passed.*

C. Fill in the blank with the correct word: pass, passed, past.

1. The _____ in front of the dying man.
2. I _____ my test. Did you _____ yours?

LESSON 34 (Continued)

write, right, wright, rite
wright

Wright looks a little like a combination of *write* and *right*. When it's a person's name, it is capitalized: *Wright*. The **Wright** brothers flew in North Carolina.

Without being capitalized, it's a term for someone who makes something, as a play**wright** or a ship**wright**. Wheel**wright** Pond is near my home. Do you suppose it was named after someone who made wheels?

write

But the two words you mix up most of the time are *write* and *right*, not the word *wright*. Not just you—lots of people do.

Write has to do with fingers and pencils.

write, wrote, written

    write: The final silent **e** makes the **i** long.

      I *write* my grandmother every Tuesday.

    wrote: The **i** changes to **o** for the past tense.

      I just *wrote* my grandmother yesterday.

    written: Note the double **t** after the **i** in *written*.

      I have written her a long letter each time.

The **w** is silent in each of these words. Pronounce the words incorrectly to remember the **w**. Say: **w**rite, **w**rote, **w**ritten.

Look at some other **wr** words with a silent **w**:

I have *written* the *wrangler* about the *wrench*.

If I break my *wrist*, I may not have to *write* so much.

right

One meaning of *right* is "the opposite of left." Some people use their left hands; some use their **right** hands.

Another meaning for *right* is "the opposite of wrong." Some people get their spelling words all **right**. Some get them all wrong.

The fact that *wrong* starts with **wr** is not particularly helpful in spelling *right*—which obviously starts with just an **r**. It's easy to think that *wrong* and *write* belong together. But they don't.

Think: *right, wrong* (all *right*, all *wrong*)

     write, wrote, written

rite

Now, what's *rite*? A **rite** is a ceremony. We talk about marriage **rites**. You may know the word *ritual*, which has a similar meaning. If you want to talk about the spelling words you got right, or about writing a letter, you don't want the word *rite*.

D. Use the correct word in each sentence: *write, wrote, writing, written*. (These all have to do with using a pencil and paper—or your heel in the beach sand!)

1. I think I'll _____ my grandfather a letter about our new puppy.

2. I have not _____ him since last month.

3. His _____ is very fancy and fun to read.

E. Use *right, rite, write,* or *Wright*:

4. My math was all _____ . My spelling is all _____ , too.

5. Don't _____ me the wrong answers. Give me the _____ answers.

6. Mr. _____ _____ (s) the marriage _____ (s) with his _____ hand.

7. The play _____ , Mr. _____ , _____ (s) his plays _____ here.

LESSON 34
Additional Activities

1. Choose the correct word in each sentence:

    a. That's the (write, right) answer.

    b. (Write, Right) your grandmother a letter.

    c. A wheel (right, rite, wright) made wheels.

    d. A (wright, right, rite) is a ceremony.

2. Write these words: *wright, right, write, rite*. Cross out all the silent letters in each word. What letters are you left with in each word?

3. Write *science* in syllables. What is the pronounciation of the first **c**? the second?

4. Write *since* in a sentence.

5. Choose the correct word:

    a. This is (are, our) house.

    b. When (our, are) we moving into it?

6. Are *our* and *are* homonyms?

7. Use *passed* and *past* in the same sentence.

Answers

LESSON 34

A. 1. Science, since
   2. **-nce**
   3. s<u>cience</u>
   4. since
   5. science
   6. since

B. 1. Our, are
   2. Our, are, hour

C. 1. past, passed
   2. passed, pass

LESSON 34 (Continued)

D. 1. write
   2. written
   3. writing

E. 4. right, right
   5. write, right
   6. Wright, write, rite, right
   7. wright, Wright, write, right

LESSON 34: Additional Activities

1. a. right
   b. Write
   c. wright
   d. rite

2. wright, right, write, rite
   rit

3. *sci ence*
   The first **c** is silent. The second **c** sounds **s**.

4. Sample sentence: **Since** it has been many years **since** I last wrote you a letter, I will write you one now.

5. a. our
   b. are

6. No, not if they are pronounced correctly.

7. Sample sentence: I **passed past** the shoe store without buying shoes.

178

LESSON 35

suggest, suggestion
Pronunciation: səg jĕst´ ; səg jəs´ chən
    two syllables: *sug gest*
    The pronunciation of **g** rule:
        When **g** is followed by **e, i,** or **y,** it is pronounced **j.**
        When **g** is followed by **a, o, u,** a consonant, or nothing, it is pronounced **g.**
    Watch, when you have two **g**'s in a word. The first one, followed by another **g,** will always be pronounced **g,** but the second one will vary according to what letter follows it.
    suggest   -   **gj**
    giggle   -   **gg**
    What are your **suggestions** for success? I **suggest** you keep a list of all the words with double consonants that you mi**ss**pell. The list will give you a**ss**istance for a**cc**uracy on many an o**cc**asion.

buried
Pronunciation: bĕr´ ēd
    bury, buries, buried, burying
    We don't hear the **u** in this word; people pronounce it with a short **e** (or a long **a**). Try pronouncing it with a **u** as you spell it.
    The **y** in *bury* changes to **i** before adding **-es** or **-ed** (consonant before **y** rule). You keep the **y** before the **-ing** suffix, however.

A.   Insert the correct form of *bury* (*bury, buried, burying*) in the blanks in each sentence:

1. Gramp helped Martha _____ her pet squirrel after it died.

2. The _____ beetle _____ a dead mouse in our back yard.

3. If you _____ the hatchet, you aren't mad at someone anymore.

4. Don't confuse _____ with *berry* as in *strawberry* and *raspberry.*

5. My spelling homework was _____ under the pizza box.

6. I need to _____ some trash.

B.   Substitute *buried* or *suggest* for the italicized words:

1. What do you *recommend*?

2. My shoes are *concealed* by the junk in my room.

keep, kept
    There are a few **-eep** words with a similar pattern of present to past tense:
      keep, kept   *weep, wept*   *sleep, slept*   *creep, crept*
    Rather than adding **-ed** to the present tense double **e** word, you make the double **e** into a single **e** with a **-pt** at the end of the word.

doctor
Pronunciation: dŏk´ tər
    The **k** sound is spelled with a **c.**
    The schwa **r** ending is spelled **or.** Quite a few words denoting people do end in **-or.**
    What do you want to be when you grow up? A doct**or,** an act**or,** an edit**or,** an investigat**or,** a janit**or,** a sculpt**or,** a senat**or,** a prospect**or,** a realt**or,** a profess**or,** a sail**or,** an ambassad**or,** an auth**or,** an educat**or,** or an arbitrat**or**? How about being a visit**or,** too?

C.   Fill in the missing vowels: d__ct__r, k_____p, k__pt, b__ried.

LESSON 35 (Continued)

raspberry

Pronunciation: **răz′ bĕr ē**

rasp - you don't hear the **p**, but it's there. It is silent before the **b** — as in *cupboard*, also.

berry - double **r** after the **e**.

A **raspberry** is made up of a cluster of druplets, or beads. When a **raspberry** is ripe, it is easily separated from the "standard" that it grows around. The blackberry does not separate from its standard.

Plural: **y** after a consonant, so change the **y** to **i** before adding **-es**.

What other berries do you know? blueberries, strawberries, huckleberries?

We make razzleberry juice at home. We mix grape juice and orange juice to make razzleberry juice. It's just the color of razzleberries.

suppose, supposed, supposing

Pronunciation: **sə pōz′**

Two **p**'s: *su***p** *p***ose**

The word has two syllables. Sometimes we pronounce the word so fast that we say "spose," especially when we say "I suppose so" as "spose so." But the word does have a first syllable: **sup-**.

The final silent **e** makes the **o** long. The **s** sounds like a **z**.

Are we **supposed** to **sup** (eat **sup**per) before we leave, or will we eat on the way?

purpose

Pronunciation: **pûr′ pəs**

The first syllable is spelled the way it sounds. In the second, you might think that the final silent **e** would make the **o** long, but it doesn't. It is an unaccented syllable, and you don't hear that **o** clearly. It sounds more like a short **u**.

When you spell it, say: *purp***ose** as in *supp***ose**, *r***ose**, and *ch***ose**.

I supp*ose* you ch*ose* that r*ose* on purp*ose*!

Have you heard little children, hurt on a playground, turn to supp*ose*dly offending playmates and say, "You did that on **purpose**!"

D. Use the following words to fill in the crossword puzzle: *chose, berries, rose, hose, supposing, purpose, raspberry.*

Across

2. You water the garden with this.
4. a red berry that comes off its standard easily when ripe
6. intent (noun)
7. plural of *berry*

Down

1. selected
3. guessing, assuming
5. a) a flower
   b) got up yesterday

LESSON 35
Additional Activities

1. How are the following words supposed to be spelled?
    spose, sposed, sugjest, keept, docter, baries, rasberry, purpus

2. What colors are raspberries? Answer in a complete sentence using both the words *colors* and *raspberries*.

3. How are the words *purpose* and *suppose* alike?

4. What suggestions do your mother or father make about your room?

5. In the question above, write each word and the vowel sounds in each. (Example —What/short **u**.)

                   Spelling Demons Week by Week

Answers

LESSON 35

A.
1. bury
2. burying, buried
3. bury
4. bury
5. buried
6. bury

B.
1. suggest
2. buried

C. **o, o; ee; e; u**

LESSON 35 (Continued)

D. Crossword Puzzle:

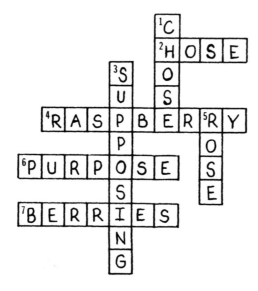

LESSON 35: Additional Activities

1. suppose, supposed, suggest, kept *or* keep, doctor, buries, raspberry, purpose
2. Sample sentence: Most **raspberries** are red, but their **colors** can also be dark purple, yellow-orange—and green, if they are not ripe.
3. They both end in **pose**.
4. That I clean it—clean it up and clean it out.
5. what/ short **u**; suggestions/ short **u** or schwa, short **e**, short **u** or schwa; do/ o͞o; your/ ô or o͝o; mother/ short **u**, schwa; or/ ô; father/ ä, schwa; make/ long **a** and silent **e**; about/ schwa, ou; your/ ô or o͝o; room/ o͞o.

LESSON 36

it's, its

Its is the possessive form of the pronoun **it**.

The dog hurt **its** paws.

There is no apostrophe as in *Jenny's*: this is *Jenny's* book.

The possessive pronouns do not have apostrophes:

my (mine)	our (ours)
your (yours)	your (yours)
his, her (hers), its	their (theirs)

If you use the *it's* with the apostrophe, you are using a contraction of two words: *it is*—a pronoun and a verb.

If you were to say: the dog hurt **it's** paw, you'd really be saying: The dog hurt **it is** paw.

Your/you're and **its/it's** are similar doubles.

You're (you are) late.   This is **your** book.

It's (it is) late.   This is **its** boundary.

It's and **its** rank in the top ten of misused words. Children's school papers and local newspapers show **its** and **it's** incorrectly used many times. See if you can find it in the newspapers—maybe even in your school papers!

A. Fill in the correct word: *it's* or *its*.

1. _____ time to go home.

2. The team played _____ best.

3. The fabric lost _____ colors in the bright sun.

4. Our town celebrated _____ bicentennial last August.

5. I like the bay, but I don't like _____ fishy odor.

your, you're

Pronunciation: *you're* **yŏor**
                your **yŏor, yôr, yōr**
                yours **yŏorz, yôrz, yōrz**

The pronunciation can be the same for both *you're* and *your*, though most people give *your* a longer o sound, as **yôr** or **yōr**, than they use in *you're*.

You're is the contraction for the words *you are*. As such, it is a pronoun and a verb—used as the subject and verb of a sentence.

You're late! = **You are** late.

Your is a possessive pronoun, used as an adjective before a noun.

Is this *your* box of raspberries?

Yours can be used without a noun following it. Is this **yours**?

We often sign letters: **Yours** truly,

yourself, yourselves

Don't use these when a simple *you* would be better.

Correct: Do it **yourself**!
            Give **yourself** a break!
            I asked Jimmy and **you** (not *yourself*) to come.

B. Use *your* or *you're* in each sentence:

1. Are _____ hands clean?

2. _____ all ready to go, aren't you?

3. Give me _____ hand, please.

4. _____ mother is here.

5. _____ both mother and father to that child!

LESSON 36 (Continued)

there
Pronunciation: **thâr**
Meanings:
1) opposite of *here*
    I am here; you are *there*
2) to start off a sentence
    There is a turtle in my pocket.
    There are two turtles in my swimming pool.
        If the **thâr** you want is followed by *is* or *are*, you want *there*.
3) used as an expletive
    There! I have finished mowing the lawn.
    Watch out for contractions with *there:*
    There's (There is) a turtle in my desk.
    There'll (There will) be trouble for the person who put a snapping turtle in my desk.

they're
Pronunciation: **thâr**
Meaning: contraction for *they are*
    It is not a contraction for *there are;* it is a contraction for *they are.* If you can substitute *they are* for the **thâr** you want, use *they're.*

their
Pronunciation: **thâr**
Meaning: *Their* means "belonging to them."
This is *their* book. It belongs to them.
Their is always followed by a noun (although there may be an adjective between the *their* and the noun). It has to be **their** "something or other."
Theirs is *their* plus a noun all rolled together.
It is *theirs.* (It belongs to them; it is *their* book.)We're talking Big Ten—Most Wanted criminals with these words:
their **the**y're **the**re
All three **thâr**'s begin with the letters **the**. You will never have "**thier**" as a word.

C. Fill in the blanks with *there, their,* or *they're:*
1. _____ are fourteen heifers in that field.
2. _____ not in _____ barn.
3. _____ _____ in the field because _____ barn burned down.
4. _____ staring at the next field. _____ wondering what is in it.
5. _____ is one weird animal in the next field.
6. It has very shaggy hair. Is it a bear? No. A buffalo? No, it is a musk ox.

D. Write your own sentences using *there, they're,* and *their.* Put more than one in a sentence if you can. Ask someone to check them for you.

E. Circle the correct spelling; one in each group is correct:
1. thier, their
2. they're, they'er, there'er
3. there, thair, thier

LESSON 36
Additional Activities

1. Write sentences:
   a. Use *its* and *it's* in one sentence.

   b. Use *your* and *you're* in one sentence.

   c. Use *their* and *they're* in one sentence.

2. Three of the words above are contractions. Write them and then write the words from which they are made.

3. What is the plural of *yourself*?

4. Choose the correct word:
   a. The team won (its, it's) first state championship.

   b. (They're, There) the winners this year.

   c. (There, Their) coach is pleased.

Answers

LESSON 36

A.
1. It's
2. its
3. its
4. its
5. its

B.
1. your
2. You're
3. your
4. Your
5. You're

LESSON 36 (Continued)

C.
1. There
2. They're, their
3. They're, there, their
4. They're, They're
5. There

D. Sample sentences:
1. Where **there's** a musk ox, **there** must be a reindeer.
2. **They're** all walking toward the fence.
3. **Their** heads are down.
4. **They're** walking **there** with **their** friends the polar bears.

E.
1. their
2. they're
3. there

LESSON 36: Additional Activities

Sample sentences:
1.
   a. **It's** a nice day for the team and **its** game.
   b. **You're** the one who left **your** sweater out in the rain.
   c. **They're** coming to our house in **their** airplane.

2. it's/it is
   you're/you are
   they're/they are

3. yourselves

4.
   a. its
   b. They're
   c. Their

LESSON 37

want, wanted
Pronunciation: **wŏnt, wŏnt′əd**
Maybe it's not pronounced carefully. Perhaps people don't realize *wanted* is the past tense of *want* and therefore calls for an **-ed** on the end.
I *wanted* to get a higher grade on the test than I did.
I went to soccer practice; then I rode my bike; after that I *wanted* to go home to take a nap.

when
When is a question word, asking what time. It is spelled **wh** (and pronounced **hw**) like other question words: *when, where, why, which, what.*
Don't confuse it with *went*, the past tense of *go*.
I went to the library.
When did you go?
I went Tuesday.

went
    go, goes, going, went, gone
Pronunciation: **wĕnt**
This word is spelled just as it sounds. Don't spell it "whent." If you do, you're mixing up *when* and *went*. *When* is a question word.
Went is the past tense of the verb *go*. Think how difficult this verb must be for people who haven't always spoken English!
I *go* today, I *went* yesterday, I have *gone* every day of my life.
    (not: I have went. Correct: I have *gone*.)

than, then
Than (**thăn**) is a comparison word.
I am more clumsy *than* you are.
Then (**thĕn**) is a time word.
I'll do the dishes. *Then* I'll have my dessert when I've finished the dishes.
    Pronounce the words carefully, distinguishing between the two. Say them out loud, really emphasizing the vowels. Say them, right now: *than, then.*
    Think of *then* and *when* together; they are both time words and are both spelled with an **e**.
The summer went by more quickly *than* I wanted it to. I had just begun to work on the rock garden *when* the weather grew too cold to work outside. First I tried to work every day. *Then* I decided to garden only *when* the sun was shining.

A. Replace the dictionary-spelled words in each sentence with their real spelling: *when, want, wanted, than, then, went.*

1. (**Hwĕn**) do you (**wŏnt**) to go?

2. I (**wŏnt′əd**) to go earlier (**thăn**) this.

3. Jim (**wĕnt**) already.

4. I know. (**Thĕn**) we should go, too.

B. Use the correct word from the two in parentheses at the end of each sentence:

1. He is smarter_____ I am. (then, than)

2. He called me; _____ I called him. (then, than)

3. I'll go _____ you call. (then, when, went)

4. I _____ to go soon. (went, want)

LESSON 37 (Continued)

machine
Pronunciation: mə shēn´
  The **a** is unaccented. Sound it as an **a** when you spell it.
  The **ch** sounds **sh**, as in *Chicago, Lake Michigan, Chevrolet.*
  The i sounds long **e** as in *gasoline, routine, police.*
Related word: *machinery*

That motorcycle is a beautiful *machine.* So is that *Ch*evrolet you bought in *Ch*icago on Lake Mi*ch*igan.

onion, union
Pronunciation: *onion*   ŭn´yən
              union   yo͞on´yən
  Except for the first letter, the words are spelled the same. They end in **-nion.**
  The **i** after the **n** has a consonant **y** sound that you also have in *William* and *million.*
  The **o** before the final **n** is a schwa sound.
  The **n**'s do sound like **n**'s!
Onion, beginning with an **o,** is pronounced with a short **u,** the sound that you have in so many **o** words: *mother, brother, some, tongue, nothing, above. Union,* spelled with a **u,** is pronounced with a long double **o** with a consonant **y** sound in front of it.
Every time I peel *onions* my eyes tear.
The United States is a *union* of 50 states.
Does your father or mother belong to a labor *union* at work?
During the Civil War, the southern states seceded from the *Union.*

animal
Pronunciation: ăn´ə məl
  You hear the first **a.** The next two vowels are unaccented. When you pronounce the word for spelling, say it in a way to help you remember the vowels: **ăn ĭ măl.** Listen to the consonants, too, so you put the **n** before the **m. Anim**als have natural en**em**ies.
  An animal got in my garden and ate my broccoli and brussels sprouts and squash. My son cheered for the **animal**—probably a woodchuck. When the **animal** ate my melons, my son stopped cheering.

C. Answer the questions and fill in the blanks:
1. What is the sound of the **ch** in *machine*?
2. The United States is a _____ of 50 states.
3. *United* and *union* have the same initial sound. What is it?
4. What is the sound of the first **o** in *onion*? What is an onion? Can you draw a picture of one? What do fried onion rings look like?
5. What is the sound of the **i** in *onion* and *union*?
6. What is the sound of the **i** in *machine*?
7. Underline the words that rhyme: *machine, twine, gasoline.*
8. *Onion, union, machine:* Pronounce each word as it is spelled, not as it is really sounded.
9. What do the spelling of *animal* and *enemy* have in common?
10. How many ways can you spell *animals* wrong? How is it really spelled?

problem
Pronunciation: prŏb´ləm
  Sometimes people mispronounce the word as "prob'm," and then they transpose the **l** and the **e** and spell it "probelm." It is *problem.*

LESSON 37
Additional Activities

1. Which word is a comparison word: *then* or *than*?

2. Which word is a time word: *than* or *then*?

3. Which word is a question word: *when* or *went*?

4. Which word is a verb: *when* or *went*?

5. Draw a picture of any machine, real or imaginary.

6. What are the sounds of the **a, ch,** and **i** in *machine*?

7. What letters are the same in *onion* and *union*? What letter is different?

8. Choose the correct spelling: *animals, aminals.*

9. Draw any animal, real or unreal.

10. Choose the correct word in each sentence:
    a. I (wanted, whanted) the blue team to win.
    b. I (want, went) to the game.
    c. I (want, went) more popcorn.
    d. I don't know (when, then, went) he's coming home from the game.

Answers

LESSON 37

A. 1. When, want
    2. wanted, than
    3. went
    4. Then

B. 1. than
    2. then
    3. when
    4. want

LESSON 37 (Continued)

C. 1. **sh**
    2. union
    3. **yo͞o**
    4. short **u**

An onion is a bulbous plant cultivated as a vegetable.

Sample drawings:

 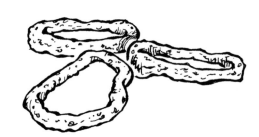

    5. the consonant **y**
    6. long **e**
    7. machine, gasoline
    8. **ŏn ĭ ŏn**; the letter **u**, **nĭ ŏn**; **mă chĭ ně**
    9. The **n** is the first consonant, and the **m** is the second consonant in each word.
    10. Sample misspellings: annimals, aminals, annimmals, annimmalls, animalz, anymolz; need any more? It is really spelled *animals*.

LESSON 37: Additional Activities

1. than
2. then
3. when
4. went
5. Sample drawing:

6. **a**—schwa; **ch**—**sh**; **i**—long **e**
7. **-nion**; the first letter is different

8. anim**a**ls
9. Sample drawing:

10. a. wanted
    b. went
    c. want
    d. when

LESSON 38

enjoy, enjoyed, enjoys, enjoyment, enjoying
We finally learn the consonant before **y** rule, and then along come words with a *vowel* before the **y**. They're like other ordinary words:
If you want to make a plural, just add **s**.
To make the third person singular of the verb, just add **s**.
If you want to make the past tense by adding **-ed**, just add **-ed**.
If you want to add other suffixes—whether they begin with a vowel or a consonant—just add them.
If you changed that **y** to **i** before adding a suffix beginning with a vowel, see how funny it would look: *boy*, "boies."

journey, journeys, journeying, journeyed
Rule: When a vowel comes before the **y**, there are no changes to be made before adding any suffix.
I continued my *journeys* from the vall**eys** to the mountains.
Pronunciation: **jûr′nē**
The **ûr** sound is spelled **our**. The long **e** sound is spelled **ey**.

A.   Circle the correctly spelled word in parentheses:
1.   I am (enjoying, enjoiing, enjoing) my vacation.
2.   I like (journeing, journeying, journing) to distant places.
3.   He (enjoys, enjoies) (plaiing, pling, playing) softball.

turkey, turkeys
one turkey, two turkeys
There is a vowel before the **y**, so you simply add **s** to make the plural. You don't change the **y** to **i**. ("Turkeies" looks funny, doesn't it?) Remember the **e** before the **y**.
The boys were chasing the wild *turkeys* in the vall**eys**. They thought they saw monk**eys**, but there are no monk**eys** in our vall**eys**. In fact, I'm not sure we even have any wild *turkeys*.

alley, alleys
Pronunciation: **ăl′ē**
Meaning: a narrow street or passageway
The garages were located off the *alley* between the properties.
The bowling *alley* was filled on Friday night.
Don't confuse *alleys* with *allies*. *Alley*, with a vowel before the **y**, adds **s** for the plural; *ally*, with a consonant before the **y**, changes the **y** to **i** before adding **-es**.

B.   List the following words in two categories:
attorney, baby, lady, essay, journey, city, chimney, strawberry, sky, donkey, alley, honey, try, cry, study, enemy, money, key, boy, library, country, joy, play, turkey, copy, county, monkey, valley, family
Consonant before y

Vowel before y

C.   Now write the plurals for the above words, following these rules:
Consonant before **y**:   Vowel before **y**:
   change **y** to **i**   just add **s**
   before adding **-es**   for plural
   for plural

LESSON 38 (Continued)

who, whom;   who, how;   who's, whose;   who'll

who

    Who is another question word. A mystery story is often called a *whodunit* ("Who done it?"). But the **wh** is not pronounced **hw** like the other question words: *where, when, which, what.* You hear just an **h** sound. That's true for these words: *who, whom, who's, whose, who'll,* and *whole* and *wholly.* Remember the book *Horton Hears a Who?* All **h**'s.

    The **o** in all those *who* words is pronounced ōō as in *food.*

whom

    Whom is pronounced **hōōm**.

    Use *who* for subjects of sentences. Use *whom* for objects.

Who is going for the ice cream?
    (subject of verb *is going*)
To *whom* did you give my in-line skates?
    (object of preposition *to*)
Whom did you give my chocolate ice cream to?
    (still object of preposition *to*; phrase is just split)
Whom did you hit with that wild pitch?
    (object of verb *hit*)

how

    Don't mix up the word *who,* which has a beginning **h** sound, with *how. How* is another question word, meaning "in what manner." It rhymes with *cow* and *now.*

How are you?
Who, me? I'm fine. *How* are you?
Just peachy, thanks.

whose, who's

    Who's is a contraction for *who is* (or perhaps *who has*)—the pronoun *who* and the verb.

    Whose is a possessive pronoun (like *my, her, his, their*), and it has no apostrophe.

Whose coat is that?
Who's (who is) at the door?

who'll

    Don't mix up *who'll* with *whole.* When you write the contraction, write *who,* then stop. Next, write the apostrophe in the space. Finally, write the double **l** from *will.* You'll write contractions more accurately if you make yourself break the word in writing it.

D.   Use the correct word from the two in parentheses at the end of each sentence:

  1. _____ cares? (Who, Whom)

  2. _____ did you call? (Who, Whom)

  3. _____ did you say would be chairman? (Who, Whom) [The pronoun will be the subject of the verb *would be.*]

  4. _____ in charge here? (Who's, Whose)

  5. _____ lunch is this? (Who's, Whose)

  6. _____ like to clean the litter pan? (Who'd, Who'll)

  7. _____ is there? (Who, How)

  8. _____ is your brother since his accident? (Who, How)

  9. With _____ did you go to the dance? (who, whom)

10. _____ did you go to the dance with? (Who, Whom)

11. _____ did you write? (Who, Whom)

LESSON 38
Additional Activities

1. Circle the correct spelling(s):
   enjoiement, journeiing, turkys, turkies
   alleys, alleies, attornies, attorneys

2. What is the difference between the following two sentences?
   To whom did you give my three doughnuts?
   Whom did you give my three doughnuts to?

3. How is *whose* like the word *her*?

4. How is *who's* like the word *she's*?

5. Write a sentence using *who*.

6. Write a sentence using *whom*.

Answers

LESSON 38

A. 1. enjoying
2. journeying
3. enjoys, playing

B. and **C.**

Consonant before y		Vowel before y	
baby	babies	attorney	attorneys
lady	ladies	essay	essays
city	cities	journey	journeys
strawberry	strawberries	chimney	chimneys
sky	skies	donkey	donkeys
try	tries	alley	alleys
cry	cries	honey	honeys (*or* honies)
study	studies	money	moneys (*or* monies)
enemy	enemies	key	keys
library	libraries	boy	boys
country	countries	joy	joys
copy	copies	play	plays
county	counties	turkey	turkeys
family	families	monkey	monkeys
		valley	valleys

LESSON 38 (Continued)

D. 1. Who
2. Whom
3. Who
4. Who's
5. Whose
6. Who'd
7. Who
8. How
9. whom
10. Whom
11. Whom

LESSON 38: Additional Activities

1. alleys, attorneys
2. The preposition and its object (*to whom*) are together at the beginning of the first sentence. In the second sentence, the object (*whom*) is at the beginning of the sentence, and the preposition (*to*) is at the end.
3. They are both adjectives: *whose* coat, *her* coat.
4. They are both contractions: *who's* = *who is; she's* = *she is.*
5. Sample sentence: Who broke the croquet mallet?
6. Sample sentence: I don't know **whom** you mean.

194

LESSON 39

decide, decision

The words *decide, decision, concise, precise, homicide, suicide, incision,* and *scissors* all have a common root: **cid** or **cis**, meaning "to cut."

If you make a *precise* statement, you say exactly what you mean. You have cut out extraneous details. If your statement is *concise,* you have cut out anything extra.

Homicide and *suicide* refer to killing someone else or oneself. *Genocide* refers to the planned killing of a whole racial or cultural group.

What things do *insecticides, pesticides,* and *fungicides* kill?

An *incision* is a cut like the one the doctor makes to get at the appendix he is going to take out.

When you *decide* something, you make up your mind; you cut off other ideas. A *decision* cuts off alternatives; you have chosen one.

You use *scissors* to cut; a **chisel** helps you cut.

It is the **cid** or **cis** that refers to the cutting.

Pronunciation: *decide:* **dĭ sīd′**   *decision:* **dĭ sĭzh′ən**

You don't hear the **e** because it is unaccented. The **c** sounds **s**. If you remember **cut**, that may help you to remember the **c**.

In *decision,* the **s** sounds **zh**. The vowel combination in the last syllable is pronounced as an unaccented schwa, so you don't really hear the **io**. The common ending **-ion** is pronounced **ən**.

Caesarean section

Pronunciation: **sĭ zâr′ē ən   sĕk′shən**

A **Caesarean** or (**Caesarian**) **section** is a surgical incision through the abdominal wall and uterus, performed to extract a fetus.

The story is that the Roman ruler Julius **Caesar** was born by this operation and named after the term *a* **caeso** *matris utero,* "from the incised womb (uterus) of his mother."

Caeso is from **caesus,** past participle of *caedere,* "to cut." Caesar was named after the operation; not the operation after Caesar. Now the spelling is often **cesarean** or **cesarian** section.

scissors

Pronunciation: **sĭz′ərz**

Why don't you pronounce the word the way it is spelled to help you learn to spell it: **skĭssors.**

Science and *scenery* have a silent **c** also, as do a few other words.

Do you know another name for **scissors**? Shears.

You know what **scissors** are—they cut. Remember they cut, and you can remember the silent **c**. With four **s**'s (scissors), you wouldn't think that you'd also need a silent **c**!

A.   Answer the questions:

1.   What is a Caesarean (also spelled Caesarian, cesarean, or cesarian) section?

2.   What do *scissors, Caesarian,* and *decision* have in common?

3.   What do *scissors, scenery, scepter, scent,* and *science* have in common?

4.   Can you make up some word with the ending **-cide** (like spelling "instructorcide")?

5.   What is the plural of *scissors*? Where will you find out?

LESSON 39 (Continued)

afraid, among, across, above

Usually, when you have a single unaccented vowel as the first syllable of a word, it is spelled with an **a**. It sounds a little like the short **u** sound.

Notice that the **a** is a syllable by itself. A consonant starts the second syllable: *one* consonant, not doubled. With a double consonant, one of the two consonants would be in the first syllable, one in the second.

afraid

Pronunciation: ə frād′

The first syllable, the **a** alone, is unaccented. It has a schwa sound which is almost a short **u**.

The long **a** sound in the second syllable is spelled **-ai**, like the **ai** in *aid, raid, paid*.

If you have fear, you are **afraid** of something.

among

Pronunciation: ə mŭng′

The first syllable, the **a** alone, is unaccented. It has a schwa sound which is almost a short **u**.

The accented **o** is pronounced short **u** as in *glove, above, mother*.

Mother wears garden gloves when she works *among* the flowers.

across

Pronunciation: ə krôs′

The first syllable, the **a** alone, is unaccented. It has a schwa sound which is almost a short **u**.

Think of the original meaning of the word: "in the form of a cross." Can you spell the word *cross*? You wouldn't spell it "ccros" or "cros," would you? Spell it correctly, and then put an *a* in front of it: *across*. That way you won't double the wrong letter.

The **o** sounds ô as in *boss*.

Ross, the boss, tossed the ball *across* the ocean to me.

above

Pronunciation: ə bŭv′

the first syllable, the **a** alone, is unaccented. It has a schwa sound which is almost a short **u**.

The **o** has the short **u** sound as do *among* and *another*.

Cornell University's song begins "Far **above** Cayuga's waters..." because the university sits on hills **above** Lake Cayuga.

B.   Draw pictures to show the following, and label each drawing with the correct underlined word.

1.   The rabbit ran *around* the tree.

2.   It is *about* four o'clock.

3.   The white house is *across* Elm Street.

4.   The squirrel is *among* the flowers.

5.   I am all *alone*.

6.   I am *apart* from the others.

7.   He is leaning *against* the tree.

8.   The little prince is far *away* from home.

9.   The sun shines *above* the house.

10. Flowers grow *along* the road.

LESSON 39
Additional Activities

1. What is the sound of the the first vowel in *afraid, among, across,* and *above*? How do you spell that sound in each word?

2. What is the sound of the **o** in *among* and *above*?

3. How does thinking of the word *cross* help you to spell *across* correctly? How many **c**'s, **r**'s, and **s**'s?

4. What Latin root meaning "to cut" is used to make *decide, decision,* and *scissors*?

5. What are the sounds of the **c** in each word?

6. Divide *scissors* into syllables. How many syllables? How many **s**'s in that word?

7. Draw a picture of a pair of scissors. Label the picture.

8. Draw pictures showing the meaning of *among, across,* and *above*.

Answers

LESSON 39

A. 1. A Caesarean section is a surgical incision through the abdominal wall and uterus, performed to extract a fetus.

2. They all have something to do with "cut," and they come from the Latin root **cid-** or **cis-**, meaning "to cut."

3. They all begin with the consonants **sc**, and the **c** is silent.

4. Sample word: If I keep snarling at cats, someone will accuse me of **caticide.**

5. *Scissors* is already plural in form. My **scissors** are sharp. You could say you had one pair of scissors or two pairs of scissors. You would find plurals in the dictionary.

LESSON 39 (Continued)

B.   Sample drawings:

Answers (Continued)

LESSON 39:   Additional Activities

1. schwa; **a**
2. short **u**
3. You wouldn't start spelling *cross* with two **c**'s, and you probably would not spell it with two **r**'s, either. So if you can spell *cross* and add an **a** to the beginning, you will have the word *across*. One **c**, one **r**, and two **s**'s.
4. *cid,* or *cis*
5. It sounds **s**. In *scissors*, the **c** could be considered silent.
6. *scis sors;* two; four **s**'s
7. Sample drawing:

    Scissors
8. Sample drawings:

among   across   above

LESSON 40

where, wear, were (plus **ware** and **we're**)

These are not homonyms. They are "spellonyms" or "spellonummies." The pronunciation is so similar that you may think they're homonyms. Then you confuse the spelling. Maybe you only *think* you know the meaning of the words. Maybe your pronunciation is careless. Maybe you're in too much of a hurry to play soccer.

where

Pronunciation: **hwâr**

Where is a question word asking in what place something or someone is.
Where are my mittens? *Where* is he?

It is used in the middle of sentences, too, to answer a question of place:
I don't know *where* my mittens are or *where* he is.

It is spelled **wh**, but it is pronounced **hw**. Try saying it. The ending of the word (**-ere**) sounds like the air you breathe. Put those two sounds together and you get **hwâr**

wear

Pronunciation: **wâr** (no **hw** sound as in *where*)
Meaning: There are lots of meanings. Here are two:
        1) to be clothed in: I **wear** mittens when my hands are cold.
        2) to produce by constant use: I may **wear** a hole in my mittens.
There is a homonym for *wear: ware.*
        Pronunciation: **wâr**
        Meaning: articles of the same general kind, such as glass**ware**, hard**ware**, soft**ware**

were

Pronunciation: **wûr**
Meaning: a part of the verb to be used in the past tense with you, we, they, or plural nouns.
Where *were* you wearing mittens in June?

It can be used with other pronouns when what you are saying is contrary to fact (not true):
If I *were* you, I would put those mittens away for the summer.

we're

Pronunciation: **wîr**
Meaning: contraction for *we are.*
We're going to buy mittens to wear next winter.

Without the apostrophe and that little space it takes, *we're* looks like *were.* If you always break the word when you put the apostrophe in, there will be less confusion.

A.   Use *where, wear, were, ware,* or *we're* in the following sentences:

1. I would like to _____ a werewolf costume for Halloween.

2. Did you look at the hard _____ store?

3. _____ ?

4. At the hard_____ store. _____ going there now. Want to come?

5. My brother and I _____ going to the magic store.

6. _____ is that?

7. It's _____ the pizza place used to be.

8. _____ going right by there now.

              Spelling Demons Week by Week

LESSON 40 (Continued)

believe
Pronunciation: bĭ lēv′
  i before **e**
  Look at the first syllable: *be.*
  Look at the rest of the word: *lieve.*
  b, then one **e**, **l**, THEN THE **IE**, then **v**, then silent **e**
  Look at the same pattern in other words:

> *re ceive*
> *de ceive*
> *con ceive*
> *per ceive*

Those are "after **c**" words, so they are spelled **ei**, but the pattern of the prefix and then the syllable with the **ie** or **ei** is the same.
  belief bĭ lēf′   *beliefs* bĭ lēfs′
  believing bĭ lēv′ ĭng (change the **f** to **v**: *drop the e before adding* -ing)
  Believe and *believing* are MOST WANTED WORDS. **BE** careful. **BE**lieve.

B. Fill in the blanks with one of the following words: *believing, piece, belief, believe.*
      I _____ I'll have a bowl of buttered popcorn. My _____ is that
    popcorn is delicious. Have you ever tried to eat one _____ of popcorn at a
    time? Try it. I don't _____ you can do it. You won't catch me
    _____ you can do it unless I see you. Seeing is _____ .

friend
  It sounds like **frĕnd**, but that's not the way it's spelled. It's an **i** before an **e** word.
  Can you think of another **ie** word in which that vowel combination sounds like a short **e** (ĕ)? Let me know if you can.

Wrong	**Right**
frend	*friend*
freind	

He is your *fri*end until the **end**.

piece
i before **e**
Pronunciation: pēs
THINK: **pie**ce of **pie**. It'll give you the right *piece*, and you'll remember the **i** before **e** in both *piece* and *pie*.
  I will cut this **pie** into two **pieces**—one for you and one for me. I believe that will be enough for each of us. I'd like my friend to have some **pie**, but no more than half. That will keep the peace.

C. What hard spots, memory aids, and rules will you use to remember each of these words:
    1. friend
    2. believe
    3. piece

D. Circle the one correct spelling in each group:
    1. beilieve, believe, bielieve, belive
    2. friend, freind, frend

LESSON 40
Additional Activities

1. Of the following words, which are homonyms: *where, wear, were, ware, we're*?

2. One word in the above list is a contraction. What is it? For what two words does it stand?

3. What is the vowel sound in *where*?

4. How are the words *here* and *where* and *there* alike? different?

5. What word is a past tense of *are*? Use it in a sentence.

6. *Believe* follows the **i** before **e** rule. What is that rule?

7. Where does the **ie** come in the word *believe*?

8. What is the first syllable of *believe*?

9. What is the final letter of *believe*?

10. What will help you to remember the spelling of *friend*? Does the word follow the rule? What little word is in friend?

11. Does the spelling of *piece* follow the rule? What small word is in *piece*? How will that help you to spell *piece*?

12. Use *believe, piece*, and *friend* in the same sentence.

Answers

LESSON 40

A. 1. wear
   2. ware
   3. Where
   4. ware, We're
   5. were
   6. Where
   7. where
   8. We're

LESSON 40 (Continued)

B. believe, belief, piece, believe, believing, believing

C. 1. *friend*—hard spot: **ie**; memory aid: **friend** until the **end**; rule: **i** before **e** word
   2. *believe*—hard spots: **e**, then **ie**, then **e**; memory aid: **e** is the first and last vowel, **ie** in the middle; rule: **i** before **e** word
   3. *piece*—hard spots: **ie**, **c** rather than **s** when it has the **s** sound; memory aid: **piece** of **pie**—the phrase shows two words beginning with the letters **pie**; rule: **i** before **e** word

D. 1. believe
   2. friend

LESSON 40: Additional Activities

1. wear; ware
2. we're; we are
3. â (r)
4. Each ends with the letters **here**. *Here* has just those four letters, *there* starts with a **t**, and *where* starts with a **w**. *Where* and *there* have the same vowel sound, different from the sound in *here*.
5. *were;* Sample sentence: We **were** traveling down the coast of Oregon to reach California.
6. The rule: **i** before **e** except after **c** (unless the **c** sounds **sh**), and except in words that sound long **a**, and in a lot of other exceptions.
7. The **ie** comes in the second syllable, between the **l** and the **v**.
8. *be*
9. silent **e**
10. Help: **i** before **e**; it follows the rule; it ends with the word *end*, so you can think "a **friend** is your **friend** until the **end**."
11. Rule: yes. *Pie* is in *piece*. Think: "a **piece** of **pie**."
12. Sample sentence: I **believe** I will have a **piece** of pie with my **friend**. Whoops! My **friend** already ate the whole pie. What kind of a **friend** is that? A **friend** just until the end of the pie!

Fourth Quarter Quizzes

This section starts with a choice of oral quizzes to dictate to your students for this quarter of the work: 10 words, 20, 50, or 100. Choose the one or ones best suited to the individual needs of your students, the time you have, and how many words you feel are important for each quarter. If the word is a homonym or a near homonym, I have provided a sentence.

The oral quizzes are followed by two reproducible written quizzes: Sound to Spelling and General.

Oral Quizzes

Test I: 10 Words

1. Independence Day
2. brought
3. America
4. science
5. supposed
6. their (Their pond is frozen.)
7. animals
8. who's (Who's going to the pond?)
9. scissors
10. believe

Test II: 20 Words

1. Independence Day
2. brought
3. America
4. science
5. supposed
6. their (Their pond is frozen.)
7. animals
8. who's (Who's going to the pond?)
9. scissors
10. believe
11. Lincoln
12. lying
13. before
14. write (Can you write your name on the ice?)
15. suggest
16. its (The school closed its doors.)
17. than (It's colder now than in January.)
18. journeys
19. decide
20. friend

Test III: 50 Words

1. Independence Day
2. brought
3. America
4. science
5. supposed
6. their (Their pond is frozen.)
7. animals
8. who's (Who's going to the pond?)
9. scissors
10. believe
11. Lincoln
12. lying
13. before
14. write (Can you write your name on the ice?)
15. suggest
16. its (The school closed its doors.)
17. than (It's colder now than in January.)
18. journeys
19. decide
20. friend
21. Halloween
22. Veterans Day
23. Memorial Day
24. bought
25. thought
26. lain
27. chosen
28. stopped
29. laughed
30. since
31. passed (I passed my geometry test.)
32. right (I got every one right.)
33. doctor
34. raspberry
35. purpose
36. you're (You're the silly one.)
37. there (Is your bike here or over there at the field?)
38. they're (They're all going to the field now.)
39. wanted
40. then (We'll go to the field; then we'll go to the gym.)
41. onion
42. enjoyed
43. alleys
44. turkeys
45. across
46. among
47. decision
48. piece (Cut me a large piece of pie, please.)
49. were (Were you going to eat the whole thing?)
50. we're (No, we're going to save some for you.)

Oral Quizzes (Continued)

Test IV: 100 Words

1. Independence Day
2. brought
3. America
4. science
5. supposed
6. their (Their pond is frozen.)
7. animals
8. who's (Who's going to the pond?)
9. scissors
10. believe
11. Lincoln
12. lying
13. before
14. write (Can you write your name on the ice?)
15. suggest
16. its (The school closed its doors.)
17. than (It's colder now than in January.)
18. journeys
19. decide
20. friend
21. Halloween
22. Veterans Day
23. Memorial Day
24. bought
25. thought
26. lain
27. chosen
28. stopped
29. laughed
30. since
31. passed (I passed my geometry test.)
32. right (I got every one right.)
33. doctor
34. raspberry
35. purpose
36. you're (You're the silly one.)
37. there (Is your bike here or over there at the field?)
38. they're (They're all going to the field now.)
39. wanted
40. then (We'll go to the field; then we'll go to the gym.)
41. onion
42. enjoyed
43. alleys
44. turkeys
45. across
46. among
47. decision
48. piece (Cut me a large piece of pie, please.)
49. were (Were you going to eat the whole thing?)
50. we're (No, we're going to save some for you.)
51. Abraham
52. ideas
53. Columbus Day
54. Indian summer
55. autumn
56. buy (I'll buy my lunch today, I think.)
57. laid
58. lied
59. lay
60. lie
61. fished
62. asked
63. choose
64. chose
65. tongue
66. our (Our history test was hard.)
67. are
68. rite (A ceremony may be called a rite.)
69. Wright (A person's last name may be spelled Wright, as in "the Wright brothers' airplane.")
70. past (We study the past in history.)
71. suggestion
72. supposing
73. buried (The pirates buried their treasure.)
74. kept
75. burying (My dog is always burying bones.)
76. it's (It's a long way home.)
77. your (How far is your house?)
78. yourself
79. yourselves
80. theirs (Theirs is a half mile away.)
81. union
82. machine
83. machinery
84. when (When are you going?)
85. went (I went to Florida last year.)
86. problem
87. who
88. whom
89. whose (Whose dirty boots are those?)
90. how
91. who'll
92. afraid
93. above
94. Caesarean (cesarian, cesarean, caesarian)
95. section
96. believing
97. where (Where is my teddy bear?)
98. wear (Wear your boots today; it's cold.)
99. ware (Walk to the [hard]-ware store with me.)
100. believed

FOURTH QUARTER
Sound to Spelling Quiz

In the following test, spell the word correctly from the sound of the word given by the dictionary markings.

1. lĭng´kən
2. īdz
3. ô´təm
4. Hăl ð ēn´
5. mə môr´ ē əl
6. thôt
7. brôt
8. bī (Do you want to bī my car?)
9. bôt
10. lī (I think I'll lī down on the grass.)
11. stŏpt
12. fĭsht
13. lăf
14. lăft
15. ăskt
16. cho͞oz
17. chŏz´ən
18. chŏz
19. bĭ fôr´
20. ə mĕr´ĭ kə
21. tŭng
22. sĭns
23. sī´ ĕns
24. är
25. our (Our house is for sale, too.)
26. our (The our is three o'clock.)
27. păst (It's half păst three.)
28. păst (I păst her the popcorn.)
29. rīt (Mary can rīt with either hand.)
30. rīt (The rīt turning signal is out.)
31. rīt (Mr. Rīt taught our shop class.)
32. rīt (The marriage rīt was short.)
33. səg jĕst´
34. bĕr´ĕd (I bĕr´ĕd my dead cat.)
35. kĕpt
36. dŏk´tər
37. răz´ bĕr ē
38. sə pŏz´
39. sə pŏzd´
40. pûr´ pəs
41. sŭg jĕs´chən
42. bĕr´ē ĭng (We are bĕr´ē ĭng the dead squirrel.)
43. bĕr´ēz (The dog bĕr´ēz its bone.)
44. ĭts (The dog wagged ĭts tail.)
45. ĭts (ĭts green.)
46. yo͝or (yo͝or going to have the car fixed.)
47. yo͝or (yo͝or right front light is out.)
48. yo͝orz (Is this scarf yo͝orz?)
49. yo͝or´sĕlf
50. thâr (Is thâr something wrong?)

FOURTH QUARTER
Sound to Spelling Quiz (Continued)

51. thâr (**Thâr** late.)

52. thâr (**Thâr** bus was late.)

53. thârz (**Thârz** was, too.)

54. wŏnt

55. wŏnt´əd

56. hwĕn

57. wĕnt

58. thăn

59. thĕn

60. mə shēn´

61. ŭn´yən

62. yo͞on´yən

63. ăn´ə məl

64. ĕn joi´

65. ĕn joid´

66. jûr´nē

67. jûr´nē ĭng

68. jûr´nēd

69. jûr´nēz

70. tûr´kē

71. ăl´ē

72. ăl´ēz

73. ho͞o

74. ho͞om

75. ho͞oz (**Ho͞oz** on first?)

76. ho͞oz (**Ho͞oz** dirty mitten is this?)

77. ho͝ol (**Ho͝ol** clean the mitten?)

78. hou (**Hou** old are you now?)

79. dĭ sīd´

80. dĭ sĭzh´ən

81. sĭ zâr´ē ən

82. sĕk´shən

83. sĭz´ərz

84. ə krôs´

85. ə bŭv´

86. ə gĕnst´

87. ə frād´

88. ə mŭng´

89. bĭ lēv´

90. bĭ lēv´ĭng

91. bĭ lēf´

92. bĭ lēvd´

93. frĕnd

94. pēs (I need a **pēs** of pie.)

95. pēs (We need **pēs** in the world.)

96. hwâr

97. wâr (I **wâr** jeans every day.)

98. wûr (**Wûr** you at the game?)

99. wîr (**Wîr** going tomorrow night.)

100. wâr (His father runs a [hard]**wâr** store.)

FOURTH QUARTER
General Quiz

1. Fill in the proper word where indicated by the blank lines in the tense columns. The present tense is now; the past tense is before now; the past perfect tense or the past participle shows action completed before the past tense.

Present Tense	Past Tense	Past Perfect Tense
Example: *pay*	*paid*	*paid*
a. think	_____	thought
b. _____	sought	sought
c. bring	_____	brought
d. _____	bought	bought
e. say	_____	said
f. lie (recline)	_____	_____
g. lie (not tell the truth)	_____	_____
h. lay	_____	_____
i. stop	_____	stopped
j. fish	_____	fished
k. choose	_____	_____
l. pass	_____	passed
m. write	_____	_____
n. want	_____	wanted
o. go	_____	_____
p. enjoy	_____	_____

2. Put in the apostrophes where they should be:
   a. April Fools Day
   b. Lincolns Birthday
   c. Veterans Day

3. From what two words are the following contractions made?
   a. it's
   b. you're
   c. they're
   d. we're
   e. who's
   f. who'll

4. What rule do you follow when you spell *believe, friend,* and *piece*?

5. If a word ends in a vowel before the consonant, what do you do before making the plural of a noun or adding suffixes to a verb?

6. Write the singular form of *allies, alleys,* and *raspberries*.

FOURTH QUARTER
General Quiz (Continued)

7. Choose the right homonym:
   a. (write, right) Do you _____ with your _____ or your left hand?
   b. (Wright, right, write) Mr. _____ _____ (s) with his _____ hand.
   c. (hour, our) What _____ are _____ cousins arriving for dinner?
   d. (it's, its) _____ time for our team to win _____ first championship.
   e. (your, you're) _____ not using _____ head!
   f. (there, they're, their) _____ they are, waving _____ arms at us. _____ acting silly, aren't they?
   g. (piece, peace) I'd like a little _____ and quiet now. Can you play that tuba _____ some other time?
   h. (who's, whose) _____ playing the drums? _____ stereo is blasting? I'm not the only noisy one.
   i. (very, vary) It is _____ noisy in here. Can't you _____ your practicing time?
   j. (passed, past) It's _____ my bedtime. Time _____ quickly this evening.

8. Mark the hard spots in the following words:
   a. tongue   f. doctor
   b. before   g. decide
   c. Lincoln   h. across
   d. suggest   i. piece
   e. supposed

9. The following are not homonyms, but they are close enough in pronunciation to be confused. Choose the correct word.

   a. (our, are) _____ cousins _____ coming, aren't they?

   b. (buries, berries) A squirrel _____ its acorns, doesn't it? What about _____ ? Do squirrels eat _____ ?

   c. (when, went) _____ I _____ to Alaska, I drove the Alaska Highway.

   d. (were, we're) _____ going next summer. _____ you there in July?

   e. (then, than) No, in September. It's cooler _____ _____ it is in July.

   f. (whole, who'll) _____ take care of your _____ garden while you're gone?

Answers to Fourth Quarter Quizzes

Sound To Spelling Quiz

1. Lincoln
2. ides
3. autumn
4. Halloween
5. memorial
6. thought
7. brought
8. buy
9. bought
10. lie
11. stopped
12. fished
13. laugh
14. laughed
15. asked
16. choose
17. chosen
18. chose
19. before
20. America
21. tongue
22. since
23. science
24. are
25. our
26. hour
27. past
28. passed
29. write
30. right
31. Wright
32. rite
33. suggest
34. buried
35. kept
36. doctor
37. raspberry
38. suppose
39. supposed
40. purpose
41. suggestion
42. burying
43. buries
44. its
45. it's
46. you're
47. your
48. yours
49. yourself
50. there
51. they're
52. their
53. theirs
54. want
55. wanted
56. when
57. went
58. than
59. then
60. machine
61. onion
62. union
63. animal
64. enjoy
65. enjoyed
66. journey
67. journeying
68. journeyed
69. journeys
70. turkey
71. alley
72. alleys
73. who
74. whom
75. who's
76. whose
77. who'll
78. how
79. decide
80. decision
81. Caesarean (or cesarian, cesarean, or Caesarian)
82. section
83. scissors
84. across
85. above
86. against
87. afraid
88. among
89. believe
90. believing
91. belief
92. believed
93. friend
94. piece
95. peace
96. where
97. wear
98. were
99. we're
100. ware

General Quiz

1. a. think, thought, thought
   b. seek, sought, sought
   c. bring, brought, brought
   d. buy, bought, bought
   e. say, said, said
   f. lie, lay, lain
   g. lie, lied, lied
   h. lay, laid, laid
   i. stop, stopped, stopped
   j. fish, fished, fished
   k. choose, chose, chosen
   l. pass, passed, passed
   m. write, wrote, written
   n. want, wanted, wanted
   o. go, went, gone
   p. enjoy, enjoyed, enjoyed

2. a. April Fools' Day
   b. Lincoln's Birthday
   c. Veterans Day (usually written with no apostrophe)

3. a. it's = it is
   b. you're = you are
   c. they're = they are
   d. we're = we are
   e. who's = who is
   f. who'll = who will

4. **i** before **e**

5. nothing

6. allies—ally
   alleys—alley
   raspberries—raspberry

7. a. write, right
   b. Wright, write, right
   c. hour, our
   d. It's, its
   e. You're, your
   f. There, their, They're
   g. peace, piece
   h. Who's, whose
   i. very, vary
   j. past, passed

8. a. tongue
   b. before
   c. Lincoln
   d. suggest
   e. supposed
   f. doctor
   g. decide
   h. across
   i. piece
   (or any other hard spots)

9. a. our, are
   b. buries, berries, berries
   c. when, went
   d. We're, Were
   e. then, than
   f. Who'll, whole

SUBJECT QUIZZES

Contractions Quiz

Lessons 14, 17, 36, 38

1. *It's, its; you're, your; they're, their* (and *there*) are confusing to many people. Each time you pick up a newspaper you can find a mistake someone has made with these words. The mistake I see in the local newspaper the most frequently is *it's* for *its*.

    If you use *it's*, you are using a pronoun (*it*) and a verb (*is*). If you can substitute *it is* in your sentence for *it's*, then you are using the correct word. If you want the possessive pronoun instead, then you want *its*.

    For each of the following uses of *it's*, try to substitute *it is* in the sentence. If that doesn't make sense, then you want *its*. Write the correct word in front of the sentence and cross out each wrongly used *it's*.

    a. _____ The school lost *it's* soccer team.

    b. _____ The high school chorus loaned *it's* risers to the church for their Christmas program.

    c. _____ Jim thought the department had lost *it's* accreditation.

    d. _____ The store opened *it's* doors for the sale at 9 A.M.

    e. _____ *It's* sale was the first of the year.

    f. _____ This department has not taken *it's* inventory yet.

    g. _____ Our dog hates *it's* bath.

    h. _____ Our cat gives itself *it's* own bath.

    i. _____ What does this mean? "Virtue is *it's* own reward."

    j. _____ The hippopotamus opened *it's* mouth.

    k. _____ That state has had more than *it's* share of troubles.

2. *Their* is a possessive pronoun that acts as an adjective. Your sentences will say: "their house," "their mittens," "their football," "their something." *They're* is a contraction for *they are*.

    There can be used to mean the opposite of *here*. It is also frequently used to introduce a sentence. If your sentence starts off with *There is* or *There are*, then you will want *there*, not *they're* or *their*. Listen closely to hear whether you want *There are* or *They're* (for *they are*). Sometimes contractions are made with *there* and *is* or *will*.

    Write the correct spelling before each of the following sentences. Each of the homonyms is written in dictionary pronunciation: **thâr**.

    a. _____ **Thâr** are three puppies left in the litter.

    b. _____ **Thâr** are two males and one female.

    c. _____ **Thârz** only one female.

    d. _____ I'm afraid **thâr'll** be crying tonight.

    e. _____ **Thâr** won't be any crying at my house.

    f. _____ **Thâr** goes the black and white one out of the box!

217   *Spelling Demons Week by Week*

Contractions Quiz (Continued)

g. _____ How many puppies were **thâr** in the whole litter?

h. _____ **Thâr** were nine.

i. _____ Were you **thâr** when they were born?

j. _____ I was **thâr**, but not the children.

k. _____ Where were they? **Thâr** with **thâr** father.

l. _____ **Thâr** sorry they missed it.

m. _____ **Thâr** will be another time.

3. Make contractions from these imaginary words and the negative *not*. Example: *noes, noes not, noesn't.*

    a. foes, foes not, _____

    b. zad, zad not, _____

    c. tave, tave not, _____

    d. os, os not, _____

    e. nus, nus not, _____

    f. shill, shill not, _____

4. *Its* acts as an adjective and will be followed by a noun (with perhaps an adjective in between). In Exercise 1 above, write the noun that each *its* modifies in the sentences.

    a. _____   g. _____

    b. _____   h. _____

    c. _____   i. _____

    d. _____   j. _____

    e. _____   k. _____

    f. _____

5. In Exercise 3 above, what real word is similar to each of the imaginary ones? Write the contraction of the real one and the word *not*.

    a. _____   d. _____

    b. _____   e. _____

    c. _____   f. _____

6. We say: *I'd've, he'd've, you'd've,* and *they'd've.* Have you ever seen them written like this? What's the problem?

7. Write the words that the following contractions are made from:

    I'm _____   *who'll* _____

    I'd _____   *let's* _____

    I'll _____   *you're* _____

    I've _____   *you'd* _____

    who's _____   *you'll* _____

    who'd _____   *you've* _____

Doubling Final Consonants Quiz

Lessons 8, 16, 17

1. Write the rules for doubling consonants at the end of words before adding suffixes:
   a. for one-one-one words before a suffix beginning with a vowel.

   b. for one-one words of more than one syllable when the accent is on the final syllable before a suffix beginning with a vowel.

   c. for one-one words of more than one syllable when the accent is not on the final syllable before any suffix.

2. What must you be careful about:
   a. when a consonant is doubled in the middle of the word?

   b. when the accent is not on the last syllable and the word ends in l?

3. When you add the suffix **-ence** to these words: *refer, prefer, transfer, concur,* and *occur,* what happens to the final **r**? What does the change in accent have to do with the spelling?

4. If you decide to double the **l** in *traveled,* as in the British spelling, what must you be careful not to do with every other word that ends in **l** following a single consonant that has the accent on the first syllable?

5. A word may end in a double consonant to begin with (*miss, marshall*). When you take off the suffix from words like *marshalled* and *missing,* what must you be careful to do?

6. Many words end in a final silent **e**. What must you be careful to do with those words as opposed to one-one-one words?

7. Circle the correctly spelled words:
   a. occurence, preference
   b. traveled, differed
   c. cancellation, excellence
   d. committment, benefiting
   e. transference, begining
   f. reder, paralleled
   g. occured, modeled
   h. forgotten, swiming
   i. happened, preferred
   j. conferrence, biger

Doubling Final Consonants Quiz (Continued)

8. Why do you not double the **t** in *commitment* and do double it in *committed*?

9. State two reasons that people double the **l** in *traveled.*

10. In 100 years, do you think people will double all **l**'s or not double any? Why?

11. What is one practical reason for doubling the final consonant in a word like *hop* or *tap*?

12. Take the following nonsense words that have the accents marked and add the suffixes with the correct spelling according to the rules:
    Example: *fi dad'*   *fidadded*   *fidadness*

Add the prefix

a.	**er sot'**	-ed _____	-ment _____
b.	**ar' wad**	-ing _____	-ful _____
c.	**bi fer'**	-er _____	-ness _____
d.	**whan' nel**	-ing _____	
e.	**chrav' el**	-ed _____	
f.	**wum'**	-ed _____	-ing _____
g.	**tri der'**	-ed _____	-ing _____

13. Here are some real words, not in your lessons, but ones you will use. Follow the rules to add suffixes to each. The accents in the words are marked.

a.	**de fer'**	-ed	_____
b.	**dis pel'**	-ed	_____
c.	**ad mit'**	-ance	_____
d.	**al lot'**	-ment	_____
e.	**for bid'**	-en	_____
f.	**o mit'**	-ed	_____
g.	**per mit'**	-ing	_____
h.	**pro pel'**	-or	_____
i.	**re mit'**	-ance	_____
j.	**trans mit'**	-er	_____

Words Ending in Final, Silent E Quiz

Lessons 3 and 16; also 13, 18, 19, 35, and 40

1. What is the rule for adding **-ed** to a verb ending in final, silent **e**?

2. What is the rule for forming the third person singular of a verb ending in final, silent **e**?

3. What is the rule for adding **-ing** to a verb ending in final, silent **e**?

4. What is different about dealing with words ending in final, silent **e** from dealing with one-one-one words?

5. Add **-ed** and **-ing** to the following words:

   a. believe _____ _____

   b. judge _____ _____

   c. suppose _____ _____

   d. close _____ _____

   e. receive _____ _____

   f. decide _____ _____

   g. practice _____ _____

   h. hope _____ _____

   i. surprise _____ _____

   j. invite _____ _____

   k. arrive _____ _____

   l. prepare _____ _____

   m. please _____ _____

6. Add **-ing** to the following words:

   a. live _____   f. make _____

   b. write _____   g. give _____

   c. come _____   h. lose _____

   d. have _____   i. love _____

   e. take _____   j. choose _____

7. What words do the following come from?

   a. hoping _____   e. taped _____

   b. starring _____   f. ridding _____

   c. stared _____   g. riding _____

   d. tapping _____   h. hopping _____

Homonyms Quiz

In many lessons; especially 2, 34, 36

1. Write one sentence or more to show your understanding of the meanings of the following homonyms:

   a.   two, to, too

   b.   write, rite, Wright, right

   c.   your, you're

   d.   it's, its

   e.   who's, whose

   f.   piece, peace

   g.   principle, principal

   h.   all ready, already

   i.   knew, new

   j.   no, know

   k.   rein, reign

   l.   their, they're, there

   m.   passed, past

2. In the following paragraph, substitute the correctly spelled word for the sound of the word in parentheses.

   I (hûrd) _____ (sŭm) _____ sounds (wŭn) _____ (our) _____ ago. They came from that (hōl) _____ in the back yard as (ī) _____ (pǎst) _____ (bī) _____ . Is that where I (bĕr´ēd) _____ the (blo͞o) _____ (pēs) _____ or the (rĕd) _____ (pēs) _____ of hard (wâr) _____ ? I think I'll tell my school (prĭn´sə pəl), _____ who will be (hō´lē) _____ mystified, but he may want to have the newspaper (rīt) _____ a (pēs) _____ about it. Maybe I'll just (clōz) _____ the (hōl) _____ with (āt) _____ (wāts) _____ . (Rīt) _____ now, I'm going to (brāk) _____ into a run and go (wā) _____ far away to find (pēs) _____ from that noise.

Spelling Demons Week by Week

"I before E" Rule Quiz

Lessons 5, 9, 12, 13, 36, 40

Tests I and II are oral; dictate them to your students. Test III can be oral or written. Tests IV and V are written; reproduce them for your students.

Test I: 10 Words

1. believe
2. neighbor
3. ceiling
4. weird
5. eight (Count to eight.)
6. friend
7. receive
8. kaleidoscope
9. their (Their team lost.)
10. chief

Test II: 25 Words

1. believe
2. neighbor
3. ceiling
4. weird
5. eight (Count to eight.)
6. friend
7. receive
8. kaleidoscope
9. their (Their team lost.)
10. chief
11. piece (I ate a piece of pie.)
12. ancient
13. rein (Hold the horse's rein.)
14. companies
15. weigh (How much do you weigh?)
16. Fahrenheit
17. conceited
18. efficient
19. belief
20. reign (The king will reign for life.)
21. studied
22. tried
23. conscience
24. deceitful
25. foreign

Test III

Write the full **i** before **e** rule.

"I before E" Rule Quiz (Continued)

Test IV

Under the following categories, place words from the list below:

i before e   **except after c**   **unless c sounds sh**

EXCEPTIONS

except when sounds long a   **German long i sound**   **other exceptions**

believe, efficient, ceiling, friend, freight, deceive, receive, rein, deceitful, ancient, belief, conceited, neighbor, perceive, piece, conceive, weird, chief, conscience, eight, species, glacier, reign, kaleidoscope, foreign, reveille, their, Fahrenheit, weigh, Einstein, reindeer, Eisenhower, sleigh, neither, seize, heifer, leisure, either

Test V

Choose the correct spelling:

1. beleive, believe
2. freind, friend
3. receive, recieve
4. anceint, ancient
5. neighbor, nieghbor
6. peice, piece
7. weird, wierd
8. cheif, chief
9. eight, ieght
10. reign, riegn
11. foreign, foriegn
12. their, thier
13. weigh, wiegh
14. efficeint, efficient
15. freight, frieght

16. rein, rien
17. beleif, belief
18. consceince, conscience
19. speceis, species
20. glaceir, glacier
21. kaleidoscope, kaliedoscope
22. reveille, revielle
23. Fahrenheit, Fahrenhiet
24. ceiling, cieling
25. deceive, decieve
26. deceitful, decietful
27. conceited, concieted
28. perceive, percieve
29. conceive, concieve

Plurals Quizzes

Lessons 6, 7, 15, 17, 22, 38

Several units have considered the special plurals of words ending in **f, y,** and **o** (plus *circus*). Here are a few reminders:

Words ending in **y** follow one of two rules depending on whether they end in consonant/**y** or vowel/**y.** There are virtually no exceptions (proper names?), so it is worth learning the two rules.

The plurals for some words ending in **o** follow the rules; others do not. I think the rules are worth noting, but special individual lists may be in order. (They are for me.) Otherwise, it's dictionary time.

Words ending in **f** form their plurals in one of two ways. There are some patterns to the groups, but exceptions exist. Again, I suggest learning the two methods of forming the plural, but do not consider them to be rules. Make your own lists.

Words ending in **o** or **f** are not that numerous. We are talking about lists with around ten words in each.

Plurals Quizzes

Test I: Plurals of Words Ending in Y

1. What is the rule for forming the plurals of words that end in a consonant before the final **y**?

2. What is the rule for forming the plurals of words that end in a vowel before the final **y**?

3. Write the plurals of the following:

   a. study _____   g. try _____

   b. county _____   h. boy _____

   c. journey _____   i. enemy _____

   d. baby _____   j. library _____

   e. turkey _____   k. worry _____

   f. valley _____   l. monkey _____

4. Write the singular form of the word from these plurals:

   a. allies _____   i. companies _____

   b. stories _____   j. boys _____

   c. attorneys _____   k. keys _____

   d. replies _____   l. plays _____

   e. alleys _____   m. chimneys _____

   f. counties _____   n. valleys _____

   g. flies _____   o. essays _____

   h. families _____   p. copies _____

5. What is wrong with the following words? (Give the rule.)

   a. attornies _____

   b. countryes _____

   c. flys _____

   d. companys _____

   e. monkeies _____

Spelling Demons Week by Week

Plurals Quizzes (Continued)

Test II: Plurals of Words Ending in O

Like **y** words, **o** words can be divided into vowel/**o** and consonant/**o** words.

1. What is the rule for forming the plurals of words that end in a vowel before the **o**? Give examples.

2. Several divisions of consonant/**o** words just add **s** for the plural. Give examples for each division:

    a. Italian music words

    b. foreign words

    c. shortened, clipped forms of words

3. Now consider the **o** words that add **-es** for the plural.

    a. What are the words that always add **-es**?

    b. What are the words that you may use either **-es** or **s** for ?

    What will *you* use, **-es** or **s**? Why?

4. Circle the correct plurals in the following list:

    a. celloes, cellos
    b. ponchoes, ponchos
    c. ratioes, ratios
    d. buffaloes, buffalos, buffalo
    e. tomatoes, tomatos
    f. pianoes, pianos
    g. studioes, studios
    h. echoes, echos
    i. radioes, radios
    j. mottoes, mottos
    k. altoes, altos
    l. mosquitoes, mosquitos
    m. vetoes, vetos

    n. zooes, zoos
    o. sopranoes, sopranos
    p. torpedoes, torpedos
    q. tacoes, tacos
    r. volcanoes, volcanos
    s. photoes, photos
    t. potatoes, potatos
    u. gauchoes, gauchos
    v. heroes, heros
    w. autoes, autos
    x. memoes, memos
    y. cargoes, cargos

5. What is wrong with the spelling of the following plurals: "potato's," "tomato's"?

6. What plural **o** words should *you* have on a list?

Plurals Quizzes (Continued)

Test III: Plurals of Words Ending in F

1. Give examples of the word patterns that change the **f** to **v** and add **-es**, and write the plurals for each of these types of words:

   a. ending in **-lf**:

   b. ending in two vowels/**f**:

          exception:

   c. ending in **-fe**:

2. Give examples of the word patterns that keep the **f** before the plural **s** (ending), and write the plural for each of these types of words:

   a. ending in **-oof**:

   b. double **f** ending:

3. For which words do you have a choice?

4. What words will you put in *your* special list?

Test IV: Plurals of Words Ending in S, Z, X, CH, SH, SS, and ZZ

The rule states that for these words, you form the plural by adding **-es**. This makes it possible to pronounce the words.

1. Write the plurals of the following according to the above rule:

   a. circus   f. thermos

   b. rhinoceros   g. bonus

   c. campus   h. census

   d. sassafras   i. trellis

   e. hippotamus

2. Write the plurals of the following words according to the above rule:

   a. mess   e. buzz

   b. church   f. fox

   c. crush   g. box

   d. fizz

3. Not many one-syllable words end in one **s** or one **z**. Those that do may not follow the rule, or there may be choices for the plural. Use your dictionary to find the plurals for *bus, gas, whiz,* and *quiz.* (How about *Liz*?)

Plurals Quizzes (Continued)

Test V: All Plurals

Write the plurals for the following:

1. country

2. mosquito

3. belief

4. tomato

5. attorney

6. family

7. roof

8. life

9. buffalo

10. sheriff

11. study

12. chief

13. leaf

14. dwarf

15. thief

16. monkey

17. turkey

18. potato

19. try

20. knife

Spelling Demons Week by Week

Quiz For Y Words

Lessons 7, 15, and 38

1. What is the rule for forming the plural of consonant/**y** nouns? for vowel/**y** nouns? Write the correct plural of both *study* and *turkey*.

2. The second consideration is adding **-es**, **-ed**, **-er**, and **-ing** to verbs ending in **y**.

    a. If a verb ends in consonant/**y**, how do you form the third person singular and the past tense of the verb? What do you do before adding **-er** to the verb? If the verb ends in vowel/**y**, how do you add these endings?
        Make *copy* into the third person singular and the past tense and also add **-er** to the word. Do the same for *play*.

    b. If a verb ends in **y**, what do you do before adding **-ing**?

        Show that with the words *copy* and *play*.

3. Finally, adding suffixes to nouns or adjectives: What do you do to consonant/**y** words before adding the suffixes **-ly**, **-ness**, **-ful**?

    Add the suffix indicated to each of the following words:

	Word	Add suffix
a.	happy	-ly _____
b.	sloppy	-ness _____
c.	busy	-ness _____
d.	beauty	-ful _____

Verb Tense Quiz

Lessons 7, 8, 11, 14-17, 32, 33, and others

1. Regular verbs form the past tense by adding **-ed** (*walk, walked*). Sometimes you have to change the spelling before adding the **-ed** (change **y** to **i**, drop the final **e**, or double the final consonant).

    Write the past tense for each of the following:

    a. study _____
    b. travel _____
    c. plan _____
    d. carry _____
    e. hope _____
    f. try _____
    g. hop _____
    h. label _____
    i. journey _____
    j. prefer _____
    k. cancel _____
    l. reply _____
    m. occur _____
    n. worry _____
    o. refer _____
    p. benefit _____
    q. model _____
    r. cry _____
    s. commit _____
    t. marry _____
    u. control _____
    v. transfer _____
    w. suppose _____
    x. enjoy _____
    y. happen _____
    z. play _____
    aa. ask _____
    bb. pass _____
    cc. want _____
    dd. channel _____
    ee. lie (to tell a falsehood) _____

2. Some words don't add **-ed**; their form is changed. Write the past tense of the following:

    a. lose _____
    b. build _____
    c. mean _____
    d. hear _____
    e. catch _____
    f. teach _____
    g. think _____
    h. bring _____
    i. buy _____
    j. say _____
    k. pay _____
    l. lay _____

3. Some words have two different forms for the past tense: One for the simple past and one for the past perfect. Write both those forms for the following:

    a. choose _____ _____
    b. know _____ _____
    c. fly _____ _____
    d. begin _____ _____
    e. forget _____ _____
    f. do _____ _____
    g. go _____ _____
    h. lie (recline) _____ _____

231   *Spelling Demons Week by Week*

SUBJECT QUIZ ANSWERS
Contractions Quiz

1. Every one is *its*.

2.
   a. There
   b. There
   c. There's
   d. there'll
   e. There
   f. There
   g. there
   h. There
   i. there
   j. there
   k. They're, their
   l. They're
   m. There

3.
   a. foesn't
   b. zadn't
   c. taven't
   d. osn't
   e. nusn't
   f. shon't (based on *will not/won't*; otherwise, *shilln't*)

4.
   a. team
   b. risers
   c. accreditation
   d. doors
   e. sale
   f. inventory
   g. bath
   h. bath
   i. reward
   j. mouth
   k. share

5.
   a. does, doesn't
   b. had, hadn't
   c. have, haven't
   d. is, isn't
   e. was, wasn't
   f. will, won't

6. I've seen them written in stories with a lot of informal conversation. They can be difficult to read.

7. I am, I had *or* I would, I will, I have; who is *or* who has, who had *or* who would, who will; let us; you are, you had *or* you would, you will, you have

Doubling Final Consonants Quiz

1. a. Double the final consonant of a one-one-one word before adding a suffix beginning with a vowel.
   b. For one-one words of more than one syllable when the accent is on the final syllable, double the final consonant before adding a suffix beginning with a vowel.
   c. For one-one words of more than one syllable when the accent is not on the final syllable, do not double the final consonant before adding any suffix.

2. You must be careful:
   a. that you do not mistake that double consonant for the final consonant in the word.
   b. that you do not double the final l.

3. When the accent reverts to a syllable other than the last syllable, you do not double the final consonant: *reference, preference, transference*; when the accent stays on the last syllable, you double the final consonant: *concurrence, occurrence*.

4. Be careful not to double every final l in a word that is not accented on the last syllable.

5. Leave the final double letters on the word.

6. Drop the e before adding a suffix beginning with a vowel and do not double the consonant.

7. a. preference   f. paralleled
   b. traveled, differed   g. modeled
   c. cancellation, excellence   h. forgotten
   d. benefiting   i. happened, preferred
   e. transference   j. (neither)

8. You double the final consonant only before a suffix beginning with a vowel.

9. They have seen the British spelling with two l's; they have learned about doubling the final consonant and incorrectly apply the rule to words with the accent on the first syllable.

10. I think they will double all of them. *Traveled* has been doubled for some time; now I am beginning to see the l in *model* doubled. It is easier to think about doubling them all rather than distinguishing between words accented on the last or another syllable.

11. So it is not incorrectly pronounced: *hoped* with a long o is a different word from *hopped* with a short o.

12. a. ersotted, ersotment   e. chraveled
    b. arwading, arwadful   f. wummed, wumming
    c. biferrer, biferness   g. triderred, triderring
    d. whanneling

13. a. deferred   f. omitted
    b. dispelled   g. permitting
    c. admittance   h. propellor
    d. allotment   i. remittance
    e. forbidden   j. transmitter

233

Words Ending in Final, Silent E Quiz

1. Just add **d**.

2. Just add **s**.

3. Drop the **e** before adding **-ing**.

4. With final, silent **e** words, you drop that **e** before adding **-ing**, or you just add **s** or **d** rather than **-es** or **-ed**; you do nothing with the consonant preceding the silent **e**. With one-one-one words, you double the final consonant before adding **-ed**, **-es**, or **-ing**.

5. a. believed, believing
   b. judged, judging
   c. supposed, supposing
   d. closed, closing
   e. received, receiving
   f. decided, deciding
   g. practiced, practicing
   h. hoped, hoping
   i. surprised, surprising
   j. invited, inviting
   k. arrived, arriving
   l. prepared, preparing
   m. pleased, pleasing

6. a. living
   b. writing
   c. coming
   d. having
   e. taking
   f. making
   g. giving
   h. losing
   i. loving
   j. choosing

7. a. hope
   b. star
   c. stare
   d. tap
   e. tape
   f. rid
   g. ride
   h. hop

Homonyms Quiz

1. Answers will be students' own sentences.

   a. two, to, too: Lesson 2

   b. write, rite, Wright, right: Lesson 34

   c. your, you're: Lesson 36

   d. it's, its: Lesson 36

   e. who's, whose: Lesson 38

   f. piece, peace: Lesson 40

   g. principle, principal: Lesson 18

   h. all ready, already: Lesson 25

   i. knew, new: Lesson 11

   j. no, know: Lesson 11

   k. rein, reign: Lesson 5

   l. their, they're, there: Lesson 36

   m. passed, past: Lesson 34

2. **I heard some** sounds **one hour** ago. They came from that **hole** in the back yard as I **passed by**. Is that where I **buried** the **blue piece** or the **red piece** of hard**ware**? I think I'll tell my school **principal**, who will be **wholly** mystified, but he may want to have the newspaper **write** a **piece** about it. Maybe I'll just **close** the **hole** with **eight weights**. **Right** now, I'm going to **break** into a run and go **way** far away to find **peace** from that noise.

"I Before E" Rule Quiz

Test III.   **I** before **e** except after **c** unless that **c** sounds **sh**; then spell the word **cie**. If the vowel sounds long **a**, it is **ei**. There are other exceptions—like *weird, either, leisure*—and exceptions that are derived from German words where the **ei** sounds long **i**.

Test IV.

i before e	except after c	unless c sounds sh
believe	ceiling	efficient
friend	deceive	ancient
belief	receive	conscience
piece	deceitful	species
chief	conceited	glacier
	perceive	
	conceive	

EXCEPTIONS

except when sounds long a	German long i sound	other exceptions
freight	kaleidoscope	weird
rein	Fahrenheit	foreign
neighbor	Einstein	reveille
eight	Eisenhower	neither
reign		seize
weigh		either
reindeer		heifer
sleigh		leisure

Test V.

1.	believe	11.	foreign	21.	kaleidoscope
2.	friend	12.	their	22.	reveille
3.	receive	13.	weigh	23.	Fahrenheit
4.	ancient	14.	efficient	24.	ceiling
5.	neighbor	15.	freight	25.	deceive
6.	piece	16.	rein	26.	deceitful
7.	weird	17.	belief	27.	conceited
8.	chief	18.	conscience	28.	perceive
9.	eight	19.	species	29.	conceive
10.	reign	20.	glacier		

Plurals Quizzes

Test I: Plurals of Words Ending in Y

1. To form the plural of consonant/**y** words, change the **y** to **i** before adding **-es**.

2. To form the plural of vowel/**y** words, just add **s**.

3.
   a. studies
   b. countries
   c. journeys
   d. babies
   e. turkeys
   f. valleys
   g. tries
   h. boys
   i. enemies
   j. libraries
   k. worries
   l. monkeys

4.
   a. ally
   b. story
   c. attorney
   d. reply
   e. alley
   f. county
   g. fly
   h. family
   i. company
   j. boy
   k. key
   l. play
   m. chimney
   n. valley
   o. essay
   p. copy

5.
   a. "attornies": The plural is formed as if the singular were "attorny." It is not; it is *attorney*, and the plural should be *attorneys*.

   b. "countryes": The **y** should have been changed to **i** before the **-es**.

   c. "flys": The **y** should be changed to **i** and an **e** inserted before the **s**.

   d. "companys": The **y** should be changed to **i** and an **e** inserted before the **s**.

   e. "monkeies": The **y** at the end of *monkey* should be kept, not changed to **i** with another **e** added. It is spelled *monkeys*.

Plurals Quizzes (Continued)

Test II: Plurals of Words Ending in O

1. Just add **s**; (sample examples): radio, radios; rodeo, rodeos; ratio, ratios; zoo, zoos; studio, studios

2. a. *Italian music words*:   cello, cellos; alto, altos; soprano, sopranos; piano, pianos

   b. *foreign words*:   taco, tacos; gaucho, gauchos; poncho, ponchos

   c. *shortened words*:   photo, photos; auto, autos; memo, memos

3. a. potato, potatoes; tomato, tomatoes; echo, echoes; hero, heroes; torpedo, torpedoes; veto, vetoes

   b. mosquito, mosquitoes, mosquitos
   volcano, volcanoes, volcanos
   motto, mottoes, mottos
   no, noes, nos
   buffalo, buffaloes, buffalos, buffalo
   cargo, cargoes, cargos

   (I will probably use **-es** because it is easier to remember **-es** for all of them. I will probably use *buffalo* for more than one *buffalo*.)

4.
a.	cellos	i.	radios	r.	volcanoes, volcanos
b.	ponchos	j.	mottoes, mottos	s.	photos
c.	ratios	k.	altos	t.	potatoes
d.	buffaloes, buffalos, buffalo	l.	mosquitoes, mosquitos	u.	gauchos
		m.	vetoes	v.	heroes
e.	tomatoes	n.	zoos	w.	autos
f.	pianos	o.	sopranos	x.	memos
g.	studios	p.	torpedoes	y.	cargoes, cargos
h.	echoes	q.	tacos		

5. You don't use an apostrophe for the plural. That would mean something belonging to the tomato or the potato: the potato's vine; the tomato's blossom. It should be *tomatoes, potatoes.*

6. Suggested answer: the ones that have a choice of **-es** or **s** for the plural.

Plurals Quizzes (Continued)

Test III: Plurals of Words Ending in F

1. a. half, halves; elf, elves; shelf, shelves; self, selves; wolf, wolves
   b. leaf, leaves; loaf, loaves; thief, thieves
      exception: belief, beliefs
   c. life, lives; wife, wives; knife, knives

2. a. roof, roofs; proof, proofs
   b. bluff, bluffs; skiff, skiffs; sheriff, sheriffs

3. hoof, hoofs, hooves; scarf, scarfs, scarves; wharf, wharfs, wharves

4. Suggested answer: the ones for which I have a choice.

Test IV: Plurals of Words Ending in S, Z, X, CH, SH, SS, and ZZ

1. a. circuses
   b. rhinoceroses
   c. campuses
   d. sassafrases
   e. hippopotamuses
   f. thermoses
   g. bonuses
   h. censuses
   i. trellises

2. a. messes
   b. churches
   c. crushes
   d. fizzes
   e. buzzes
   f. foxes
   g. boxes

3. bus, buses, busses; gas, gases, gasses; whiz, whizzes; quiz, quizzes; Liz, Lizzes

Test V: All Plurals

1. countries
2. mosquitoes, mosquitos
3. beliefs
4. tomatoes
5. attorneys
6. families
7. roofs
8. lives
9. buffaloes, buffalos, buffalo
10. sheriffs
11. studies
12. chiefs
13. leaves
14. dwarfs
15. thieves
16. monkeys
17. turkeys
18. potatoes
19. tries
20. knives

Quiz for Y Words

1. To form the plural of consonant/**y** nouns, change the **y** to **i** and add **-es**. To form the plural of vowel/**y** nouns, just add **s**.

   studies, turkeys

2. a. If the verb ends in consonant/**y**, change the **y** to **i** before adding **-es** for the third person singular and **-ed** for the past tense. Change the **y** to **i** before adding **-er** to a consonant/**y** word. Just add **s**, **-ed**, or **-er** to a vowel/**y** word.

   copies, copied, copier
   plays, played, player

   b. If a verb ends in **y**, keep the **y** before adding **-ing** whether there is a consonant or a verb before the **y**.

   copying, playing

3. Before adding the suffixes **-ly**, **-ness**, or **-ful** to consonant/**y** words, change the **y** to **i**.

   a. happily
   b. sloppiness
   c. business
   d. beautiful

Verb Tense Quiz

1.
a. studied
b. traveled
c. planned
d. carried
e. hoped
f. tried
g. hopped
h. labeled
i. journeyed
j. preferred
k. canceled
l. replied
m. occurred
n. worried
o. referred
p. benefited
q. modeled
r. cried
s. committed
t. married
u. controlled
v. transferred
w. supposed
x. enjoyed
y. happened
z. played
aa. asked
bb. passed
cc. wanted
dd. channeled
ee. lied

2.
a. lost
b. built
c. meant
d. heard
e. caught
f. taught
g. thought
h. brought
i. bought
j. said
k. paid
l. laid

3.
a. chose, chosen
b. knew, known
c. flew, flown
d. began, begun
e. forgot, forgotten
f. did, done
g. went, gone
h. lay, lain

FINAL TESTS

I have provided 12 final tests. Tests I and II are oral, for you to dictate to your students. You can choose a 50-word or a 100-word test. Tests III through XII are written, for you to reproduce and hand out to your students.

Oral Quizzes

Test I (Oral): 50 Words

1. probably
2. separate
3. answer
4. people
5. tongue
6. science
7. suggest
8. supposed
9. purpose
10. it's (It's a nice day.)
11. hoping
12. February
13. they're (They're going to play tennis.)
14. I (I don't play tennis.)
15. Wednesday
16. excellent
17. countries
18. its (The cat is chasing its tail.)
19. your (Where's your tennis racquet?)
20. believe
21. beginning
22. quite
23. surely
24. there (My racquet is over there, by the door.)
25. stomach
26. judgment
27. hopping
28. practice
29. alleys
30. you're (You're not serious, are you?)
31. occurred
32. forty
33. doesn't
34. receiving
35. sincerely
36. could've
37. women (Forty women were there.)
38. who's (Who's going for ice cream?)
39. which
40. certain
41. wasn't
42. studied
43. because
44. vacuum
45. allies
46. committed
47. Tuesday
48. broccoli
49. their (They left their racquets at the court.)
50. library

Oral Quizzes (Continued)

Test II (Oral): 100 Words

1. probably
2. separate
3. answer
4. people
5. tongue
6. science
7. suggest
8. supposed
9. purpose
10. it's (It's a nice day.)
11. hoping
12. February
13. they're (They're going to play tennis.)
14. I (I don't play tennis.)
15. Wednesday
16. excellent
17. countries
18. its (The cat is chasing its tail.)
19. your (Where's your tennis racquet?)
20. believe
21. beginning
22. quite
23. surely
24. there (My racquet is over there, by the door.)
25. stomach
26. judgment
27. hopping
28. practice
29. alleys
30. you're (You're not serious, are you?)
31. occurred
32. forty
33. doesn't
34. receiving
35. sincerely
36. could've
37. women (Forty women were there.)
38. who's (Who's going for ice cream?)
39. which
40. certain
41. wasn't
42. studied
43. because
44. vacuum
45. allies
46. committed
47. Tuesday
48. broccoli
49. their (They left their racquets at the court.)
50. library
51. happiness
52. potatoes
53. America
54. than (You had more cake than I did!)
55. clothes (Don't wear your best clothes to the picnic).
56. awful
57. past (What is the past tense of *bring*?)
58. tries
59. excitement
60. lose
61. efficient
62. bigger
63. used to
64. doctor
65. neighbor
66. privilege
67. pleasant
68. thought
69. acknowledgment
70. enjoyed
71. decide
72. across
73. tomato
74. toward
75. all right
76. turkeys
77. about
78. daughter
79. forgotten
80. buried (My great-grandfather was buried Saturday.)
81. a lot
82. jewelry
83. Lincoln
84. tonight
85. scissors
86. they
87. foreign
88. truly
89. planning
90. birthday
91. until
92. passed (I passed through Chicago on my way to Los Angeles.)
93. close (Close the door quietly.)
94. tired
95. hadn't
96. tomorrow
97. then (We'll make the popcorn; then we'll eat it.)
98. weird
99. studying
100. soldier

Test III: Pronunciation

A. Write the pronunciation of the following:

1. chihuahua
2. colonel
3. woman
4. Wednesday
5. one

6. whether
7. biscuit
8. soldier
9. many
10. of

B. Write the pronunciation of the **ou** in the following:

1. enough
2. through
3. although
4. thought
5. trouble
6. about
7. cough
8. doughnut
9. country
10. county

11. silhouette
12. could
13. would
14. should
15. brought
16. bought
17. journey
18. your
19. you're

C. Write the pronunciation of **au** in:

1. laugh
2. daughter
3. autumn

D. Write the pronunciation of **o** in:

1. among
2. across
3. above
4. onion (both o's)
5. suppose
6. purpose
7. chose
8. of
9. do
10. woman

11. women
12. gone
13. conceited
14. come
15. one
16. only
17. to
18. forty
19. off
20. some

Test III: Pronunciation (Continued)

E.   What is the pronunciation of **e** in the following:

1. quiet

2. quite

3. America

4. there (both **e**'s)

5. certain

6. begin

7. pretty

8. been

F.   What is the pronunciation of **a** in:

1. any

2. a lot

3. already

4. average (both **a**'s)

5. have

6. are

G.   What is the pronunciation in the following words of the:

1. **c** in *decide*

2. **s** in *sugar*

3. **ch** in *machine*

4. **kn** in *knew*

5. **oes** in *does*

6. **w** in *answer*

7. **p** in *raspberry*

8. **w** in *who*

9. **wh** in *while*

10. **d** in *fished*

Test IV: Usage

A. Write sentences using the following words and contractions:

1. its, it's

2. your, you're

3. there, they're, their

4. we're, were

5. who's, whose

B. Write sentences using the following words:

1. lie, lay, lain, lying (to recline, rest)

2. lay, laid, laid, laying (to place—takes an object)

3. lie, lied, lied, lying (to tell a falsehood)

Test V: Contractions

A. Write the words from which the following contractions are made:

1. let's

2. who's

3. who'll

4. who'd

5. we're

6. they're

7. it's

8. you're

9. won't

10. I'm

B. Write the contractions for the following:

1. I will

2. I would *or* I had

3. does not

4. do not

5. did not

6. was not

7. had not

8. have not

9. is not

10. cannot

11. could have been

Test VI: Abbreviations

A. Write the abbreviations for the following:

1. et cetera

2. ounce

3. ounces

4. pound

5. pounds

Test VII: Spelling

A. Circle the correctly spelled words:

1. certain,   poka dotted,   sincerely,   conscience

2. straigt,   childern,   collonel,   excelent

3. forty,   ancient,   across,   Wednesday

4. brought,   journeyed,   wierd,   perceive

5. mayonaise,   surprise,   principle,   passed

6. beliefs,   committed,   it's,   benefiting

7. write,   sposed,   pichur,   whether

8. tonighte,   beautyful,   traveled,   seperate

9. hadn't,   although,   onomotapoeia,   happyer

10. scissors,   companies,   ninty,   befor

Test VIII: Rules

1. Write the rules for the consonant/**y** words:

    a. to form the plural of nouns.

    b. to form the third person singular of verbs.

    c. to form the past tense of the verb.

    d. to add **-ing**.

2. Write the rules for vowel/**y** words:

3. Write the full **i** before **e** rules.

Test VIII: Rules (Continued)

4. Plurals:

    a. How do you form the usual plural of a noun?

    b. How do you form the plural of words ending in **o**?

    c. How do you form the plural of words ending in **s**, **x**, **ch**, **sh**, **ss**, **z**, and **zz**?

    d. How do you form the plural of words ending in **f**?

5. What is meant by the term one-one-one word?

6. What do you do with one-one-one words?

7. What do you do with the final consonant before adding a suffix beginning with a vowel when:

    a. the word has more than one syllable, it ends with a single consonant preceded by a single vowel, and it has the accent on the last syllable?

    b. the word has more than one syllable, it ends with a single consonant preceded by a single vowel, and it does not have the accent on the last syllable?

8. What is the rule for words ending in final silent **e** when you want to add **-ing** to the word?

Test IX: More Rules

What rules do the following illustrate?

1. *worry* (singular noun) to *worries* (plural noun)

2. *monkey* (singular noun) to *monkeys* (plural noun)

3. *marry* (verb) to *marrying* (adding **-ing**)

4. *study* (first person verb) to *studies* (third person singular verb)

5. Name the parts of the **ie** rule that each of the following represents:

    a. *believe*

    b. *ceiling*

    c. *efficient*

    d. *neighbor*

    e. *Einstein*

    f. *weird*

Test IX: More Rules (Continued)

6. *hop* to *hopped*

7. *hope* to *hoping*

8. *refer* to *referred*

9. *prefer* to *preference*

10. *circus* to *circuses*

11. *channel* to *channeling*

12. *life* to *lives*

13. *radio* to *radios*

14. *tomato* to *tomatoes*

15. *study* (verb) to *studied* (past tense of verb)

16. *chief* to *chiefs*

Test X: Misspellings

How is each word misspelled? Circle the site(s) of the misspellings.

1. ect.	35. isen't	68. intresting
2. somthing	36. gess	69. brang
3. libary	37. nickle	70. stopt
4. Febuary	38. bilt	71. fisht
5. fourty	39. wimmen	72. laff
6. hunderd	40. vanilla folder	73. laffd
7. surtin	41. Wenzday	74. choosen
8. onle	42. Toosday	75. america
9. comeing	43. wasen't	76. tungue
10. writeing	44. potatoe	77. sinse
11. sincerly	45. i	78. siense
12. usualy	46. haden't	79. sugjest
13. brocolli	47. becuz	80. docter
14. colliflour	48. cann't	81. should of been
15. foriegn	49. alot	82. spose
16. studyes	50. alright	83. purpus
17. countryes	51. awfull	84. thier
18. emenies	52. truely	85. whanted
19. begining	53. tward	86. beleive
20. committment	54. exitement	87. Linkon
21. enuf	55. shure	88. deside
22. truble	56. shuger	89. eazy
23. jewerly	57. childern	90. acke
24. wierd	58. ment	91. stummick
25. recieve	59. urly	92. picknicking
26. dosen't	60. tonite	93. poka dot
27. Augst	61. tomorow	94. exept
28. useto	62. probly	95. excelent
29. looze	63. probely	96. wheather
30. beutyful	64. anser	97. praktise
31. marryed	65. pepol	98. livs
32. happend	66. seperate	99. tryd
33. occured	67. diffrent	100. bigest
34. cloze		

Spelling Demons Week by Week

Test XI: Memory Tricks

How do the following memory tricks ("mnemonics") help you to spell the words? What other tricks work for you?

1. *piece* of *pie*

2. *friend* until the *end*

3. **the** starts *there*, *they're*, and *their*

4. **a** *rat* in *separate*

5. *reign* in *foreign*

6. *pal* in *principal*

7. *all wrong* is two words; so is *all right*

8. *a little* is two words; so is *a lot*

Test XII: Related Words

What do these words have in common?

a lot, all right, all ways, polka dot, used to, all ready, a little, all wrong

Answers to Final Tests

Test III: Pronunciation

A.
1. chə wä′ wä
2. kûr′ nəl
3. wŏŏ′ mən
4. wĕnz′ dā
5. wŭn
6. whĕth′ ər
7. bĭs′ kət
8. sōl′ jər
9. mĕn′ ē
10. ŭv

B.
1. short **u**
2. long double **o**
3. long **o**
4. ô
5. short **u**
6. **ou**
7. ô
8. long **o**
9. short **u**
10. **ou**
11. schwa
12. short double **o**
13. short double **o**
14. short double **o**
15. ô
16. ô
17. ûr
18. short double **o** or ōr *or* ôr
19. short double **o**

C.
1. short **a**
2. ô
3. ô

D.
1. short **u**
2. ô
3. short **u**
4. short **u**, schwa
5. long **o**
6. schwa
7. long **o**
8. short **u**
9. long double **o**
10. short double **o**
11. short **i**
12. ô
13. schwa
14. short **u**
15. consonant **w**/short **u**
16. long **o**
17. long double **o**
18. ôr
19. ô
20. short **u**

E.
1. schwa
2. silent
3. short **e**
4. âr/silent
5. ûr
6. short **i**
7. short **i**
8. short **i**

F.
1. short **e**
2. schwa
3. ô
4. short **a**/schwa
5. short **a**
6. ä

G.
1. **s**
2. **sh**
3. **sh**
4. silent **k**/**n**
5. short **u**/**z**
6. silent
7. silent
8. silent
9. **hw**
10. **t**

Test IV: Usage

Sentences will vary.

Test V: Contractions

A.
1. let us
2. who is/who has
3. who will
4. who would/who had
5. we are
6. they are
7. it is
8. you are
9. will not
10. I am

B.
1. I'll
2. I'd
3. doesn't
4. don't
5. didn't
6. wasn't
7. hadn't
8. haven't
9. isn't
10. can't
11. could've been

Test VI: Abbreviations

1. etc.
2. oz.
3. oz.
4. lb.
5. lbs.

Test VII: Spelling

1. certain, sincerely, conscience
2. (none)
3. forty, ancient, across, Wednesday
4. brought, journeyed, perceive
5. surprise, principle, passed
6. beliefs, committed, it's, benefiting
7. write, whether
8. traveled
9. hadn't, although
10. scissors, companies

Test VIII: Rules

1. a. To form the plural of consonant/**y** nouns, change the **y** to **i** and then add **-es**.
   b. To form the third person singular of consonant/**y** verbs, change the **y** to **i** and then add **-es**.
   c. To form the past tense of consonant/**y** verbs, change the **y** to **i** and then add **-ed**.
   d. To add **-ing** to consonant/**y** verbs, keep the **y** and add the **-ing**.

2. For vowel/**y** words, you keep the vowel/**y** before all suffixes.

3. **I** before **e** except after **c**, unless the **c** sounds **sh**, and then you spell the word **cie**. **I** before **e** except in words that sound long **a**. Other exceptions are words of German derivation in which the **ei** sounds long **i**. There are also other exceptions such as *weird*, *either*, and *leisure*.

4. Plurals:
   a. You form the usual plural of a noun by adding **s** to it.
   b. Words ending in **o**:
      i. Some words ending in **o** just add **s**:
         1) words ending in vowel/**o** (*radio*).
         2) Italian or musical terms (*cello*).
         3) clipped words (*auto*, *photo*).
         4) foreign words (*taco*, *poncho*).
      ii. Some words ending in consonant/**o** always add **-es** (*tomato*).
      iii. Some words ending in consonant/**o** add **s** or **-es** (*volcano*, *volcanos*, *volcanoes*).
   c. To words ending in **s**, **ch**, etc., add **-es** for the plural.
   d. To some words ending in **f**, just add **s**. To others, change the **f** to **v** and add **-es**.
      chief, chiefs; life, lives

5. A one-one-one word is a one-syllable word ending in one consonant preceded by one vowel.

6. Before adding a suffix beginning with a vowel to a one-one-one word, you double the final consonant.

7. Multi-syllable words:

   a. If the accent is on the last syllable, you double the final consonant.
   b. If the accent is not on the final syllable, you do not double the final consonant.

8. You drop the final, silent **e** before adding **-ing**.

Test IX: More Rules

1. Consonant/**y** words change the **y** to **i** before adding **-es** for the plural.

2. Vowel/**y** words don't change the spelling before suffixes.

3. Keep the **y** of a consonant/**y** word before adding **-ing**.

4. Change the **y** of a consonant/**y** word to **i** before adding **-es** for the third person singular verb.

5.
   a. **I** before **e**;
   b. except after **c**;
   c. unless the **c** sounds **sh**; then spell it **cie**.
   d. If it sounds long **a**, it is spelled **ei**;
   e. Words of German derivation sounding long **i** are spelled **ei**.
   f. There are unexplained exceptions; *weird* is one of them.

6. Double the final consonant of a one-one-one word before adding a suffix beginning with a vowel.

7. Drop the final silent **e** before adding **-ing**.

8. In a two-syllable word ending in one consonant preceded by one vowel with the accent on the last syllable, double the final consonant before a suffix beginning with a vowel.

9. If, in adding the suffix **-ence**, the accent reverts to a syllable other than the last one, do not double the final consonant.

10. For the plural, add **-es** to words ending in **s**.

11. If the multi-syllable word ending in one consonant preceded by one vowel has the accent not on the last syllable, you do not double the final consonant before a suffix.

12. Some nouns ending in **f** change that **f** to **v** before adding **-es** for the plural.

13. A noun ending in vowel/**o** just adds **s** for the plural.

14. Some words ending in consonant/**o** add **-es** for the plural.

15. To make the past tense of a consonant/**y** word, change the **y** to **i** before adding **-ed**.

16. Some nouns ending in **f** just add **s** for the plural.

Test X: Misspellings

1. ect. (etc.)
2. somthing (something)
3. libary (library)
4. Febuary (February)
5. fourty (forty)
6. hunderd (hundred)
7. surtin (certain)
8. onle (only)
9. comeing (coming)
10. writeing (writing)
11. sincerly (sincerely)
12. usualy (usually)
13. brocolli (broccoli)
14. colliflour (cauliflower)
15. foriegn (foreign)
16. studyes (studies)
17. countryes (countries)
18. emenies (enemies)
19. begining (beginning)
20. committment (commitment)
21. enuf (enough)
22. truble (trouble)
23. jewerly (jewelry)
24. wierd (weird)
25. recieve (receive)
26. dosen't (doesn't)
27. Augst (August)
28. useto (used to)
29. looze (lose *or* loose)
30. beutyful (beautiful)
31. marryed (married)
32. happend (happened)
33. occured (occurred)
34. cloze (close)
35. isen't (isn't)
36. gess (guess)
37. nickle (nickel)
38. bilt (built)
39. wimmen (women)
40. vanilla folder (manila folder)
41. Wenzday (Wednesday)
42. Toosday (Tuesday)
43. wasen't (wasn't)
44. potatoe (potato)
45. i (I)
46. haden't (hadn't)
47. becuz (because)
48. cann't (can't)
49. alot (a lot)
50. alright (all right)

Test X: Misspellings (Continued)

51. awfull (awful)
52. truely (truly)
53. tward (toward)
54. exitement (excitement)
55. shure (sure)
56. shuger (sugar)
57. childern (children)
58. ment (meant)
59. urly (early)
60. tonite (tonight)
61. tomorow (tomorrow)
62. probly (probably)
63. probely (probably)
64. anser (answer)
65. pepol (people)
66. seperate (separate)
67. diffrent (different)
68. intresting (interesting)
69. brang (brought)
70. stopt (stopped)
71. fisht (fished)
72. laff (laugh)
73. laffd (laughed)
74. choosen (chosen)
75. america (America)

76. tungue (tongue)
77. sinse (since)
78. siense (science)
79. sugjest (suggest)
80. docter (doctor)
81. should of been (should have been)
82. spose (suppose)
83. purpus (purpose)
84. thier (their *or* there)
85. whanted (wanted)
86. beleive (believe)
87. Linkon (Lincoln)
88. deside (decide)
89. eazy (easy)
90. acke (ache)
91. stummick (stomach)
92. picknicking (picnicking)
93. poka dot (polka dot)
94. exept (except)
95. excelent (excellent)
96. wheather (whether *or* weather)
97. praktise (practice)
98. livs (lives)
99. tryd (tried)
100. bigest (biggest)

Test XI: Tricks

1. The letters **pie** start both words, and you do think of *piece* with *pie*.

2. The word *friend ends* with the letters **-end**, and you want a friend to last forever.

3. *Their* is frequently misspelled as "thier." If you can remember that all the tha5r's start with **the-**, it may help.

4. The first **a** is the problem in this word; *a rat* may help you to remember it.

5. Sound the last syllable of *foreign* with a long **a** as in *reign*; they are both spelled the same way.

6. Your *principal* is supposed to be your *pal*.

7. You wouldn't spell *all wrong* as one word, so don't spell *all right* as one word.

8. You wouldn't spell *a little* as one word; so don't spell *a lot* as one word.

Test XII: Related Words

They are all two words.

Index to Demons

NOTE: Numbers refer to lesson in which each word is presented.